SAP® NetWeaver BI Accelerator

SAP® Essentials

Expert SAP knowledge for your day-to-day work

Whether you wish to expand your SAP knowledge, deepen it, or master a use case, SAP Essentials provide you with targeted expert knowledge that helps support you in your day-to-day work. To the point, detailed, and ready to use.

SAP PRESS is a joint initiative of SAP and Galileo Press. The know-how offered by SAP specialists combined with the expertise of the Galileo Press publishing house offers the reader expert books in the field. SAP PRESS features first-hand information and expert advice, and provides useful skills for professional decision-making.

SAP PRESS offers a variety of books on technical and business related topics for the SAP user. For further information, please visit our website: *www.sap-press.com*.

Marc O. Schäfer, Matthias Melich
SAP Solution Manager Enterprise Edition
2nd edition 2009, approx. 550 pp., hardcover
ISBN 978-1-59229-271-4

Armin Kösegi, Rainer Nerding
SAP Change and Transport Management
3rd edition 2009, approx. 900 pp., hardcover
ISBN 978-1-59229-247-9

Thomas Schneider
SAP Performance Optimization Guide
5th edition 2008, 638 pp., hardcover
ISBN 978-1-59229-202-8

Frank Föse, Siegrid Hagemann, Liane Will
SAP NetWeaver ABAP System Administration
3rd edition 2008, 646 pp., hardcover
ISBN 978-1-59229-174-8

J. Andrew Ross

SAP® NetWeaver BI Accelerator

Bonn • Boston

ISBN   978-1-59229-192-2

© 2009 by Galileo Press Inc., Boston (MA)
1st Edition 2009

Galileo Press is named after the Italian physicist, mathematician and philosopher Galileo Galilei (1564–1642). He is known as one of the founders of modern science and an advocate of our contemporary, heliocentric worldview. His words Eppur si muove (And yet it moves) have become legendary. The Galileo Press logo depicts Jupiter orbited by the four Galilean moons, which were discovered by Galileo in 1610.

Editor Florian Zimniak
Copy Editor Julie McNamee
Cover Design Silke Braun
Photo Credit Getty Images/Martin Harvey
Layout Design Vera Brauner
Production Iris Warkus
Typesetting SatzPro, Krefeld (Germany)
Printed and bound in Canada

Contents

Contents

1   Introduction

We are entering an era where the overwhelming majority of information will not be hand-crafted. It will be stamped out by machines. This is inevitable. It has already begun to change the computing marketplace: most organizations of size now realize they can afford to save and mine all their logs, and are looking for inexpensive ways to do so.
Joe Hellerstein, University of California, Berkeley, October 2008

Billions of billions of bits of potentially useful information surround us. They form an ocean of resources in which companies can sink or swim. Business opportunities abound in this ocean for anyone with the intelligence to grasp them. To find these opportunities, a smart entrepreneur will deploy the latest analytic tools as intelligence multipliers.

A new generation of fast and flexible tools for analytic reporting on vast volumes of business data is now available. Compared with the opportunities they open up, these tools are surprisingly inexpensive. Any well organized company can deploy them to extract the hidden value of its own data. The result is nothing less than a revolution in business intelligence.

Not so long ago, knowledge workers had to request analytic reports from their IT departments and wait for days or weeks to receive them. The task of extracting actionable information from business data and converting the information into useful knowledge was so slow as to be inapplicable to the real-time control of business processes.

Today, users typically generate their own reports from portal views and control processes embedded in business applications from their desktops. This enables companies to apply the knowledge the users generate to adapt their business processes on a daily or hourly basis.

Given the ever-increasing amount of data that business users and knowledge workers are expected to handle, this enhanced reporting capability is a big step forward. But it raises new challenges.

In business as a whole, the volume of data generated is estimated to double every two years. Also, the number of users of business intelligence (BI) productivity tools will likely continue to increase year on year, as the tools improve and as companies learn to leverage their potential for increasing the efficiency and agility of business processes. As a consequence, in a modern company, the IT team is constantly busy deploying BI tools to cope with more and more users and data, all the while trying to keep costs within budget. So the workload of the IT department has changed, but it is no easier than before.

At SAP®, we considered this whole situation and decided we could offer our customers something better. Some years earlier, within the SAP NetWeaver development group, we had developed a search engine called TREX (for text retrieval and information extraction) that could now be extended to perform searches over large volumes of structured data. Moreover, we saw how we could implement the new engine on distributed hosts to perform parallel selection of results and aggregation of key figures, using modern scalable hardware to execute the operations on data held entirely in memory. Because memory reads are orders of magnitude faster than disk reads (microseconds rather than milliseconds), this makes a difference.

With parallel processing in memory, a performance advantage is achieved that can trigger a revolution in business intelligence. The SAP NetWeaver Business Intelligence Accelerator, based on TREX technology, achieves order-of-magnitude improvements in response times for many of the queries that are part of the typical workload of a BI user in a modern company.

Marketed as a preconfigured package (in industry jargon an *appliance*), the SAP NetWeaver BI Accelerator is optimized for performance and ease of deployment, and represents a new departure in SAP product philosophy. The BI accelerator was developed in close cooperation with Intel® engineers to run specifically on Intel processors in a Linux environment. With these platform choices fixed in advance, accelerator deployment becomes much smoother and the product can be more highly optimized to offer what SAP NetWeaver BI users really need. The result is a product that any company with the current release of SAP NetWeaver BI can attach to their existing landscape and within a short time be using productively to accelerate a wide range of BI queries.

The value proposition for a company that deploys the BI accelerator has two sides: it increases user productivity, and it reduces the overall lifetime cost of an

SAP NetWeaver BI solution compared with other ways to enhance the performance of analytic queries.

User productivity is raised for several reasons. Not only are many existing queries executed much faster than before but also a wider range of queries can be executed with good response times. Unlike traditional performance tuning for a BI system, which enabled specific queries to run faster but left other queries as slow as before, deployment of the accelerator gives users new flexibility to ask any queries and get answers fast. This encourages BI system users to work more freely and extract more value from company data, which translates to a competitive advantage for the company.

On the other side of the proposition, the total cost of owning the solution is reduced for several reasons, too.

Until recently, the standard way to improve the performance of an existing SAP NetWeaver BI system was to tune the system manually, which was skilled work that constantly needed to be checked and revised. By contrast, the approach embodied in the accelerator is to make full use of increasingly inexpensive hardware resources to eliminate the need for skilled tuning. The accelerator contains enough main memory and enough processors working in parallel to handle the data quickly anyway, regardless of how tricky the data model and the query may be.

Another reason for reduced costs is that because the accelerator is delivered as a preconfigured appliance, the latest platform ideas are implemented coherently to reduce integration and maintenance demands and increase reliability and availability. The accelerator is delivered on the latest blade server hardware, which not only liberates administrators from many routine tasks but also offers incremental scalability at low marginal cost.

Costs are also reduced because deployment of the accelerator takes load off other system components, especially the database. By taking the analytic reporting load off the database, the accelerator reduces pressure to invest heavily in additional database capacity, where manual performance tuning is still necessary, in favor of an automated solution tailored precisely for the analysis of mass data.

To see how fundamentally the relative costs of hardware and skilled personnel have changed in the past two decades, it is enough to look at Figure 1.1. The cost in US dollars of random access memory (RAM) per gigabyte has fallen by a factor of almost a thousand, and of hard disk drives by several tens of thousands, whereas it hardly needs saying that the dollar costs of skilled IT staff have risen. Given this transformation, the proper response is to save much more raw data on disk than before and to invest much more generously than before in memory-based resources. With those resources, companies can mine that wealth of data and analyze it to find both new market opportunities and new potential for optimization to increase the productivity of company staff. The return on investment (ROI) in such resources can quickly cover the total cost of ownership (TCO) of solutions that leverage them. Certainly, it would be irrational to remain with the same allocations of hardware and personnel costs as in the past century.

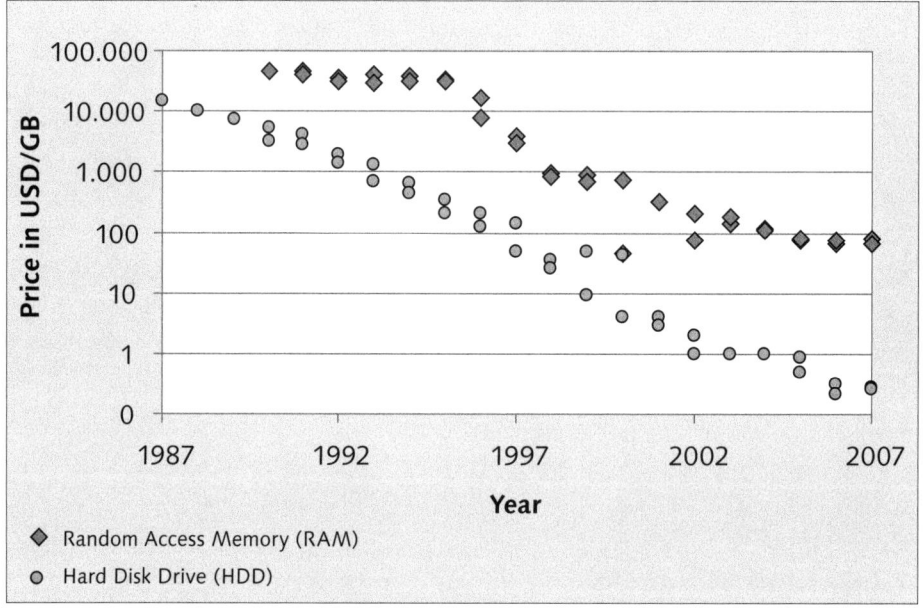

Figure 1.1 Falling Costs of Random Access Memory and Hard Disk Drives, 1987–2007 (Source: John C. McCallum/Pascal Schmidt-Volkmar)

The bottom line is that the SAP NetWeaver BI Accelerator enables the companies that deploy it to realize an order of magnitude improvement in their SAP NetWeaver BI analytic reporting. Compared with previous options, the accelerator offers an unprecedented combination of increased performance and flexibility, reduced total cost of operation, and support for new levels of business analytics. The new accelerator technology can be a game changer.

About This SAP Essentials Guide

This book is designed to help anyone involved with introducing and running the SAP NetWeaver BI Accelerator in a company. It is addressed to two main groups of readers:

▸ For decision makers and business managers, it outlines a vision of the new business opportunities that the accelerator opens up and gives a fair impression of the deployment and administration effort required.

▸ For technical managers and system administrators, it provides the basic facts needed in order to plan and prepare for the practical work involved in setting up the BI accelerator and running it on a day-to-day basis.

How to Use This Book

It would be hard to read this book from cover to cover like a novel. Few readers will be interested in all of it, and most readers will skip or skim parts. But the book has been designed to be read selectively. The following hints may help you plan your reading.

Chapter 2 offers an overview of the impact of the accelerator. For busy readers, it includes an executive summary of the impact of the accelerator from a business perspective. The more technical parts introduce some of the main functional concepts behind the accelerator.

Chapter 3 describes the architecture of the accelerator in more depth. Still the emphasis is on ideas and principles. It outlines the main features of the accelerator and the main processes and activities involved in putting it to productive use.

Chapter 4 presents the basic knowledge that an administrator will need for everyday administration of an SAP landscape that includes a BI accelerator. This chapter is not meant to replace other sources of the same information and may become outdated in detail as the accelerator continues to evolve. However, it provides a relatively digestible overview.

Chapter 5 presents the more advanced knowledge that an administrator should have ready at hand but will not need every day. Details are offered that can help the IT staff to stay cool even in the more challenging situations that can occasionally arise. For extreme cases, the details may help them work with SAP Service engineers.

Chapter 6 returns to business and presents a few success stories. The first story tells how collaboration with hardware partner IBM proved the extreme scalability of the accelerator. The second story shows how collaboration with a leading company led to a breakthrough advance in the handling of some performance-critical queries. The other stories underscore the message that many early adopters of the accelerator are very satisfied with the results.

Chapter 7 offers a deeper technical insight into how the accelerator works. Readers can use it to learn what makes the accelerator tick. The emphasis is on ideas, concepts, and processes, including patented innovations, rather than on exactly how they are implemented.

A final glossary is intended to help anyone for whom some of the technical terms are unfamiliar and who prefers not to have to reach too far or go online for definitions.

Acknowledgments

We thank all the companies named in this book for working with us to ensure that the accelerator did in fact live up to its early promise.

We thank alliance partner Intel Corporation for ongoing collaboration to implement and enhance the accelerator core functionality.

We thank the initial hardware partners Hewlett-Packard and IBM® for their continuing cooperation in refining the accelerator deployment concept.

We thank Winter Corporation for permission to cite details from their report on Project Jupiter (see Section 6.1).

We thank the Colgate-Palmolive Company for permission to tell the story of our collaboration to extend the scope of the performance boost delivered by the accelerator (see Section 6.2).

We also thank Bayer AG, the German Defense Forces, Rabobank Group, Kimberly-Clark Corporation, and WACKER Group for permission to tell their success stories (see Chapter 6).

We thank SAP NetWeaver colleagues Klaus Nagel, Alex Peter, Mathias Poehling, Daniel Schneiss, and Arne Schwarz for reviewing drafts of the book and suggesting numerous improvements.

We thank SAP NetWeaver colleagues Roland Kurz and Franz Färber for their courage and vision in driving the accelerator project.

We also thank all the other SAP NetWeaver colleagues who helped improve this book. Their contributions were substantial, but the colleagues are too numerous to mention by name.

We thank Florian Zimniak and his team at SAP PRESS for the smooth and professional collaboration in preparing the book.

Most of the technical information in this guide is also available from other SAP sources, such as the SAP Developer Network (SDN, which with over a million members is the largest of the SAP Communities of Innovation). For professional administrators, the *Technical Operations Manual* for SAP NetWeaver BI Accelerator (version 1.4 in October 2008) includes further detail on many topics described in this guide and is strongly recommended if you plan to work technically with the accelerator on a daily basis.

Behind the contents presented in this book stand the SAP NetWeaver Extensions Information Management teams BI and TREX, who are responsible for developing the SAP NetWeaver BI Accelerator. The named author of the book is a member of the TREX team. The SAP NetWeaver teams share the credit for the quality of the book, and the named author takes the customary blame for any errors in it. Please send us any feedback you may have via SAP PRESS at *contact@galileo-press.com*.

2   Impact

The SAP NetWeaver Business Intelligence Accelerator is a new and powerful approach to the challenge of delivering high-performance online analytic processing robustly and inexpensively in an existing IT landscape.

The SAP NetWeaver BI Accelerator delivers enhanced business intelligence functionality by boosting the performance of existing analytic functions in SAP NetWeaver BI. It is delivered as a preconfigured appliance that connects to a system landscape without the need for extensive customization or integration.

The BI accelerator software runs on commodity blade servers. To deploy it productively, the IT team plugs the servers into an existing SAP NetWeaver BI component infrastructure, the administration team uses a wizard to index the appropriate InfoCubes, and the business team goes to work with the new performance and flexibility.

The BI accelerator can index even the largest InfoCubes in an SAP NetWeaver BI landscape to create highly compressed — but not aggregated — index structures. If the accelerator is correctly sized, these structures are loaded automatically into main memory on startup, in readiness for when users need fast access to the data. The accelerator uses highly optimized aggregation algorithms to execute queries directly on these index structures entirely in memory, without any disk reads. It then delivers the results to the attached BI system's analytic engine for output to users.

The SAP NetWeaver development team has not only enhanced both the performance and the flexibility of analytic processing on large data cubes but also, crucially, succeeded in reducing the total cost of ownership (TCO) of the accelerator compared with other ways to improve productivity.

The TCO is reduced because the accelerator eliminates the need to devote scarce resources to the task of preaggregating data for storage in multiple smaller cubes because now the data is aggregated directly from even the largest cubes during query execution. The accelerator lets users drill down on the cube data to the finest granularity entirely within memory, without manual preparation of intermediate data structures and without having to wait for the experts in the IT department to fine-tune the backend database. As a result, the accelerator enhances the performance of all queries on the indexed data cubes, not just those selected for manual tuning. This new approach gives users wider scope than ever before to interrogate their data creatively, to drill down to the facts, and to extract previously hidden business value.

To help SAP realize this vision, SAP technology partner Intel Corporation collaborated with SAP in the development of the BI accelerator by using advanced Intel software and hardware technology optimizations to maximize performance and scalability and create a robust and inexpensive solution running on standard Intel Xeon processors in a 64-bit SUSE Linux environment.

As the outcome of this collaboration, the BI accelerator is delivered as a preconfigured package (also called an appliance) by certified hardware partners. Currently, the certified partners are Hewlett-Packard, IBM, Fujitsu Siemens, and Sun Microsystems. The hardware partners are responsible for exact specification of the hardware landscapes while SAP ensures that the configuration as a whole is correctly sized to meet the customer company's data volume and user load requirements.

Although the BI accelerator is a technical innovation, it is also tailored specifically to satisfy the business needs of corporate users. The value proposition represents a judicious balance of benefits and costs. Maximized performance and flexibility make up one side of the balance. Minimized total cost of operation makes up the other. To ensure that it survives close budgetary scrutiny, the accelerator:

▶ Complements but does not replace existing hardware and software, to protect existing investments

▶ Includes self-configuration and self-management functionality, to reduce administration costs

▶ Features linear scalability, to enable incremental expansion at low marginal cost

The bottom line: TCO is held to a minimum.

Historic Moment: A Billion Rows in Seconds

At SAPPHIRE 2005 in Boston, Shai Agassi, then a member of the SAP Executive Board, marked a historic milestone by giving a live keynote demonstration of the brand new SAP NetWeaver BI Accelerator. From a prototype SAP NetWeaver BI analytic dashboard, he launched complex queries against a billion data records and got results back in seconds.

For the demonstration, the BI accelerator ran under 64-bit SUSE Linux on eight Hewlett-Packard BladeSystem blade servers, each mounting dual Intel Xeon processors and 8 GB of memory. The blades were mounted above an HP ProLiant server equipped with four Intel Itanium processors running SAP NetWeaver BI under HP-UX, and an HP StorageWorks file server with a capacity of 1 TB (terabyte). All this hardware was in a single standalone cabinet set visibly on the stage.

In September 2006, Winter Corporation published a 22-page white paper entitled *The SAP NetWeaver BI Accelerator: Transforming Business Intelligence*. Its executive summary states the key performance-related findings as follows:

▶ The BI accelerator reduced response times for a broad range of queries and is far more practical than the process of building tuned aggregates.

▶ The BI accelerator scales as the problem size grows and as the blade chassis configuration is expanded with additional blades.

▶ Data loading and indexing onto the BI accelerator occurs at impressive rates, outperforming the construction of optimized aggregates that would be required for comparable query response.

The WinterCorp tests of the BI accelerator showed clearly enough that it transforms the SAP NetWeaver BI experience.

Since then, user experience has confirmed that even when the accelerator is deployed in challenging real-life scenarios, accelerated query response times are often tens and sometimes even hundreds of times better than working from the database with an average mix of prebuilt aggregates.

In March 2008, Winter Corporation published another white paper on the BI accelerator, this time on Project Jupiter, a joint effort by SAP and IBM to conduct large-scale scalability tests of the accelerator on IBM hardware, against user data volumes of up to 25 TB. The results demonstrated the ability of the accelerator to scale smoothly up to installations with 140 blade servers equipped with well over

2 TB of main memory (for details see Section 6.1), sufficient to serve an active user population of many thousands.

New Milestone: Project Jupiter

In 2007, SAP and IBM engaged WinterCorp to monitor and independently report on Project Jupiter, a joint effort by SAP and IBM to conduct large-scale scalability tests of the SAP NetWeaver BI Accelerator on an IBM-provided infrastructure, against user data volumes between 5 TB and 25 TB. The findings were published in March 2008. The highlights are listed here:

▶ Single user query performance scales well as the volume of data processed grows.

▶ Multiuser tests confirm linear scalability in both throughput and response time for all tested data volumes.

▶ Concurrency is sufficient to support an active user population in the thousands.

▶ Data can be loaded into the BI accelerator at rates in excess of 1 TB per hour.

▶ Query activity can be parallelized over a landscape with as many as 140 nodes.

Project Jupiter demonstrated the ability of SAP NetWeaver BI Accelerator to meet the need for more users to process much more data in increasingly unpredictable ways, quickly and efficiently.

The rest of this chapter is structured as follows. Section 2.1 outlines the technical advance that is revolutionizing business information processing. Section 2.2 zooms in on business intelligence and analytics and outlines the benefits of deploying accelerator technology for analytics. Section 2.3 briefly introduces the technology that gives an accelerator appliance its impressive performance. Section 2.4 offers a short summary.

2.1   The Platform Revolution

Business information processing is currently undergoing a revolution comparable in scope with the revolution that brought us from the mainframe world to the world of client-server landscapes. The new revolution is the appearance of service-oriented architectures (SOA), and the benefit they offer is adaptability and enhanced flexibility. In the business ecosystem that surrounds a modern enterprise, adoption of SOA is the right way to go.

To survive and prosper, a business must be able to adapt to changes in its environment. The SAP implementation of SOA is embodied in the SAP NetWeaver technology and enables a business to deliver on the core principles of adaptive business. The SAP NetWeaver platform ships with SAP NetWeaver Business Intelligence, which is the mount point for the SAP NetWeaver BI Accelerator.

Consider the past few decades of history in business information processing. The mainframe paradigm brought the benefit of enterprise-wide integration to business computing. The client-server paradigm brought scalability plus a measure of flexibility, by enabling enterprises to increase their hardware investment incrementally to scale with increasing load in their system landscapes.

With SOA, enterprises implement their business processes with the help of standardized services that can be composed and recomposed in a user-friendly modeling environment, without the need for specialized coding expertise. This ability to reconfigure business processes not only easily but also dynamically, on the fly, together with the robust quality of the Web Services that support and realize them, gives the modern enterprise a competitive advantage that will likely grow in coming years.

With Web Services, business models have changed their focus to emphasize the creation of adaptive business networks in which companies together with their partners and suppliers form a network of interdependencies that defines a business ecosystem. These new networks are built on three core principles:

▶ **Distributed decision making and action**
Under previous paradigms, decisions were made and implemented from company headquarters or from the center. But central planning limits flexibility and hinders adaptation to unexpected changes in the market. In an adaptive network, companies can react appropriately to market changes without the need for centralized decisions. Power to adapt can be distributed over the ecosystem without loss of coherence.

▶ **Fast recombination of business processes**
As changing market conditions change the environment of a company in a network, its managers can react by recombining the elements of their previous business processes to generate new composite processes. The enabler for such recombination is that all the business processes are composed from standardized services.

▶ **Co-evolution within the business ecosystem**
As evolving market conditions transform the competitive environment of the entire ecosystem, managers can react by changing their business processes not

only internally but also across the network. By analogy with biological organisms exchanging genes during reproduction, companies can exchange functions and roles in an ongoing process involving multiple partners. In this way, the companies evolve together to optimize their positioning in an evolving environment.

The core principles of adaptive business form the design principles that underlie the SOA approach. When a business model is realized as an integrated set of Web Services that can be combined and recombined in a flexible process environment, companies can distribute their decision making to match the granularity of the services and adapt to a changing business environment together with their partners and suppliers. In this way, the companies can survive transformations that would be fatal to isolated companies.

The main prerequisite for making effective use of the SOA paradigm is that a company can analyze its own data freely enough and deeply enough to adapt its business processes in response to short-term market requirements. Online business processes generate vast amounts of data, and by analyzing this data, a company can find significant new revenue opportunities. All it takes is the capacity to analyze the data streams in real time, as it is collected, and to find the facts that reveal the new opportunities. The right tool for industrial-scale data analysis is the SAP NetWeaver BI Accelerator.

The SAP implementation of SOA features a set of Web Services based on open standards, a portal-based modeling environment for business process composition, role-based portals for company employees, and support for end-to-end business processes that can be changed dynamically to achieve previously impossible levels of flexibility.

The SOA approach enables company experts to compose services freely to create end-to-end solutions that cross previous application silo boundaries. Previous custom approaches to the challenge of integrating "stovepipe" business processes were often complex and expensive. The SOA approach contributes significantly to reducing the total cost of a company's business operations, not only by reducing IT costs but also by increasing the flexibility and efficiency of the business as a whole.

A company can benefit from the new approach simply by running its SAP applications on the SAP NetWeaver 7.0 platform. It does not need to make big upfront changes to its business processes. Given the platform, the accelerator then helps the company to deliver on the core principles by providing the data transparency needed for adaptive decision making.

2.2   Business Impact

The rate of change we encounter today in world markets is unprecedented. The financial crisis of October 2008 was a striking example of how swift the changes can be. Adapting quickly and correctly to such changes, together with your partners and faster than your competitors, is key to survival. To react correctly, the first thing you need is information that is fast, accurate, and reliable. SAP provides the infrastructure and the tools for gathering this information, and SAP NetWeaver BI Accelerator is the right tool for analyzing the information.

2.2.1   SAP NetWeaver

SAP NetWeaver is the SAP technical platform for integrating three essential aspects of business life: business processes, people such as employees and customers, and information flows both within and between enterprises. Within SAP NetWeaver, SAP NetWeaver BI makes information actionable by helping companies identify, integrate, and analyze disparate business data from a variety of sources.

SAP NetWeaver integrates all the technical elements required to support the business processes both within an enterprise and between enterprises and their partners and customers. These elements include enterprise services and their underlying business objects, SAP technical components, and third-party elements. SAP NetWeaver supports the creation and operation of composite applications using those technical elements.

The SAP NetWeaver platform offers great adaptability to companies that build on it. The standard processes that run on the platform can be adapted and extended in a service-oriented framework. SAP NetWeaver provides frontend modeling tools to facilitate modeling of business processes simply by composing standardized services, without any need for coding skills. This enables business analysts to innovate by configuring and extending their own business processes.

SAP NetWeaver features openness at many levels in its architecture. The Web Services are built in accordance with industry-wide open standards. The SAP

NetWeaver platform is open and able to integrate services originating from different manufacturers. Interoperability extends to the platform itself, which can work together with IBM WebSphere, Microsoft .NET, and other platforms.

Such a technology platform enhances the productivity of business processes built on it in many ways. People productivity is enhanced by role-specific portal interfaces for company users. Embedded analytic tools enable users to extract maximum value from company data. Frontend modeling tools enable company analysts to optimize their business processes. The same modeling tools offer the analysts the flexibility to adapt business processes in real time.

As for the cost side of the equation, SAP NetWeaver enables companies that deploy it to lower the TCO of their IT landscape. Different deployment options for the platform can be selectively realized by means of simple configuration changes. Services that are used in multiple operations can be shared to minimize their resource footprint. The platform features extremely low planned downtime for routine maintenance and built-in high availability (HA) to minimize unplanned downtime.

As for technical integration, SAP NetWeaver is a platform on which all the various parts of a company's business operations interact. The platform enables users to compose their own business applications from standardized Web Services within the SAP NetWeaver Composition Environment (SAP NetWeaver CE). The platform also allows interoperation with other platforms based on open standards.

SAP NetWeaver provides three main levels of integration (see Figure 2.1):

▶ *People integration* is realized by the portal infrastructure for unified, personalized, and role-based user access; collaboration tools to promote dynamic communication and collaborative working within groups; and support for multi-channel access, including access via voice telephony, mobile devices, or radio frequency technology (such as wireless local area network, WLAN).

▶ *Information integration* is realized via infrastructure for information management, including business intelligence (BI) to integrate, analyze, and disseminate information; Knowledge Management for content management and access to other repositories; and SAP NetWeaver Master Data Management (SAP NetWeaver MDM) to store, augment, and consolidate master data.

▶ *Process integration* is realized in two main ways, by an integration broker that enables communication based on extensible markup language (XML) and the simple object application protocol (SOAP), and by business process management to model and drive processes in the dynamic IT environment of a large company with a distributed IT landscape.

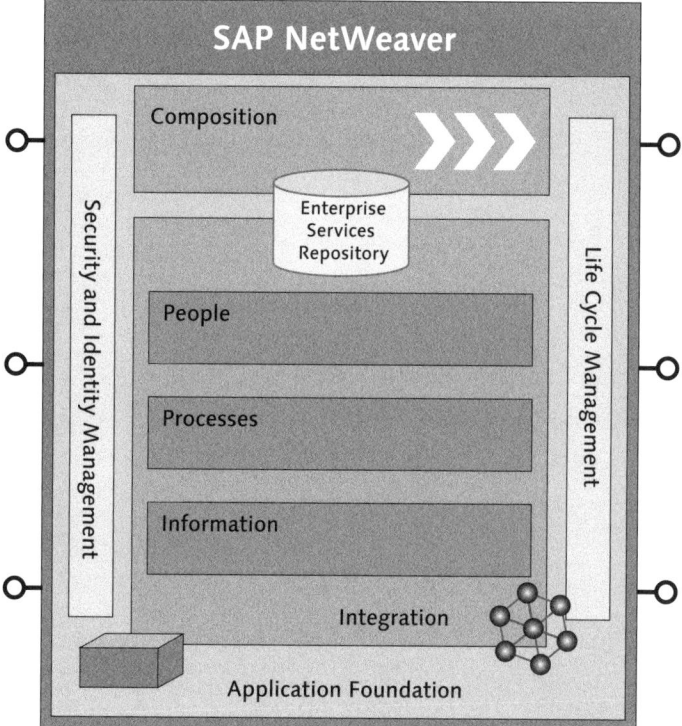

Figure 2.1 SAP NetWeaver as an Integration Platform

The application platform provided by SAP NetWeaver includes both ABAP and Java stacks, and features abstraction from specific databases and operating systems.

Within SAP NetWeaver, lifecycle management provides software logistics support for the entire technology stack, including monitoring, administration, and maintenance tools, as well as tools for managing updates and upgrades.

2.2.2 SAP NetWeaver Business Intelligence

SAP NetWeaver BI offers a powerful set of functions for online analytic processing. Companies that run SAP NetWeaver BI can accelerate their analytic queries not only by precalculating or caching queries or by precalculating aggregates but also by deploying the BI accelerator. The accelerator works with SAP NetWeaver BI 7.0 and higher, as well as with products from Business Objects, an SAP company.

SAP NetWeaver BI makes information actionable by helping companies identify, integrate, and analyze disparate business data from a variety of sources. It is an end-to-end BI solution from the extraction, transformation, and load (ETL) of the data through data warehousing to frontend tools and applications. SAP NetWeaver BI offers:

- ▶ A full range of analytic capabilities
- ▶ Portal integration with other components of the SAP NetWeaver platform
- ▶ Data warehousing for accurate and timely integration of data from all sources
- ▶ Business planning and simulation for developing custom planning applications
- ▶ Open platform supporting numerous tested and certified software products
- ▶ Business content and analytic applications based on best business practices

SAP NetWeaver BI offers data warehousing functionality for various kinds of data, including master data, volatile data in an operational data store (DataStore objects), and summarized data in multidimensional cubes (SAP NetWeaver BI InfoCubes).

Together, SAP NetWeaver BI and Business Objects offer powerful analytic functionality for business users. The products include extensive business logic for calculations, planning and forecasts, exception scanning, alerting, query precalculation and caching, and data mining. The presentation layer for this logic enables various kinds of drill-down, pivoting, *what-if* analysis, slicing and dicing, and so on.

In the context of SAP-enabled BI, analytic queries can be accelerated in various ways, not only by precalculation and caching of queries and precalculation of aggregates but also by deploying the SAP NetWeaver BI Accelerator.

Analysts working with products from Business Objects can also benefit immediately from deployment of the BI accelerator.

Business Objects, an SAP company, is the world's leading BI software company. The company offers a broad family of tools and applications to help teams optimize business performance by connecting people, information, and businesses across the business network:

▶ BusinessObjects Enterprise (BOE) is a flexible and scalable BI platform built on an SOA. The BOE platform has five tiers: client, application, intelligence, processing, and data. SAP NetWeaver BI can serve as the data tier. BOE Universes serve as the semantic layer between the upper tiers and the data tier. Universes allow business users to define dimensions and measures (corresponding to characteristics and key figures in SAP NetWeaver BI) to represent their data. Universes can connect to SAP NetWeaver BI InfoCubes and MultiProviders.

▶ For reporting, Crystal Reports is a reporting solution for designing, exploring, visualizing, and delivering reports via the web or embedded in enterprise applications.

▶ For ad hoc queries, reporting, and analysis, BusinessObjects Web Intelligence offers both self-service access to data and intuitive information analysis in one product.

▶ For advanced analysis, BusinessObjects Voyager is a web-based OLAP client with an advanced user interface based on Web 2.0 Ajax technology.

▶ For data visualization, BusinessObjects Xcelsius offers easy-to-use, dynamic, and customizable data visualization software that enables business users to create dashboards from any data source.

▶ For information discovery, BusinessObjects Polestar combines the analytic power of BI and the performance boost of the BI accelerator to provide quick answers to business questions (see Figure 2.2).

When SAP NetWeaver BI provides the data for Polestar, metadata and security are handled within SAP NetWeaver, and the BI accelerator can be deployed to index the data and boost the performance of queries in Polestar.

In January 2008, just as SAP and Business Objects were celebrating their union, a team of solution engineers working behind the scenes provided an impressive demonstration of the advantages of the union. The team connected Polestar to the BI accelerator and used the new hybrid to execute analytic queries. The prototype processed over a billion data records in less than 1 second. This is a thousand times faster than many users of BI products are accustomed to getting their results.

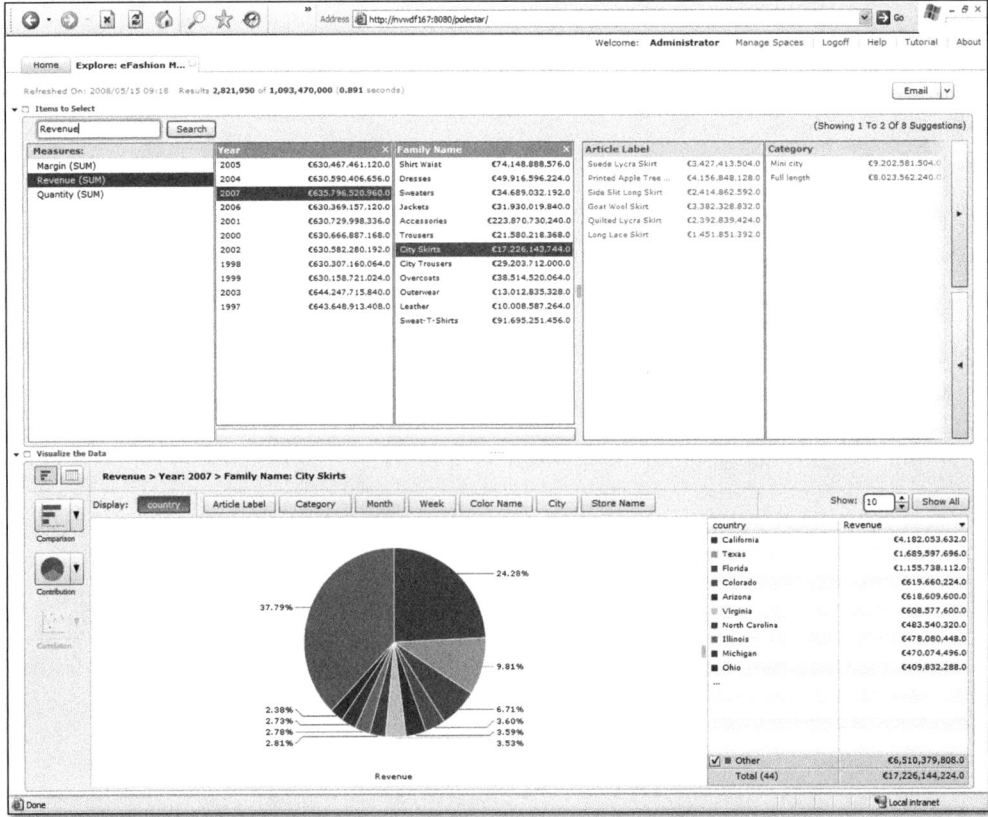

Figure 2.2 BusinessObjects Polestar User Interface

The bottom line here is that companies using BusinessObjects Polestar can now take advantage of a BI accelerator in the backend to analyze their data faster and more flexibly than ever before. In 2009, SAP will ship additional options for using the BI accelerator to enhance the analytic performance of Business Objects products.

2.2.3   The BI Accelerator Value Proposition

The BI accelerator offers two main benefits to the companies that deploy it alongside an SAP NetWeaver BI system:

▶ **Enhanced productivity**
   The increased performance and other features of the accelerator enhance the productivity of BI system users.

▶ **Reduced TCO**
   The TCO of the BI system is reduced by introducing the accelerator compared with other strategies for boosting performance.

It is worth examining these benefits in detail.

Enchanced productivity

The productivity of SAP NetWeaver BI system users is enhanced with the accelerator for several reasons:

▶ **Performance**
   Response times delivered by the BI system for analytic queries are often much faster. Even for huge InfoCubes with billions of rows, results can be returned in seconds.

▶ **Stable response times**
   The response times for repeated executions of a query or for execution of similar queries remain stable even under high system load. The response times also vary predictably under changes in data design and query design.

▶ **Scalability**
   The BIA system can easily be extended incrementally with additional hardware.

▶ **Robustness**
   The BIA blade hardware is reliable and requires much less routine administration than legacy architectures.

▶ **Usability**
   The performance and stability features encourage users to explore their data. With the accelerator, they can drill down to the facts and explore their data in an ad hoc manner, without fear of timeouts or overconsumption of system resources.

Let us look at these five reasons one by one.

Performance

Compared with typical response times for standard company SAP NetWeaver BI systems in which InfoCubes have been supplemented with manually defined aggregates, analytic query response times with the accelerator are often tens or even hundreds of times better.

Scenarios with challenging response time requirements are numerous. For example, a call center for handling customer calls needs to be able to extract relevant information from customer records within a few seconds. In such scenarios, the IT department faces demanding service level agreements, and high performance is not a luxury.

Stable Response Times

The response time improvement is consistent. If the system is not under heavy load, response times for a given query are constant whenever it is executed. Also, similar queries are answered in similar times. By contrast, response times with aggregates often vary unpredictably, depending on whether an existing aggregate exactly matches a query or whether a database optimizer finds a perfect index for the query. The problem with relying on a database optimizer is that it is a "black box" product containing proprietary algorithms that impact performance in ways a user cannot anticipate. With the accelerator, users learn to expect fast responses to new queries. This encourages ad hoc reporting and creative analysis of the data. This in turn extracts the added value hidden in the huge amounts of data generated by a modern business.

Scalability

The average response times of the accelerator for increasing amounts of data increase in proportion, with near-linear scaling. And as the number of simultaneous users increases, average response times increase gradually, again with near-linear scaling. For example, if the single-user response time for a class of queries is less than 1 second, the response time for the queries under high system load may be less than 4 seconds (Project Jupiter, see Section 6.1). In any case, good performance under increasing load is achieved without hitting a wall.

Nowadays, many companies have accumulated data repositories of several terabytes and expect to accumulate data at an increasing rate in future. Companies in the retail sector with point-of-sale (POS) data, utilities with detailed records for millions of customers, and telephone companies with billions of call records are some obvious examples. In other application areas, new technologies such as radio frequency tagging (RFID) will generate an order of magnitude more data in the near future. For such scenarios especially, good scalability is a must.

This near-linear scalability is achieved by modularization. Each blade server is a complete hardware server module in a standard and compact format. Companies deploy as many blade servers as they need to handle their user load and can later add blades one by one to handle increasing load. Because the blades are produced and sold in large numbers, they can offer massive processing power and memory capacity at commodity prices that break through previous price-performance barriers.

Robustness

The new hardware paradigm leveraged by the accelerator is a great improvement on earlier hardware. Modern blade servers require very little routine administration, are highly reliable, and offer automated failover. Thus a few administrators can be responsible for a large landscape. Further, instead of rebuilding their entire landscape to introduce new hardware, companies that deploy the accelerator begin with an encapsulated scenario where the risks are contained and the benefits are instantly visible.

On the software side, BIA indexes typically require far less maintenance effort than the aggregates they replace. Change runs and roll-ups are required only for one object per InfoCube and generally run much faster for BIA indexes than for database aggregates because the work is parallelized over the BIA blade nodes. This also allows a company to schedule much more frequent data alignments and to improve performance in scenarios where the process of building and updating aggregates would be far too cumbersome.

Usability

The opportunities opened up when the accelerator is in daily use are game changers. Knowledge workers asking analytic queries can get their answers more quickly and hence waste less time waiting, but that is only the start. With accelerator performance, complicated navigations over large data structures that were previously impractical become feasible and new patterns in the data become open to discovery. An additional benefit of accelerator deployment is that knowledge workers no longer need special training to follow the constraints of prebuilt BI aggregates.

As an example of a new opportunity, consider a retail company that uses its accelerator to perform assortment analysis at the stock keeping unit (SKU) and store level. If the accelerator is suitably sized, the company can choose to perform the analysis at point-of-sale (POS) till receipt and SKU level, for basket analysis and customer segmentation. This enables the company to pursue a much more refined and responsive assortment strategy.

Reduced TCO

Moving to the other half of the value proposition, companies can expect to enjoy reduced TCO for their SAP NetWeaver BI systems by deploying the accelerator rather than other productivity boosters for several reasons:

▶ **No aggregate maintenance**
Without aggregates to maintain, fewer resources are needed for routine administration.

▶ **System consolidation**
Dependencies between the database and reporting are relaxed, so data loads and reporting no longer need to be scheduled serially. Because the accelerator takes over the reporting load, system copies made to handle that load can be consolidated.

▶ **Longer hardware usage**
Investment in new database hardware can be delayed or avoided. Growth in reporting demand can be accommodated without adding load to the existing BI landscape.

▶ **Ease of reporting**
Long and inflexible approval processes for reporting can be replaced by shorter and more open processes. Changes in reporting requirements can often be accommodated at no additional cost.

▶ **Simplified data modeling**
Because manual performance tuning is no longer necessary, companies can afford to develop and release new analytic scenarios more quickly to their lines of business.

Again, let us look at these reasons in detail.

No Aggregate Maintenance

The accelerator creates only one BIA index for each InfoCube, so companies no longer need to waste their administration resources maintaining multiple aggregates. Because the definition and creation of aggregates is a task requiring a high skill level, and the ongoing task of maintaining them is laborious, the human resource costs for this approach to performance optimization are high. By contrast, both the initial indexing effort for an InfoCube and the subsequent maintenance effort for change runs and roll-ups are an order of magnitude lower. Furthermore, in most cases, the performance gain obtained is greater and more consistent.

System Consolidation

Some companies currently copy BI systems to manage high overall system loads. This creates new complications regarding data replication and synchronization and drives up administration costs. The costs can be avoided by deploying the accelerator to handle the reporting load on the systems. The accelerator can raise the effective capacity of a BI system sufficiently to allow multiple systems to be consolidated.

Longer Hardware Usage

Deployment of the accelerator enables companies to delay or avoid investment in more traditional hardware for increasing capacity. The lifetime of an existing database solution can be extended significantly when an accelerator is available to take some of the load. And since BIA indexes replace disk-based aggregates, the database consumes less disk space, which may be significant if database licensing is based on data volumes. Moreover, the accelerator enables companies to profit from the new hardware without premature write-down of their existing hardware investments.

Ease of Reporting

The cost reduction can be dramatic. Consider a typical scenario in a large company where the board consumes regular reports from the controlling department. Without the accelerator, a set of reports needs to be defined and prepared, then supported with tuned aggregated that must be maintained on a regular basis. This ongoing effort is a significant cost driver that severely impairs flexibility. If the board wants a new report, the workflow consequences in controlling can be disruptive. By contrast, with the accelerator, the situation is transformed. The board still gets its reports but now the controlling staff who sweated to deliver them can work much more efficiently. Also, the other company users who analyze the data more intensively can now work more creatively. They can hunt down new opportunities for optimization and raise an alarm faster if necessary. The board, too, can ask for new reports at short notice without generating excessive costs.

Simplified Data Modeling

When accelerator performance makes manual performance tuning less critical, not only can companies develop and release new analytic scenarios more quickly to their lines of business but they can also afford to be less performance-aware during the design of InfoCubes. Although good design is still important for the InfoCubes, it becomes less critical. This means in turn that the granularity of the data in an InfoCube can reach down to line item level, rendering the InfoCube sufficient for all reporting needs and allowing DataStore objects to be optimized for writes, not reads, and simplifying the modeling task in the data warehouse. In this way, accelerator deployment offers an opportunity for a company to reconsider its data warehousing practices more generally. Any companies who are starting from scratch with a new SAP NetWeaver BI project can benefit immediately from the increased flexibility in data design and modeling.

The Benefits in a Nutshell

To summarize, the SAP NetWeaver BI Accelerator value proposition is that deployment brings two main kinds of benefits:

▶ User productivity is increased due to the improved query performance, more stable response times, high scalability and robustness, and the opportunities created by enhanced usability.

▶ The total cost of operation for analytic reporting is reduced by savings in aggregate maintenance, system consolidation, longer write-downs for existing hardware, ease of reporting, and simplified data modeling.

SAP provides a tool for calculating the benefits a company can expect by deploying the accelerator. The ROI calculator for the SAP NetWeaver BI Accelerator is an easy-to-use tool to qualify and quantify the value of BI accelerator deployment by measuring the ROI to expect from introducing the accelerator into a landscape. With the right input data, the tool calculates the ROI in precise numerical terms.

The calculator is built with BusinessObjects Xcelsius as an intuitive standalone tool embedded in a Microsoft PowerPoint file that can be customized for use in larger presentations. It is available on request from SAP account executives and others.

2.2.4 Setting the Right Expectations

The accelerator dramatically improves analytic query processing at one or two steps in the process chain. To ensure that expectations remain realistic, it is worth reviewing the rest of the chain. In an SAP NetWeaver BI system, the average overall query response time depends on several factors:

▶ Time to read the data

▶ Time to perform the necessary joins and aggregations on the data

▶ Time to perform the analytic calculation

▶ Time to transfer data over the network to the frontend

▶ Time to render the result at the frontend for the user

The main impact of the BI accelerator is on the read and aggregation times. It has little impact on the analytic calculation time, which is mainly clocked up in the BI system. And the accelerator can have no impact on the network and frontend times.

If and when you embark upon a BI accelerator deployment project, you should remember these facts and take care to set the right expectations. Although you can obtain runtime performance gains for the great majority of BI analytic queries by using the BI accelerator, the current release of the accelerator does not improve the runtime of every query. At present, the accelerator is explicitly targeted at reducing the times for data selection and aggregation.

On the positive side, the BI accelerator reduces the cost of operations (in terms of aggregate design, data latency, and so on) for virtually all scenarios.

Most of the general performance rules for BI systems continue to be valid for systems with an accelerator:

▶ Keep the result sets realistically small, remembering that no user can be expected to comprehend a vast display of data.

▶ Use multidimensional navigation to drill down to details.

► Reduce complex calculations to a minimum, for example, by asking a series of simpler queries.

► Use BI compression (but the accelerator relaxes this rule because it allows fast reporting even when the data is not compressed in BI).

► Use logical partitioning to work with smaller subsets of the data.

In the ideal BI accelerator scenario, the queries feature high data read or data manager (DM) times and/or involve a high aggregation ratio, which means that even when many records are selected, only small sets are transferred back to the BI system.

Deployment of the BI accelerator can have a beneficial impact on your data modeling strategy. Once you use the accelerator for reporting, you can report directly on detailed InfoCubes (via their BIA indexes). This has the consequence that you can optimize DataStore objects for writes because you no longer need to report on them. Also, you no longer need to use the BI report-report interface because you can report directly on InfoCubes (via their BIA indexes), so your users no longer need training to use that interface.

In any case, deployment of the accelerator has a beneficial impact on your processes. Roll-ups of new data to BIA indexes are fast due to the high parallelism of the accelerator. Change runs are also fast because you no longer need to adjust transactional data after master data or hierarchy changes. Further, when the accelerator is deployed, BI compression is only needed in a few cases. The accelerator performs its own (technically quite different) compression of the data. The BIA compression reduces the volume greatly compared to a database (often by a factor of about five) and sometimes, for example, in the case of sparse data, reduces it dramatically.

2.3   Technical Impact

The insight that triggered the development of the SAP NetWeaver BI Accelerator is that sinking hardware costs and rising personnel costs have created a new opportunity for meeting the challenge posed by aggregates. The new opportunity is to calculate any aggregates required to answer a query during query runtime, in memory, without any delay for disk accesses. Solid-state memory is now inexpensive enough, and multiple processors running in parallel are fast enough, to make this the more reasonable strategy in many cases. Runtime aggregation dispenses with the need to devote skilled resources to the manual building, tuning, and updating sets of predefined aggregates.

2.3.1 The Aggregation Challenge

SAP NetWeaver BI offers prebuilt aggregates as a means to accelerate analytic queries and deliver acceptable response times to business users. Like the Info-Cubes from which they are built, aggregates are multidimensional cubes built from business data stored in relational records. Each record has a set of characteristics and one or more key figures, which are together represented as a row in a table. A subset of the characteristics forms a key for the record. The key is sufficient to identify the record when it is listed together with other records in a table.

At the center of each InfoCube is a fact table. This is a complete listing of all the records in the InfoCube. Around it, arranged in an extended star schema, are dimension tables, perhaps in addition a few supplementary tables, and at the periphery of the star schema, tables containing surrogate identifiers that represent master data as integer IDs. Section 7.4 offers a more technical description of the extended star schema. Subsets of the fact table obtained by deleting selected columns and aggregating rows with identical values for the characteristics in the remaining columns are the basis for aggregates.

Prebuilt aggregates accelerate query responses because they contain less information. Ideally, they contain only the information required to answer the query. In that case, the amount of data that has to be accessed, loaded into memory, and processed in the CPU is minimal. The art of building aggregates is to define them as small as possible so that they still suffice for answering the relevant queries.

In the SAP NetWeaver BI system, administrators can define and build as many aggregates as they need to support their users. Given an input query, the system recognizes whether aggregates are available to accelerate its response to the query and automatically selects the best aggregate for the task. The best aggregate is the one that contains the least redundant data.

The challenge for the SAP NetWeaver BI system administrator is to define and build such aggregates and then to maintain and update them. This is skilled work and hence a major cost driver.

For many companies, a proactive aggregates strategy is appropriate. System administrators study user behavior to target frequently asked queries and then build summary tables and database indexes for those queries. Because response times are improved only for the targeted queries, good judgment is required to satisfy users. Once the aggregates have been built, they have to be maintained regularly to stay synchronized with the InfoCubes from which they were derived.

To keep the work caused by creating new aggregates within bounds, a company following this strategy can adopt the management policy of restricting the number of users who are privileged to access the data and by allowing them to run only queries corresponding to predefined reports. Thus the company can ensure reasonable performance for the permitted queries at reduced cost, with the disadvantage that flexibility is also reduced. Companies following this approach need to accept a trade-off between flexibility and performance.

The basic problem with aggregates is that it is completely impractical to prebuild a set of aggregates that are optimally defined for all possible queries. As the number n of characteristics in an InfoCube increases, so the number of possible aggregates using those characteristics increases as 2 raised to the power n, that is, exponentially with n. The strategy of building more general aggregates, where each is reasonably appropriate for multiple queries, offers only limited help because it reduces the performance benefit that preaggregation offers for the queries. The problem with building too many aggregates is that they all have to be maintained.

The challenge for system administrators is to choose a strategy that optimizes their solution to these basic problems with aggregates. A dynamic business environment involves constantly changing InfoCubes and queries, so a proactive aggregates strategy needs regular review by skilled and experienced employees. This can be a viable approach as long as the data volumes involved remain manageable and the reports that need to be generated remain standardized.

The accelerator is designed to enable companies to dispense with all these enforced policies for managing aggregates. It offers the scalable power to analyze increasing volumes of data with maximum flexibility.

2.3.2 Services and Appliances

Much more business data than ever before is now online. This means the data is in a readily processed digital format, which makes it much easier for a company to extract the hidden value of that data for its own business operations. Making full use of this opportunity requires increased data warehousing capacity, which is the correct decision if the new business data is not to be wastefully discarded, and increased analytic capability, which is where the BI accelerator comes in.

A benign effect of the SOA revolution is that the need for expensive custom solutions is greatly reduced. Many companies can now meet many of their IT needs with preconfigured components, often known as appliances. As usually understood, an appliance is a hardware component with the software preinstalled so that it requires only minimal on-site configuration.

Understanding the rationale for an appliance approach is an integral part of understanding the accelerator value proposition. The benefits of delivering software as an appliance are like those of delivering software as a service. Both models make software easier to install and use. In effect, the appliance model is a way to deliver services behind a company's firewall.

The main difference between software on demand and appliances is that appliances are located on-site with the customer. The difference between a traditional on-site installation and an appliance is that the appliance has a largely preconfigured and preinstalled software stack. The vendor takes responsibility for the implementation, and the buyer configures the appliance by plugging in a network cable and opening up an interface.

The benefits of such appliances are convincing. For customers, they include the ability to avoid all the headaches of downloading, installing, configuring, monitoring, managing, securing, patching, and upgrading any open-source components that are packaged in the appliance. For SAP and the hardware partners, they include lower costs for customer support, quality assurance, and packaging of software containing multiple components.

A prepackaged appliance leverages the implementation best practices of SAP and the hardware partner and lets users focus on their business. By preinstalling the Linux operating system with the TREX code in the appliance, SAP and the hardware partners simplify versioning and patch management and reduce later support costs. For BIA customers, an appliance provides most of the benefits of a hosted SOA solution without the risk of sending sensitive business data, such as financials, credit card information, and employee data, outside the company firewall.

The essential point about appliances is not where the software resides but who takes responsibility for it and how productive it can be. Appliances are the next logical step on the journey to reducing IT costs and enabling more innovation.

For example, the functionality required to accelerate analytic processing on the SAP NetWeaver technology platform is well defined and clear in principle but complicated to implement and tricky to set up in practice. This is a classic case of a situation where everyone benefits from implementing the functionality as an appliance.

The benefits of appliance thinking are convincing. Functional code can be optimized for the hardware. The hardware specification of the appliance can be tailored exactly to suit the task, and the development effort for the appliance can be devoted to creating a finely tuned product. In the case of the BI accelerator, the result is a product that breaks through previous performance barriers.

2.3.3 An Inexpensive Solution

The BI accelerator is a logical and reasonable response to the enormous relative change in the price factors in the cost equation for data processing. As we saw, hardware costs have fallen dramatically in recent years (recall Figure 1.1), whereas the costs for skilled IT personnel have risen. This has created a new opportunity for meeting the challenge posed by aggregates, namely to calculate any aggregates required to answer a query during query runtime, on the fly, in memory. The time saved by avoiding delays for disk accesses more than compensates for the cost of installing multiple processors and many gigabytes of main memory in the hardware. In comparison with the rising cost of personnel resources, not only for IT staff but also for knowledge workers sitting waiting for their queries to execute, commodity processors and solid-state memory are now cheap enough to make this the correct strategy.

The BI accelerator is based on the SAP search and classification engine TREX ("T.rex"). This engine is technically a standalone component that is integrated in the SAP NetWeaver platform. It is not marketed as a separate product. The name TREX originally stood for text retrieval and information extraction, and the engine was originally developed for search over and within textual documents. While traces of these origins remain in the accelerator engine, the TREX ability to handle large volumes of structured data by means of massively parallel processing streams running on data held entirely in memory is fundamentally novel.

The accelerator uses the new TREX capabilities. However, it requires its own dedicated installation of TREX. A company that already has TREX installed in its landscape for search over text documents (for example in a Knowledge Management scenario) cannot simply reuse the TREX as an accelerator. The accelerator imposes special demands upon TREX, as the following thumbnail sketch of how it works may suggest.

The SAP NetWeaver BI system sends the data from an InfoCube to be accelerated to the TREX engine, which indexes the InfoCube tables to create a structure called a BIA index for that InfoCube. A BIA index is a compressed structure based on a redundant copy of the data from a BI InfoCube. The BIA index stores the data at the same level of granularity as the InfoCube. The BIA index is stored on the BIA appliance's dedicated local storage and is loaded either on startup or when required into the main memory (RAM), installed on the BIA blade servers. The TREX engine then uses the BIA index to answer any queries against that InfoCube that are forwarded from the SAP NetWeaver BI system to the accelerator. This involves joining the relevant table indexes from the BIA index together to put the requested information in the result sets. All this required the development of additional functionality above and beyond that implemented in TREX for text search.

The BI accelerator can be pictured as a standalone box sitting beside the SAP NetWeaver BI system and connected to it with a high-bandwidth SAP connection (see Figure 2.3). The box includes a file storage system with a capacity in the terabyte range to persist the BIA indexes, together with a rack containing a number of blade servers, each equipped with a number of processor cores and several gigabytes of RAM. The exact specification of the box is a matter for the hardware partners. The main SAP concern is that the sizing is correct and that the appliance is used in accordance with the licensing agreement. The main impact of the new box is to take query load off the database and reduce administration load on the BI server.

The BI accelerator creates highly compressed index structures from the InfoCubes. It does this not only to make efficient use of its memory resources but also to speed up the transfer of data from storage to memory and from memory to CPU. The indexes are normally loaded into memory on startup but can also be loaded as required to handle new queries. In cases where a large index has been split into parts, the BIA software then parallelizes the task of answering a query over all the available processor cores by allocating one part to each core and then merging the results from the split parts. The result is blazing performance, with typical response times in everyday work that are tens of times better than in a normally tuned SAP NetWeaver BI system relying on aggregates.

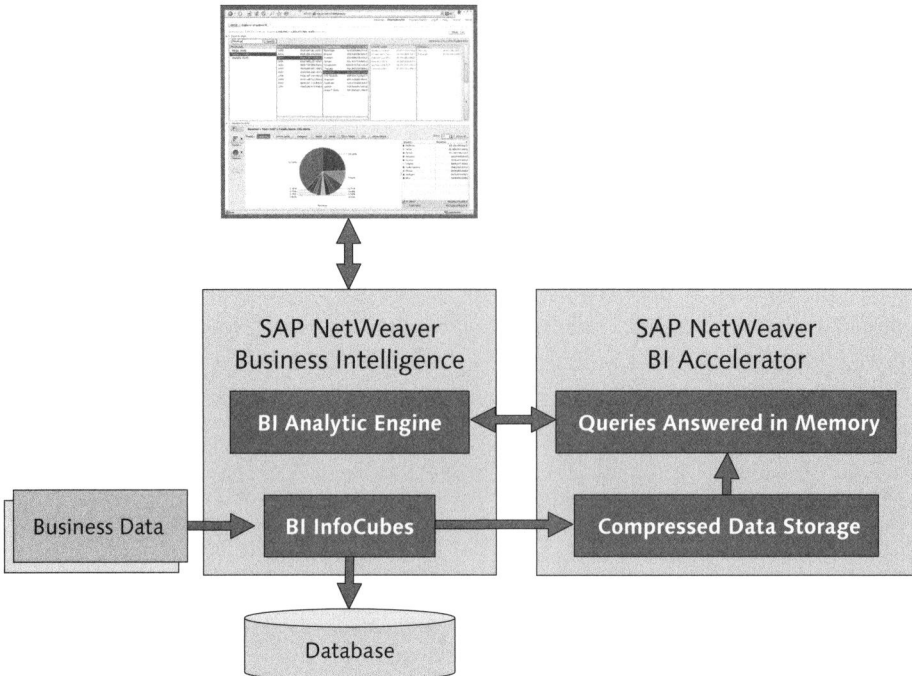

Figure 2.3 An Appliance Beside the SAP NetWeaver BI System

Once the accelerator appliance is up and running, users can call up sales data for their company's operations, aggregate the data, slice it and dice it, drill down anywhere for details, and expect exact responses in seconds or less every time, even with billions of records filling terabyte volumes on the database.

2.3.4 Ways to Respond to a Query

The concept for the BI accelerator is that it works as a backend appliance behind the SAP NetWeaver BI system and is transparent to the user, who may be unaware of it and notice only the improved performance. No additional user training or modeling efforts are required to benefit from the accelerator, and no special settings or tuning efforts are required for the BI system. So far as the BI system is concerned, the BIA index created by the accelerator for a given Info-Cube behaves just like a single all-purpose aggregate for that InfoCube.

In the BI system, an analytic query is answered using a strategy that depends on whether a BIA index exists for the query. In either case, the strategy is to ask a series of questions about the query until a "yes" answer is obtained. The BI system responds to the query using the method given by that answer. The strategy is used in any case where the answer to the query has not already been calculated in advance, as part of an information broadcasting policy, and goes as follows.

To answer a query without using the accelerator, the BI system goes through the following sequence of conditionals:

1. Is the answer still in the OLAP cache from having been recently calculated? If it is, the answer is returned. If not:

2. Does a suitable aggregate exist for answering the query. If so, the aggregate is used to calculate the answer. If not:

3. The BI system accesses the InfoProvider directly. This involves a disk access and is not quite so fast.

To answer a query using the accelerator, the BI system instead uses the following sequence of conditionals:

1. Is the answer still in the OLAP cache from having been recently calculated? If it is, the answer is returned. If not:

2. The BI system forwards the query to the accelerator. If the accelerator becomes unavailable, the BI system reverts to using aggregates, if any, and InfoProviders.

Using the BIA index is often faster than using an aggregate and always faster than accessing an InfoProvider.

2.4   Summary

SAP NetWeaver is a technology platform that can help an enterprise to leverage the new business opportunities arising from widespread adoption of SOA. SAP NetWeaver BI with Business Objects offers an end-to-end BI solution from data warehousing to the frontend that can help an enterprise make more effective use of its own accumulating wealth of business data. The SAP NetWeaver BI Accelerator enables an enterprise to give its users substantially more online analytic processing power than was possible until recently, to extract more value from that wealth of business data. Companies using such products as BusinessObjects Polestar can also benefit from deployment of the BI accelerator. The accelerator offers enhanced user productivity and reduced TCO. User productivity is enhanced by the increased performance and other features of the accelerator, and TCO is reduced compared with other strategies for boosting performance because the accelerator is highly automated and requires no manual tuning. In any scenario featuring large volumes of data, strict response time requirements, or unpredictable user queries, a company can benefit from deploying the accelerator. The accelerator is packaged as a preconfigured appliance, which allows companies to delegate responsibility for many lifecycle management questions to their hardware partners. The technology embodied in the accelerator is innovative, powerful, and easy to deploy in an SAP NetWeaver BI landscape.

3   Architecture

The SAP NetWeaver BI Accelerator performs query processing in memory, and memory is still expensive enough to be a scarce resource. Three basic design decisions were made at the outset of accelerator development, all intended to ensure that the accelerator makes efficient use of its memory resources when working with large indexes. The decisions were to make use of sophisticated compression for BIA indexes and to perform both horizontal and vertical data partitioning of InfoCube data tables.

Because the accelerator uses advanced mathematical compression techniques to reduce the size of BIA indexes, all the data from huge InfoCubes can be loaded into installed memory for fast query processing without disk access delays. Info-Cubes held on a database are stored with supplementary structures such as table indexes and aggregates that greatly increase the footprint of the data on the database disks. By contrast, the BIA indexes are compact and self-contained and have a memory footprint many times smaller. For example, data with a terabyte footprint on the database can often be handled within the memory of a BIA appliance with, say, 14 blades and 16 GB of installed memory per blade, even when allowance is made for the extra memory space required for temporary structures.

Horizontal data partitioning of tables allows parallel processing of the separate table rows over all the available blades in the appliance for both indexing and query processing. Using a preset threshold, the accelerator splits tables with many rows horizontally into a number of parts, normally as many as there are processor cores in the BIA landscape. The parts are then indexed in parallel on all the cores. When the indexes are later accessed for query execution, the parts are searched in parallel and the partial result sets merged.

Vertical data partitioning allows individual table columns to be loaded selectively into memory if necessary. The separate columns can be read from memory and cached individually by the processor cores to reduce the amount of data touched and the time needed to process it. Instead of pipelining entire table indexes through the cores, which is unnecessary if the query to be answered addresses only certain columns, the core reads only those column indexes that are required for the task at hand. By touching only relevant columns, the engine generates less data traffic on the blade and executes queries more efficiently.

Another basic architectural decision was to ensure that the accelerator is transparent for the SAP NetWeaver BI system. The effect of this decision is that both application developers and customer companies can use the same frontend functionality as before to enable their users to enjoy the benefits of the accelerator. Indeed the users need not even be aware that an accelerator is working at the backend. This decision for transparency greatly facilitates accelerator deployment in business scenarios requiring flexible access to InfoCube data, including scenarios that feature analysis tools provided by Business Objects, an SAP company.

To leverage these basic design decisions, the accelerator appliance implements the latest hardware paradigms such as blade server architecture for high scalability, low downtime, and minimal administration.

The primary value proposition for the accelerator appliance is that it can accelerate analytic query processing in all cases where queries would otherwise be answered by full table scans in the database. And it can do so with reduced TCO in comparison with an enhanced database solution. In consequence, other strategies for accelerating such analytic queries, such as building tuned aggregates, become unnecessary.

In terms of the SAP release strategy, the BI accelerator is available for SAP NetWeaver BI in all releases from 7.0 upward.

Several enhancements are planned for future versions of the BI accelerator. The accelerator functionality will be extended to accelerate query processing for other SAP NetWeaver BI InfoProviders besides InfoCubes and also to accelerate further analytic operations in SAP NetWeaver BI. Going forward, there is obvious scope for an all-purpose BI server that supports sophisticated analysis and reporting on any data in an attached data warehouse, including volatile transactional data.

The rest of this chapter is structured as follows. Section 3.1 introduces TREX and describes the TREX services that power the accelerator. Section 3.2 discusses the main features of TREX for ensuring high availability (HA) and describes backup and recovery scenarios for the accelerator. Section 3.3 discusses scalability features and sizing tools for the accelerator. Section 3.4 introduces the highly automated administration tools developed for the accelerator. Section 3.5 summarizes the chapter.

3.1   The Appliance: TREX Engine Inside

The SAP NetWeaver BI Accelerator is packaged as a standalone appliance that uses TREX engine software running on blade hardware. As such, it is relatively easy to integrate into an existing SAP landscape.

The accelerator appliance is positioned (logically if not physically) beside an SAP NetWeaver BI system and is connected to it with a high-bandwidth connection. The hardware includes a file storage unit with a capacity in the terabyte range and a rack containing a number of blade servers. Each blade runs a clone of a TREX engine. The BI system sends the data from an InfoCube to be accelerated to the TREX engine, which indexes the data to create a BIA index for that InfoCube. The BIA index is used to answer any queries against that data.

The internal workings of the accelerator are best explained with reference to the TREX architecture. This is defined by the TREX binaries, which are installed once on the BIA storage and then cloned to all the blades in the BIA landscape. Figure 3.1 shows the TREX services inside the accelerator.

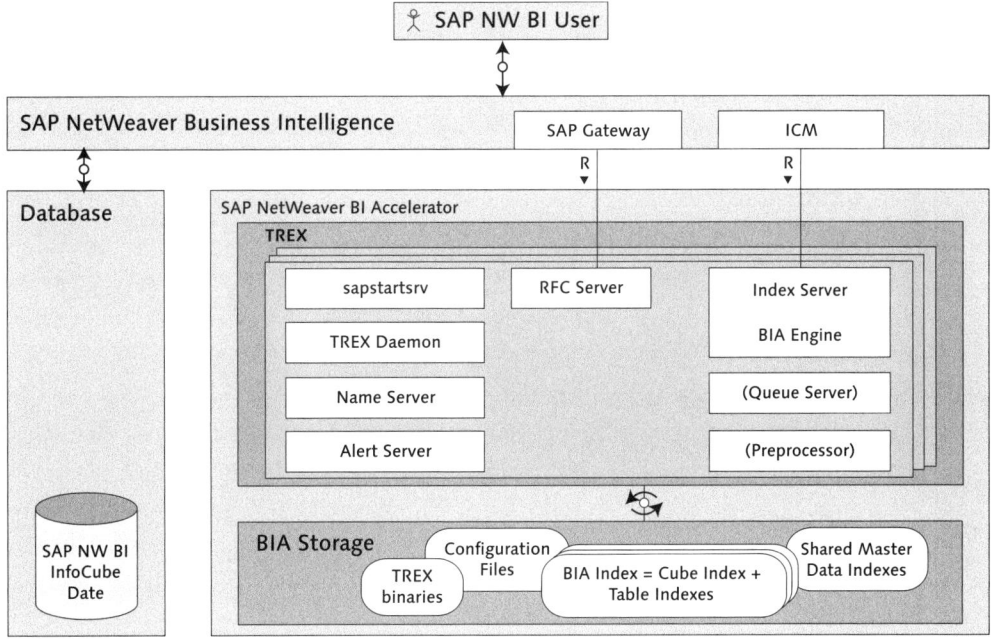

Figure 3.1 BIA Architecture with TREX Inside

3.1.1 Hardware Specification

The architecture of the BI accelerator is a new departure in the SAP world because it is packaged and marketed as a preconfigured unit. This has the benefit that the accelerator software can be optimized for a precisely defined hardware configuration to maximize performance and minimize the risk of compatibility and support issues. The accelerator software was developed in close technical cooperation with Intel, and is designed to run on standard Intel Xeon processors.

The selected hardware partners for the blade servers and file storage system and other hardware components of the BI accelerator are currently Hewlett-Packard (HP), IBM, Fujitsu Siemens, and Sun Microsystems. All four partners offer pre-tested standard configurations to meet the anticipated customer needs and all take responsibility for installing the BIA software on the hardware and delivering it to customer sites.

In all cases, the operating system for the SAP NetWeaver BI Accelerator is 64-bit SUSE Linux in the latest tested release (currently this is SUSE Linux Enterprise Server 10). A 64-bit architecture was chosen for its technical ability to address large volumes of installed memory (32 bits allow you to address only about 4 GB whereas 64 bits allow about 16 EB).

In the simplest deployment scenario, the accelerator appliance is positioned beside the SAP NetWeaver BI system (which may run on any combination of hardware and operating system supported by SAP) and connected to it with an RFC connection that must have a bandwidth of at least 1 gigabit per second (1 Gbps). The appliance contains a file storage unit with a capacity in the terabyte (TB) range, depending on the sizing, and a rack containing a number of blade servers, again depending on the sizing. Each blade server is typically equipped with two multicore Intel Xeon processors and either 16 or 32 GB of memory.

Once the BIA box has been installed and connected, operation can begin as follows. The SAP NetWeaver BI system sends the data from an InfoCube to be accelerated to the BIA engine, which creates a BIA index for the InfoCube in a preparatory indexing run. The BIA index is persisted on the BIA local storage system and loaded into memory, normally on startup. Any queries forwarded to the accelerator by the attached BI system are then executed by the BIA engine in memory.

3.1.2   TREX Client-Server Architecture

The SAP NetWeaver engine TREX is designed for client-server scenarios where TREX acts as a server responding to specific requests from a client system to perform such tasks as indexing or searching. On the client side, each application that communicates with the search engine integrates an SAP-internal TREX application programming interface (API), which provides access to TREX services. TREX offers two main APIs for use in application scenarios, which communicate via the languages ABAP and Java, respectively. To communicate with the accelerator, the BI system uses the TREX ABAP API.

The TREX software is modularized as a set of services, also known as server processes, that each performs a distinct task. The services communicate with each other using TCP/IP, and each service has its own configuration file.

The TREX daemon process starts the individual services. A configuration file called *TREXDaemon.ini* lists all the services that the daemon is responsible for starting.

3.1.3   Index Server and BIA Engine

The TREX index server plays the main role in TREX. It is responsible for indexing data and executing search requests on that data. The index server contains several specialized engines that perform the main tasks involved in executing indexing and search requests.

Within the TREX index server, the BIA engine is the heart of the accelerator. Based on the TREX attribute engine, which has the task of indexing the metadata that accompanies textual documents, the BIA engine is a powerfully extended service that enables TREX not only to index but also to aggregate large quantities of structured data. The BIA engine performs both the indexing of InfoCubes to create BIA indexes and the execution of query plans on those indexes to generate result sets for analytic queries.

The extension of TREX to handle structured data required a metamodel to specify the structure. The TREX metamodel represents BI InfoCubes in a form that TREX can work with (see Section 7.5.1). Starting with the extended star schema representation of an InfoCube as a set of joined tables, the metamodel codes all the information contained in the star schema as a set of lists that together reflect the logic of the join graph for the star schema. When the accelerator indexes an Info-Cube, it creates a logical cube index to hold this metadata.

To execute an analytic query against an InfoCube for which there exists an BIA index, the BIA engine uses the metadata in the logical cube index to create a query plan for the query (see Section 7.6). The query plan specifies which plan operations to perform to execute the query. Plan operations include elementary search, join, aggregation, and merge operations needed to assemble the required result set. Search operations find the requested attribute values, join operations join values from different column indexes to assemble result rows, aggregation operations aggregate rows with matching values, and merge operations merge partial result sets from the respective nodes that executed the query plan in parallel. The BIA engine then forwards the result set to the attached BI system.

Aggregation is the most time-consuming step, and the BIA engine runs a highly optimized and very fast aggregation algorithm. This patented algorithm minimizes not only the amount of data that is transferred on and off the processing cores but also the number of clock cycles required to build the result table. The algorithm is optimized for the hardware configuration, with its specific memory and cache architectures and its Intel chipsets, as well as for the data structures that make up the BIA indexes. This algorithm features almost linear scaling, so that response times increase gradually as the number of data records to be aggregated increases.

The BIA indexes are compressed using sophisticated integer coding techniques (see Section 7.3). A separate column index is made for each column in an Info-Cube table. If the cardinality of a column, which is to say the number of different values that appear in the column, is k, the values are represented by integers running up to k. These integers are represented using n bits, where n is the smallest integer such that $2^n \geq k$, or equivalently such that $n \geq \log_2 k$.

The individual attributes, or columns from the table indexes, are stored separately in memory. As a consequence, they can be accessed separately during query processing to minimize the amount of data that is cached or transferred to and from the processors. This approach differs from that used in databases, and it makes an essential contribution to the high performance of the accelerator.

The BI accelerator enables administrators to activate delta indexing to handle index updates. A small delta index beside the main index accepts updates so that updates do not need to be written immediately to the main index. Queries are executed against the main and delta indexes in parallel (see Figure 3.2). For some indexes in some circumstances, activation of delta indexing can improve the performance of the accelerator.

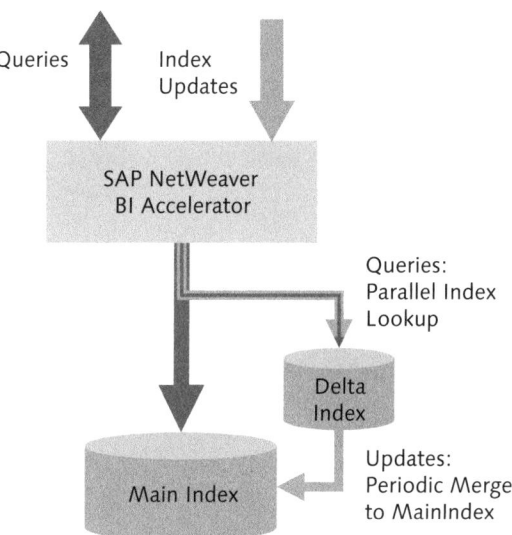

Figure 3.2 Delta Index Mechanism

The advantage of using delta indexes is that writing updates to the delta index is much faster than writing them directly to a main index. To ensure that the delta index remains much smaller than its main index, an alert check monitors the size of the delta index and triggers a message recommending a merge when necessary.

The disadvantage of using delta indexes is that query processing is more complex because both indexes have to be consulted in parallel, and therefore response times are slightly longer. For this reason, it is only worthwhile to activate delta indexing for an index that is very large (with hundreds of millions of rows) or receives frequent updates (many per day).

In the BI accelerator, both the main index files and the delta index files are written on the centrally attached storage.

3.1.4 Name Server

The TREX name server is the administrator process for an entire TREX landscape. The name server keeps track of which services are running, checks that they are all communicating with each other, and ensures that they receive the data they need to perform their tasks. The name server maintains a central configuration file called *topology.ini* that stores the key facts about the topology of the TREX landscape, including information about the available services, index allocation, task distribution, and so on. Administrators should not try to edit this file manually.

In an accelerator landscape, where a set of cloned TREX instances work together on neighboring blade servers, one of the blades hosts a single active master name server process that has exclusive write access to the topology configuration file and distributes read-only copies to the other name servers in the landscape.

In addition to administering the topology, the name server handles the load balancing of indexing and search requests. It distributes the indexes between the available hosts and coordinates the replication services. In most BIA scenarios, load balancing is not used for query execution because each BIA index is loaded only once in memory and only one (multithreaded) index server process can access its logical cube index to generate query plans. In exceptional scenarios, the logical cube indexes can be replicated between hosts to cope with very high query loads. The accelerator landscape can be configured for HA, as described in Section 3.2.

3.1.5 RFC Server

In most cases, communication between the accelerator's TREX services and the attached SAP NetWeaver BI system is routed through RFC servers. The SAP system sends requests to an RFC server via an SAP gateway. When a TREX RFC server is started, it registers at the gateways configured in TREX. The RFC server converts any requests that the attached SAP system sends via the gateway into a TREX-internal TCP/IP-based protocol and then forwards them to the appropriate TREX services.

As an initial step, before any connection can be established between SAP NetWeaver BI and TREX, the RFC destinations need to be defined on both sides. The setup of these destinations is highly automated. All that TREX needs is the usual SAP system data, such as user, password, client, system ID, and SAP system host name (see Section 4.2.2).

Internet Connection Manager

Communication between the accelerator appliance and the attached SAP NetWeaver BI system occurs primarily via the RFC server, but a further option has been implemented using HTTP. The Internet Connection Manager (ICM) offers a direct and often faster communication path between the SAP NetWeaver BI system and the TREX index server that avoids the potential bottleneck of an SAP gateway. Whether RFC or ICM is the better means of communication in a given customer scenario is difficult to decide. SAP will issue recommendations on this topic at a later date.

Like the RFC server, the ICM connects to the ABAP client of the application. When the application contacts TREX, an RFC call is first sent to the name server to get the address of the index server, then the ICM call is sent to the index server. The index server address is then cached in the application. The HTTP communication allows the application to transmit binary large objects (blobs) to the index server. The blobs are serialized into binary XML (in an SAP proprietary format).

For indexing calls, the ICM is used by default. It is installed automatically with the SAP NetWeaver Application Server (SAP NetWeaver AS) and is multithreaded to communicate with multiple SAP work processes. An HTTPS option for secure network communication via SSL is supported.

3.1.6 Alert Server

Whereas a BIA system's index servers, name servers, and RFC servers are indispensable both in principle and in practice, its alert servers are theoretically superfluous. However, alert servers are practically essential for monitoring and proactively checking the configuration and behavior of the system.

The alert server cycles regularly through a set of basic checks related to the operation of the accelerator (see Section 4.2.4). It checks for the availability of services, the consistency of indexes, RFC connection settings, and so on. For the BI accelerator, three sets of checks, called `Detect_And_Repair`, `hpa_1`, and `hpa_2`, are defined and activated by default. The administrator can reconfigure these check sets manually, or even include additional checks (which someone would need to create individually from scratch), although there is no need to do so for normal operation.

The administrator can also configure the alert server to send an e-mail notification, either in HTML format or as plain text, to one or more specified addresses. The alert server sends check results into the BI system, where they are displayed in the BIA monitoring transaction (see Section 4.1.1). Alternatively, alerts can be monitored using the CCMS infrastructure.

3.1.7 Additional TREX Servers

Three further TREX services, the web server, the preprocessor, and the queue server, are irrelevant for the BI accelerator scenario. To indicate their irrelevance, Figure 3.1 shows their names in parentheses. The services are used in the original TREX scenarios of text indexing and search. For completeness, it is worth describing them briefly.

Web Server

When TREX is used for text search, applications often communicate with TREX via HTTP. TREX is therefore equipped with a web server that offers a Java API to clients.

The BI accelerator does not use the web server. The ICM in the accelerator communicates via HTTP but does not invoke the web server to do so.

Therefore, the web server should not be installed when TREX is installed on the BIA hosts. If it were installed, it would only consume system resources to no purpose.

Preprocessor

In TREX, the preprocessor performs two main tasks. It performs the initial processing of textual documents before they are indexed in the index server. And, in cases where search requests are preprocessed, it does this, too.

As initial processing for the indexing of textual documents, the preprocessor fetches the documents to be indexed, filters the textual information from the document formatting information, and performs a linguistic analysis on the extracted text. As initial processing for text search requests, the preprocessor performs a linguistic analysis.

The BI accelerator does not receive requests formulated in natural language expressions. The accelerator does not invoke the preprocessor.

Queue Server

The queue server coordinates and controls the asynchronous indexing of textual documents. The trigger for indexing may be a numerical threshold of documents ready for indexing or a time schedule.

In an accelerator landscape, the attached BI system takes care of the scheduling of indexing requests. The accelerator appliance executes indexing requests immediately in massively parallel runs to maximize the speed of the process. The accelerator does not invoke the queue server.

Other Servers

TREX contains additional servers that are not shown in Figure 3.1. For example, the TREX Cruiser is a web crawler that can be programmed to crawl selected sites regularly in the background. Also, within the index server, there are additional engines, such as a text search engine and a text mining engine. All these services remain unused in SAP NetWeaver BI scenarios involving the accelerator. SAP does not support the use of TREX in an accelerator landscape for text search, even though the relevant TREX services are installed in an accelerator instance.

3.1.8   Attached Storage

The accelerator appliance concept includes more than TREX. The TREX blade hosts have a shared view of the BIA file hierarchy. This file hierarchy resides on hard disks in a storage solution certified by the hardware partner. At present, a range of storage solutions is supported, depending on the hardware partner, in all cases featuring redundant arrays of inexpensive disks (RAID) to increase availability. A generic Network File System (NFS) solution (see Figure 3.3) can be realized in various ways, and different hardware partners offer their own variants. The Oracle Cluster File System (OCFS, included in the Linux kernel) and General Parallel File System (GPFS, as offered by IBM) solutions (see Figure 3.4) offer different features. If you want to find out more about the current status and relative advantages of the approaches, you should contact the hardware partners.

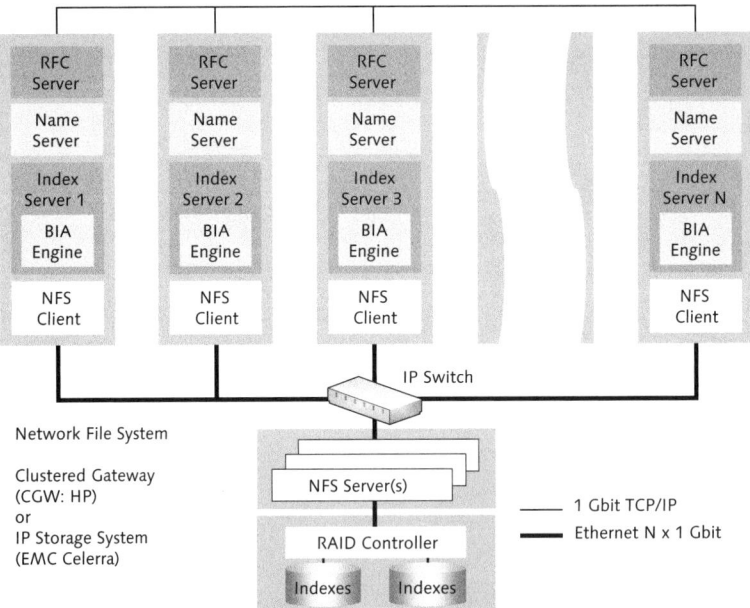

Figure 3.3 Attached Storage, Generic NFS Solution

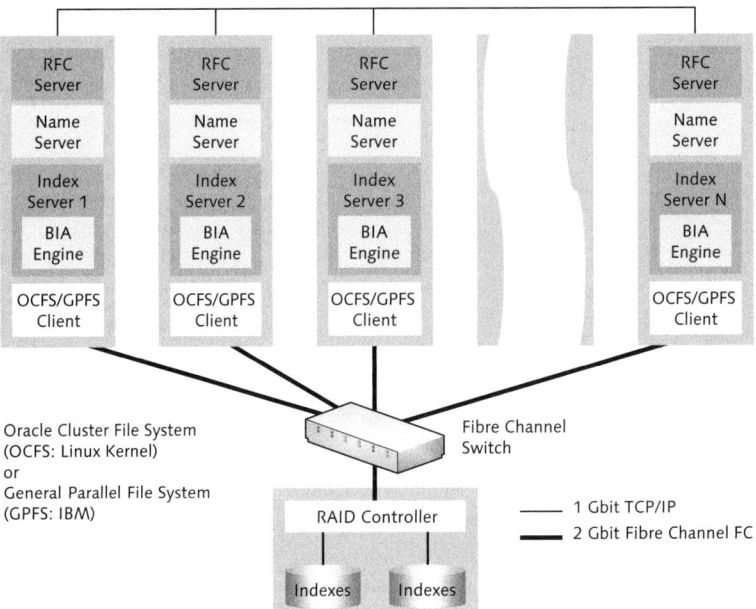

Figure 3.4 Attached Storage, OCFS or GPFS Solution

3.2   Availability

Corporate users of the SAP NetWeaver BI Accelerator demand a high level of availability, which is reflected in the basic architecture of the accelerator and its underlying software.

The TREX engine integrates mechanisms for assuring the highest possible level of availability (HA) of its services despite the occasional occurrence of errors. An important mechanism for maximizing availability is the ability to configure backup blade servers in the BIA landscape. If a blade fails and a backup blade is configured, the indexes that were loaded on the failed blade are loaded onto the backup blade, which then takes over the role of the failed blade in the landscape. The software allows any number of blades to be configured as backup, to realize any level of hardware redundancy, up to one dedicated backup blade per active blade. A dedicated backup blade can be preloaded with the relevant indexes and therefore offer fast failover.

3.2.1   Tasks Requiring Planned Downtime

Most regular tasks can be performed without downtime. However, there are still a few circumstances where an administrator will need to schedule some downtime.

Software Upgrades and Updates

The main source of planned downtime for an accelerator installation is the need to upgrade and update the software regularly. An upgrade to a new release is a major event and generally brings new functionality or visible enhancements to existing functionality. An update is the more frequent event of installing a code revision and is generally more limited in its effect. The procedure in both cases is to download the upgrade or update file from SAP Service Marketplace into a BIA directory and then run the installation script from there. The script stops the accelerator, replaces the binaries for the installation, and starts the accelerator again.

The application of a BIA revision replaces the binaries for the entire BIA installation. Bia updates, which are small changes to the coding, are not released as part of the standard SAP support packages but separately, as TREX revisions. For this reason, administrators need to check SAP Service Marketplace regularly for BI accelerator revisions in addition to any checks they make for other SAP upgrades and updates.

Each TREX revision script performs a full installation. The binaries are located centrally in the BIA storage, and all blades in the BIA landscape share access to them. This both facilitates updates and ensures that all the blades can communicate with each other because if one blade were updated separately from the others, then errors could arise. Only TREX instances of exactly the same version can work correctly together in a landscape. Therefore, downtime must be planned to install updates.

Other Maintenance Tasks

Many maintenance tasks for a BI accelerator can be performed one blade at a time, to ensure that the accelerator continues to be available to the BI system. An administrator can reassign the indexes on a blade to other blades in the landscape, then stop the blade and perform maintenance such as installing more memory or applying operating system patches. When the maintenance is completed, the blade can be restarted and the indexes reassigned. If the index reassignment was to a blade designated as a backup, the subsequent reassignment after restarting the maintained blade is automatic.

To facilitate working one blade at a time, the accelerator is designed to accept blades with different hardware specifications in one and the same landscape. For example, as long as the hardware vendor supports the combination, in a rack containing blades with dual-core processors and 16 GB memories, you can add new blades with quad-core processors and 32 GB memories. So hardware upgrades can be implemented incrementally during routine operation.

In any such maintenance scenario, the administrator should check whether the procedure can be carried out safely one blade at a time. If it can, the total downtime caused by the index reassignment for each blade in turn can be limited to a much shorter period than if the entire accelerator were stopped, maintained as a whole, and then restarted.

3.2.2   Redundancy and Backup Servers

In an accelerator landscape, redundant master servers and optional backup servers increase availability levels.

Automatic Restart of Services

To start a TREX instance, you start the TREX daemon process, which then starts all the other services. Those services are the name server, index server, RFC server, and alert server, and they are registered in the TREX daemon configuration file *TREXDaemon.ini*. The daemon is event triggered. If a TREX service stops, the operating system raises an event. The daemon reacts to the event by trying to restart the service. If the attempt fails, the daemon tries again and keeps trying until it times out (with a default timeout at 300 seconds). On timeout, it logs an error in its trace file.

In a business scenario involving the BI accelerator, several TREX instances run in parallel in a BIA landscape. However, the attached BI system abstracts from the landscape details and addresses the accelerator system as a single instance. This has the useful consequence that the BIA landscape can organize itself without causing unintended side-effects on the BI system. We say that a process is unavailable if it no longer responds to requests, even if the process itself is still running. Two main mechanisms exist and can be appropriately configured in case either a TREX name server or a TREX index server process becomes unavailable.

Master Name Servers

Each active host in the BIA landscape runs its own TREX name server. One of these name servers is designated as first master, another as second master, and another as third master. The term *master* is an inheritance from the TREX text search engine architecture and refers to the industry-wide master/slave approach. In this approach, a master server process has write access to the assigned index files, whereas a slave server process has only read access to the files.

There is only one active master name server in a given BIA landscape. The other two master name servers serve as backups for the active master. The active master process maintains the global configuration file *topology.ini* and is the only process that can write changes to that file.

Each master name server runs a watchdog process to ping the other master name servers regularly (every few seconds) and raises an alert if either of the other masters fails to respond. For example, consider a case where the first master name server currently has the role of active master. If this first master fails to respond when pinged, the second master takes over and becomes the active master, and if the second master also fails to respond, the third one takes over. In case of a failure of the third master, the first master name server takes over again. Once any one of the three master name servers becomes the active master, it retains this status until it either stops or ceases to be available for any reason. This has the consequence that in the case of a switchover, there is no automatic return to the master name server that was previously in control once it becomes available again. However, there is no need for such a return of control because any of the TREX name servers in the landscape can equally well be defined to be any of the three masters.

In the extremely unlikely case that none of the three master name servers responded, there would be something severely wrong with the installation, and it would be wise to contact SAP service support.

Backup Modes for Index Servers

During the operation of an accelerator system, it can happen that a host (that is, a blade server) fails. In that case, the TREX index server process that was running on that host no longer responds, and all requests referring to indexes assigned to this index server return an error to the user instead of the expected result.

In a multihost BIA landscape, each index server is the core service for managing all the indexing and search requests for a specified set of indexes. Any changes and searches on the specified indexes are performed by this index server, either alone in the case of a small index or as active master for the other servers in the case of a large index that has been split into multiple parts. Therefore, if a host fails and its index server becomes unavailable, the indexes assigned to that server are not available either. Because the TREX active master name server regularly pings all the hosts and services in the BIA landscape, it knows in seconds that the service is unavailable and either generates an alert message or, if a backup server has been configured, reassigns the affected indexes to the backup.

TREX supports a number of ways for backup blades to be configured in the landscape. If a blade fails and a backup blade is configured, the indexes that were loaded on the failed blade are loaded onto the backup blade, which then takes over the role of the failed blade in the landscape. New query load is then routed to the surviving blades. TREX allows any number of blades to be configured as backup, to realize any level of hardware redundancy, up to one dedicated backup blade per active blade. A dedicated backup blade can be preloaded with the relevant indexes and therefore offer fast failover. As long as the failover situation does not occur, the TREX services on the backup blades run idle.

The BI accelerator offers the following backup modes:

▶ SHARED
One blade is configured to serve as backup for all master blades, so that if any one master fails, the backup can take over.

▶ DEDICATED
One backup blade is configured for each individual master blade, so that twice as many blades are installed as are active at any given time.

▶ MULTIPLEXED
One backup blade is assigned to several master blades, so that if any one master in that set fails, the backup takes over.

▶ MUTUAL
Each master blade is backup for another master, so that every blade has a dual role, serving both as master and as backup for another master.

Figure 3.5 illustrates these modes. An administrator can select a backup mode with a single click from a drop-down menu in the TREX standalone administration tool (see Figure 5.3 in Chapter 5).

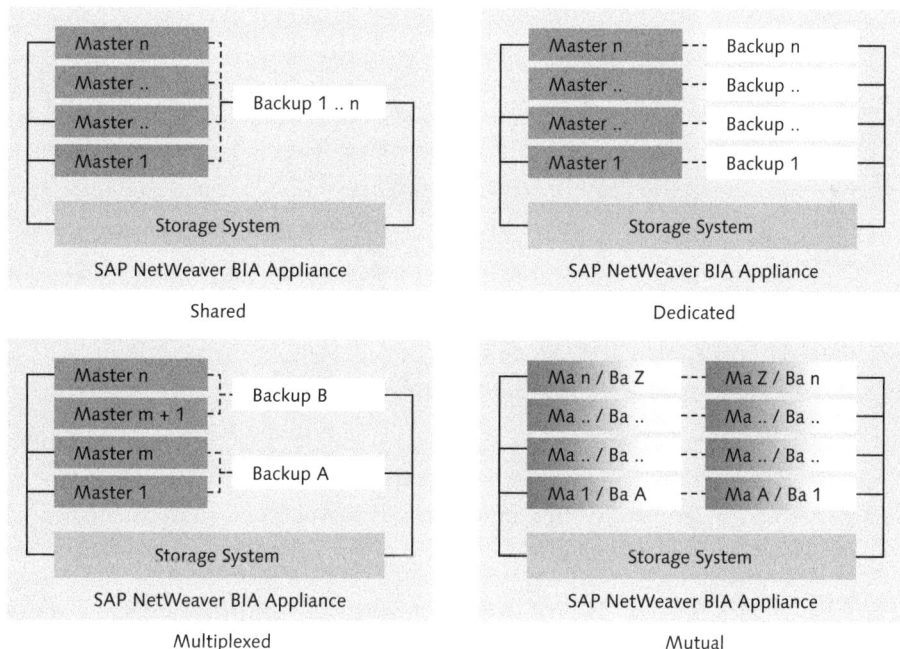

Figure 3.5 Four Ways to Configure Backup Servers

3.2.3   Backup and Recovery

A backup and recovery strategy protects your system against data loss and enables you to restore the system to a correct and consistent state. The main part of any such strategy is to back up the system at regular intervals by copying all its data to another storage medium. If your system becomes damaged, you can reload the stored duplicate to restore the system.

If data loss occurs in either SAP NetWeaver BI or the BI accelerator, you will need to recover and restore this data to its most current state within the accelerator. To do this, you can either re-index all the relevant InfoCubes or perform a BIA recovery. You may also need to perform a BI database recovery.

Depending on the age of the backup snapshot, the BIA backup and recovery process is a faster way to make the data available again than performing a complete re-index of the InfoCubes.

BIA backup and recovery is controlled from the BI system via the BIA monitoring transaction. The recovery is always in reference to the current status of the BI system. A file export (either a 1:1 backup copy or a storage snapshot) is triggered from the BI system and executed on the TREX index server. So if the BIA indexes were deleted from within the BI system, the recovery process would not restore these deleted indexes and you would need to rebuild them.

BIA backup and recovery only takes into account the index data and not the BIA software installation itself. If installation data is lost, instead of trying to repair it manually, it is both easier and more secure to reinstall the complete landscape, which takes less than 30 minutes, and then restore the indexes.

If BIA indexes are deleted in the BI system, you first need to restore the BI system to the state before the indexes were deleted and then perform a recovery. To do this, you need to have an BIA backup available that is older than the BI backup. If you do not have one, a full re-indexing is required.

SAP NetWeaver BI database backups are not synchronized with BIA backup snapshots. Database backups are synchronized with the BI system only, so restoring the accelerator triggers re-indexing of any data that was changed in the BI system after the BIA snapshot was made.

Snapshot creation is triggered from the BI system but performed by the TREX backup server. The TREX daemon starts the TREX backup server on every BIA host, but only one of the started servers is active, while the others are on standby.

The active backup server runs on the first of the backup blades (in alphanumeric order of host names). If no backup blade is defined, it runs on the blade hosting the active master name server.

To create a BIA backup, the TREX backup server can either copy all the BIA index data 1:1 to a storage directory or trigger the storage hardware to create a storage snapshot. Storage snapshots are faster to make and need less disk space.

If a copy is made, the backup data is persisted either on the accelerator storage or on any mounted external storage that is specified. All snapshots are stored there. The BIA backup snapshots can be integrated into an existing backup infrastructure.

The BI accelerator backup and recovery mechanism enables you to recover the accelerator in a variety of data loss scenarios. Four typical scenarios are described as follows.

Scenario 1

As Figure 3.6 shows, here an accelerator problem requires a recovery of the BIA indexes to the current state. It is the simplest of the scenarios in which you would otherwise have to re-index all the data.

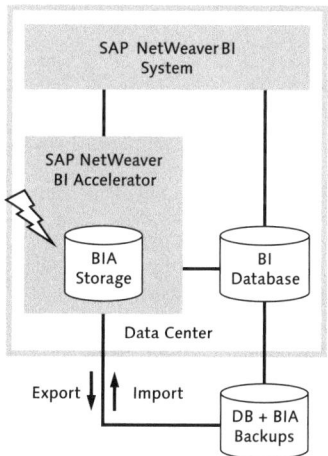

Figure 3.6 Recovery, Scenario 1

There are three main steps:

1. Fix the problem with the accelerator.

2. Select the snapshot you want to recover in the BIA monitor.

3. Start the BIA recovery process. The job executes immediately.

For details, see Section 5.2.7.

Scenario 2

Figure 3.7 shows a case where a problem with BIA 1 requires transferring operations to BIA 2, which is initially idle and may be located in a separate data center.
The transfer is initiated as soon as the failure happens, and its exact course
depends on the hardware setup. Once the transfer is completed, you can select
the snapshot you want to recover and start the recovery from the BIA monitor, as
in scenario 1.

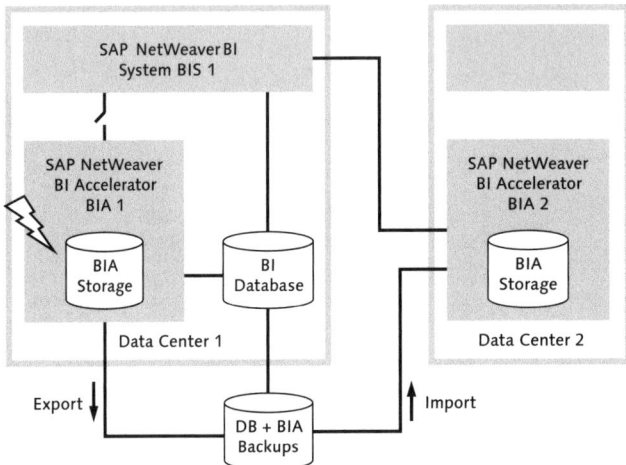

Figure 3.7 Recovery, Scenario 2

Scenario 3

In Figure 3.8, an accelerator problem requires transferring operations to BI landscape 2, which is initially idle and located in a second data center. The transfer is
initiated as soon as the failure happens, and its exact course depends on the hardware setup. Once the transfer is completed, you can select the snapshot you want
to import to BIA 2 and start the recovery from the BIA monitor in BIA 2.

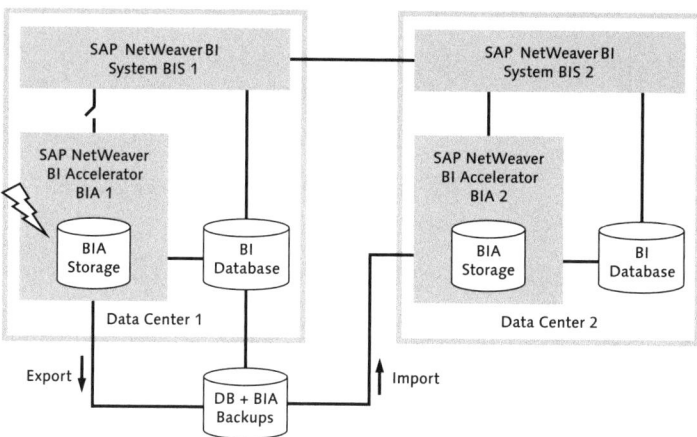

Figure 3.8 Recovery, Scenario 3

Scenario 4

The other case covered is shown in Figure 3.9. Here a database problem requires a point-in-time recovery of the database. First you need to recover the database to restore the BI system to a point in time. Then you need to import a snapshot that is older than the point in time to which the database has been recovered and start the BIA recovery process from the BIA monitor, as in the previous scenarios.

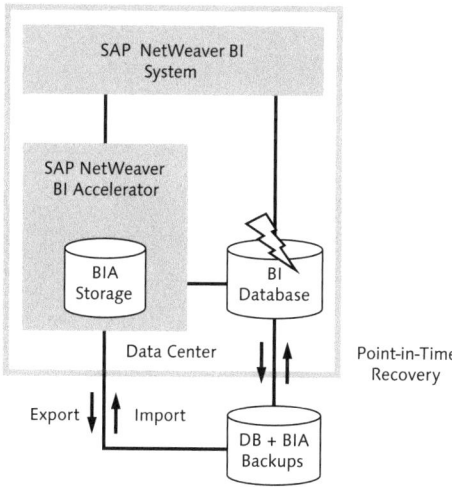

Figure 3.9 Recovery, Scenario 4

SAP tests in a typical landscape have shown that the BIA backup and recovery process is faster than a re-index in all scenarios described previously. The BIA monitor lets you simulate a recovery in advance to find out whether it would be faster than a complete re-index.

3.2.4 Disaster Tolerance

Disasters include such scenarios as gross human error, natural hazards such as fire or flood, software problems such as corrupt files or malicious software (malware), and hardware problems such as drive crashes or power failure. A disaster tolerant computing system can continue to run applications and access data following a disaster.

The practical approach to achieve disaster tolerance is to deploy redundant hardware, which may be either passive or active. In a passively redundant system, standby components are activated to take up the load of a failed component. In an actively redundant system, multiple processors running concurrently compute through the failure of a component.

Fault tolerant systems can be built from commodity servers to provide fast resumption of service following certain kinds of disaster. A disaster tolerant system provides the same high level of service as a fault tolerant system even if an entire site fails.

In case of a disaster, a "switchover" solution in addition to the BIA backup and recovery solution enables you to resume accelerator service after a brief period of downtime. During the downtime, the system load is transferred from the failed system to a redundant system at a second site. Ideally, the transfer is accomplished by simply switching from one site to the other.

Switchover complements backup and recovery in cases where service level agreements require availability within a short time following a disaster. Naturally, it cannot ensure recovery from disasters involving data loss or data corruption that affect both sites.

The essential feature of a switchover solution for disaster recovery is the availability of a second data center, with the same hardware specification as the first data center, which uses database mirroring to maintain redundant copies of all the relevant business records. The technical challenge here is to ensure that the state of the mirrored data at the moment of failover is exactly the same as that of the data in the first data center, just before it was stricken by disaster.

Two general approaches are possible here, active-passive and active-active. The active-passive approach is to set up a separate BIA landscape in the second data center, as shown in Figure 3.10. If the blade hardware is kept on cold standby, the switchover involves firing up the blades and loading the indexes from the mirrored storage, then restoring the last good state of the disaster-stricken system from the logs. This process is more than just flipping a switch. If the second BIA landscape is on hot standby, the switchover is faster.

This approach is based on storage mirroring via synchronous write from the active to the passive side for the accelerator storage. The switchover is complicated, at least in present implementations, because it requires the two BIA landscapes to have different host names. Performing a switchover involved running a script to change the host names and file paths in the topology file. For details of more recent disaster tolerant projects, contact the certified hardware partners.

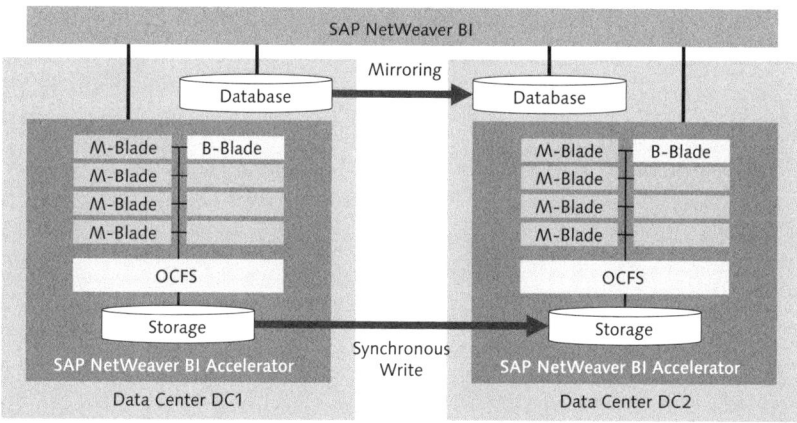

Figure 3.10 Disaster Tolerant Solution: Active-Passive Approach

The active-active approach is to set up the BIA blade servers in the second data center as part of the same BIA landscape as the blades in the first data center, as shown in Figure 3.11. All the blades in the second data center are configured within the BIA landscape as backups in dedicated mode, where each backup blade is mapped to the corresponding master blade in the first data center. To enable all the blades to function as a single landscape, there needs to be a high-bandwidth connection between the two data centers.

In this approach, there is a single virtual storage attached network (SAN) with a single mount point for both storage systems, and the file system uses GPFS. This simplifies the BIA storage mirroring. Hardware partner IBM has implemented this approach successfully as a fast switchover solution for productive BIA installations.

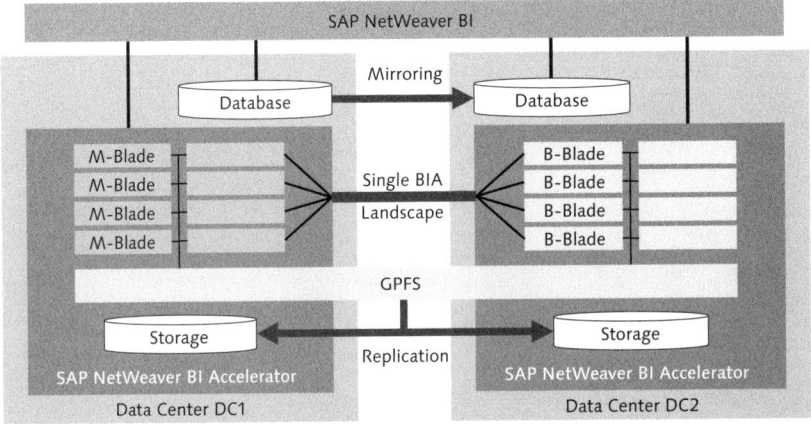

Figure 3.11 Disaster Tolerant Solution: Active-Active Approach

In both approaches, the mirroring for the BIA storage is independent of the database mirroring for the attached BI system, which may be implemented using a standard Linux cluster approach, for example. Because the accelerator in each data center communicates with the database (original or mirrored) only via the BI system, which may or may not be replicated redundantly, it imposes no particular constraint on the database mirroring technique used.

3.3 Scalability

The SAP NetWeaver BI Accelerator is designed for scalability. The accelerator runs on blade servers, and all the BIA services are cloned on each blade in the BIA appliance. Blades can be added to or removed from the landscape freely, without loss of service on the other blades, except that any queries running on a blade when it is subtracted will return an error.

Companies who deploy the accelerator can start by installing as many blades as they need to meet their initially foreseen capacity requirements, and simply purchase more blades, and clone TREX to the new blades, as required later. For this strategy to be effective, the server cabinet, enclosure, or rack for the blades needs to have the capacity to allow additional blades to be inserted without more ado, and in the initial sizing, it is wise to consider whether such free capacity should be available from the start.

The accelerator runs on a set of blade server hosts. All the BIA services are cloned on each host. One name server is designated as active master and controls the landscape as described in Section 3.2.2. The name servers on the other hosts are ready to take over if the first master goes down (see Figure 3.12). Each index server is the master for zero or more indexes. Any index server designated as backup is ready to become the master for any index assigned to a master index server if the master index server fails, and the backup takes over its function.

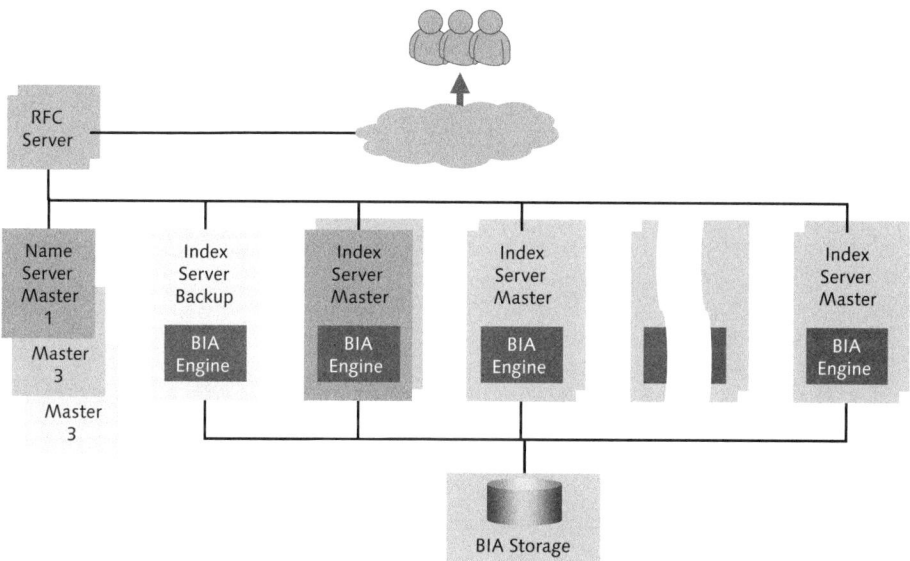

Figure 3.12 Scalability of the TREX Architecture

3.3.1 Vertical Partitioning

The BI accelerator partitions tables vertically into separate columns and indexes the columns separately. Each column index corresponds to a separate view attribute or key figure and can be accessed individually in memory, independently of the other column indexes. This pays off at least twice:

▸ Consumption of data bus bandwidth between memory and processor is reduced because during the execution of a query, only the column indexes that are relevant to that query need to be touched.

▸ Utilization of CPU resources is better because smaller data volumes are pipelined and cached, and processing those volumes is faster.

3.3.2 Splitting Indexes

The BI accelerator creates small column indexes as single flat files. Large indexes are automatically split into as many parts as there are CPU cores in the BIA landscape. This splitting enables TREX to load each index part into the memory of a different blade, so that each blade has one part of the index, and the load generated by using that index is shared equally between the blades.

The optimal size threshold for splitting indexes is strongly dependent on the customer scenario. There are two main advantages of splitting large indexes:

▸ Indexes that are too large for the memory resources of a single blade can be created and loaded in memory, as long as each split part is small enough to fit into the memory on one blade.

▸ Splitting facilitates CPU load balancing because queries can be executed separately and locally on each split part.

There is one disadvantage:

▸ Partial result sets extracted from split parts need to be merged before return to the user.

It is difficult to balance these advantages and disadvantage in advance, and test results obtained using typical indexes and queries can at best suggest locally or approximately valid threshold values.

The default index splitting threshold value is preset at 100,000,000, where this value represents the product of the number of columns and the number of rows in the table to be indexed. An administrator can change the threshold value quite easily in the TREX standalone administration tool (see Section 5.1). However, we recommend that this threshold be left unchanged unless an expert has advised changing it because the effects of changes on indexing and query runtimes are not easy to predict. Because each change requires re-indexing very large tables, the runtime cost of a poor choice of threshold is too high to allow casual experimentation.

3.3.3   Cloning BIA to New Blades

The BI accelerator was designed from the outset with scalability in mind. All the TREX services that implement the BIA capabilities are cloned on each blade server host in the BIA landscape. The architecture of a BIA installation is such that blades can be added to or subtracted from the landscape freely, without interrupting the services on the other blades (again with the proviso that any queries running on a blade at the time it is subtracted will return an error). If a blade is subtracted from the landscape, either due to a hardware failure or because an employee has pulled the blade from its rack, the active master name server monitoring the landscape registers the fact and routes new calls to other blades. Section 4.4.1 describes the cloning process in more detail.

3.3.4   Sizing and Size Restrictions

In the early stages of planning a BI accelerator implementation, you need to decide which InfoCubes you wish to accelerate and determine how big the cubes are or will become. You need this information for the sizing of the accelerator appliance.

The recommended approach is to make BIA indexes for all your InfoCubes. This can appear costly up-front, but the performance gain, the load reduction on the database, and the time saved in the nightly load window can quickly offset the costs. By sizing the accelerator for all your InfoCubes at once, you avoid the complications of scaling up your installation only after you have confirmed the value proposition for your deployment.

Some customers may prefer a staged deployment strategy where they start by indexing only those InfoCubes that have queries for which a dramatic response time improvement can be expected. These are the InfoCubes whose query statistics show a large amount of time spent in the data manager or are queried from management cockpits or dashboards. These InfoCubes show the most dramatic benefit from acceleration. Once the customer has proved the case for accelerator deployment on the basis of experience with those InfoCubes, the staged deployment can continue. Assuming the sizing is correct, the customer can proceed to index the remaining InfoCubes.

The accelerator appliance can be ordered in any size from three blades (two plus a backup) up to well over a hundred, depending on the needs of the business scenario in question and on what the selected hardware partner can deliver. The BIA software sets no particular size restriction. As experience with the hardware and software grows, it seems likely that ever larger configurations will be successfully deployed.

To investigate the scalability of the BI accelerator, SAP and IBM launched Project Jupiter in 2007. This was a joint effort to conduct large-scale scalability tests of the SAP NetWeaver BI Accelerator on an IBM infrastructure. For further details, see Section 6.1. The results demonstrate that the accelerator can meet the needs of the largest companies.

For sizing the appliance to match the deployment scenario, SAP offers a BIA sizing report that takes as input the number, size, and structure of the InfoCubes that you wish to index as well as the query throughput that needs to be supported. The report then calculates the appliance hardware specification in terms of storage and memory capacity and number of CPU cores that would be required for the scenario.

SAP NetWeaver BI Accelerator Sizing

For companies that have already deployed SAP NetWeaver BI, SAP Note 917803 explains how to estimate memory and disk space sizing for the SAP NetWeaver BI Accelerator.

As the note explains, program `zz_biamemconsumption_bw3x` analyzes a set of InfoCubes and calculates the memory consumption of their BIA indexes. The program can run in SAP BW releases 3.0+.

Before running the program, list the InfoCubes to be analyzed. Because shared master data tables are also analyzed, it is better to analyze any InfoCubes that share tables together. Then select from the following parameters:

▶ `P_DETAIL`: All the InfoCube data is analyzed, which may take a very long time.

▶ `P_SAMPLE`: Only part of the data is analyzed. This is faster but it reduces accuracy.

▶ `P_NOVIEW`: This option does not use the fact view of the database. This reduces accuracy.

▶ `P_FAST`: This is the fastest option but is also the most inaccurate.

▶ `P_ATTR`: This option outputs an additional list of all fields for each fact view.

The program estimates the memory space consumed by the BIA indexes for the selected InfoCubes. To estimate the actual memory consumption for a production system, including space for temporary files, multiply the calculated storage requirement by 3 and multiply the calculated main memory requirement by 2.

The results are only guidelines for sizing an accelerator solution.

For new implementations, the SAP Quick Sizer can give a first, approximate estimate of the hardware capacity required.

3.4   Minimized Administration

The SAP NetWeaver BI Accelerator was designed to minimize the need for routine administration. It features automated monitoring, configuration, optimization, and self-repair, and therefore needs very little administration for such a complex product.

Some hardware-dependent administration is still necessary for the appliance. Depending on the service level agreement with the hardware partner, certain more technical tasks that require specialist knowledge, such as operating system patching, can be performed by the hardware partner.

Any normal administrative tasks that need to be performed manually can be performed comfortably via the SAP transactions described in Chapter 4 (see Section 4.1).

Any more specialized tasks that require deeper interactions with the TREX engine in the BI accelerator can be performed with the TREX standalone administration tool described in Chapter 5 (see Section 5.1).

Other actions may be required on a more infrequent basis. These include fundamental reviews of sizing, service levels, and data modeling, and are best performed with or by SAP consultants.

3.5   Summary

The SAP NetWeaver BI Accelerator is based on TREX, and the code for a full set of TREX services is stored in the BIA file hierarchy. When the BIA blade servers are up and running, a cloned TREX instance runs on each of the blades to form a BIA landscape. Each blade has name server, index server, RFC server, and alert server processes running.

The landscape is controlled by an active master name server running on one of the blades. Backup master name servers on two other hosts regularly ping each other and the active master name server, and stand ready to take over if necessary.

On each blade, the index server contains the BIA engine that creates BIA indexes and executes BI queries. An RFC server on each blade handles communication with the attached BI system. On each blade, there is also an alert server, which cycles through a configured set of checks and generates an alert if an error condition arises.

Availability is ensured up to high levels by provision for redundant backup blade servers and by tools for backup and recovery that support usage of a second standby data center for disaster recovery.

Scalability is designed into the accelerator from the outset. The accelerator features near-linear scaling over a wide range of usage scenarios and can be scaled incrementally by adding blade servers. To date, the largest fully tested configuration includes 140 blades (Project Jupiter).

The BIA landscape runs with a high level of autonomy, so that manual administration tasks are kept to a minimum.

4 Administration

This chapter is a relatively practical guide to accelerator administration. It should be especially helpful for an administrator in a company that already has an SAP NetWeaver BI installation and is either considering deployment of the SAP NetWeaver BI Accelerator or is just about to introduce it.

There are three main sets of administration tasks that need to be performed in a BI accelerator installation:

▶ Initial tasks arise as soon as the accelerator is installed and need to be completed before the deployment goes live.

▶ Regular tasks need to be planned in advance and then scheduled to run regularly during routine production operation.

▶ Occasional tasks need to be performed from time to time, as and when the occasions arise that prompt them.

For more detailed and up-to-date information, check SAP Note 883726 regularly. This is the central note for the SAP NetWeaver BI Accelerator. See also the latest version of the Technical Operations Manual for SAP NetWeaver BI Accelerator.

This chapter is structured by the tasks. Section 4.1 introduces some of the most useful transactions for BIA administration. Section 4.2 describes initial tasks, Section 4.3 considers regular tasks, and Section 4.4 describes some occasional tasks. Section 4.5 summarizes the chapter. We start with the following brief overview of administration tasks.

Like relational aggregates, accelerator indexes are redundant downstream data sources that are used to improve query performance. For this reason, hierarchy and change run processes and processes for rolling up data are like those for aggregate maintenance. However, the accelerator is configured for parallel processing and can therefore perform these routine maintenance tasks much more quickly than a typical database can perform corresponding tasks on sets of precalculated aggregates.

In SAP NetWeaver BI, when you load new data packages into an InfoCube, these are not immediately available for reporting. To fill a BIA index or an aggregate with the new data from the InfoCube, you first have to roll up the new data. Once it has been rolled up, the new data can be used in the execution of queries. Because BIA indexes look like aggregates to the BI system, the roll-up process chain is the same whether the system has an accelerator attached or not. However, because there is only one BIA index per InfoCube, the process is much faster for an accelerator.

Like aggregates, BIA indexes are affected by changes to master data. They are also adjusted by attribute change runs. Again, the process chain for a change run is the same whether or not an accelerator is in use.

The BI accelerator enables you to activate delta indexing for any BIA indexes or their constituent tables that are sufficiently large (hundreds of millions of records) or frequently updated (at least daily) to benefit from the activation.

The BI accelerator plans and prepares for index reorganization and actively suggests one as soon as this would bring a sufficiently large benefit, but it does not actually reorganize the indexes without a manual intervention. This is because the reorganization causes a brief interruption of service, and an administrator can best decide when this interruption may cause the least disturbance to users.

As described in Section 3.2.2, one master name server is responsible for landscape topology, ensuring high availability, and replication of index and other data within the BIA landscape. Each blade in the BIA landscape has its own name server, which is a local clone of the active master and serves the local host. The master name servers ping each other regularly, and if the active master goes down, the next master on the list takes over. The topology information is persisted on the attached storage system.

Within each cloned BIA instance, an alert server cycles regularly through a set of checks and triggers a warning or an error message if preconfigured thresholds for any checks are exceeded. The alert messages are fed to the monitoring tools and can be sent automatically as e-mails to anyone you choose. This and other affordances built into the accelerator can ease your work as an administrator considerably.

4.1   Main Administration Transactions

The administration tools available for the SAP NetWeaver BI Accelerator are sufficient to ensure that all routine tasks can be accomplished easily, and almost all tasks can be performed within SAP transactions. The main transactions for this purpose are:

▶ The BIA monitor RSDDBIAMON

▶ BIA index maintenance via the Data Warehousing Workbench (DW Workbench) RSA1

▶ The BIA index maintenance Transaction RSDDV

▶ The BIA index check and repair Transaction RSRV

▶ The TREX administration tool TREXADMIN

4.1.1   The BI Accelerator Monitor

The standard BIA monitoring transaction is RSDDBIAMON. The BIA monitor is the primary tool for the technical administration and maintenance of the BI accelerator and provides an instant overview of its current status. It is worth taking the time to get to know it well.

The monitor also offers a detailed, technical overview of the hardware, BIA services, any trace files that exist, and the BIA indexes. However, the BIA monitor does not support maintenance at the logical level of the InfoProvider. The usual SAP NetWeaver BI transactions are available for that purpose.

The BIA monitoring transaction opens as shown in Figure 4.1. The BIA CHECK RESULTS panel on the left side of the screen displays the results of the BIA alert server checks on three tabs. If the checks reveal problems, the system automatically proposes appropriate actions.

The most basic task for the administrator of a BIA landscape is to make an overall status check from the BIA monitor, so the monitor opens with SUMMARY tab on top. The status display shows:

▶ A green (square) icon if the status is OK

▶ A yellow (triangular) icon if there are messages or warnings

▶ A red (round) icon if there are errors for the status

With status yellow and red, the system usually displays an action that can fix the problem. If the proposed action can be started from the BI system, you can execute the action from the screen area Execute Actions.

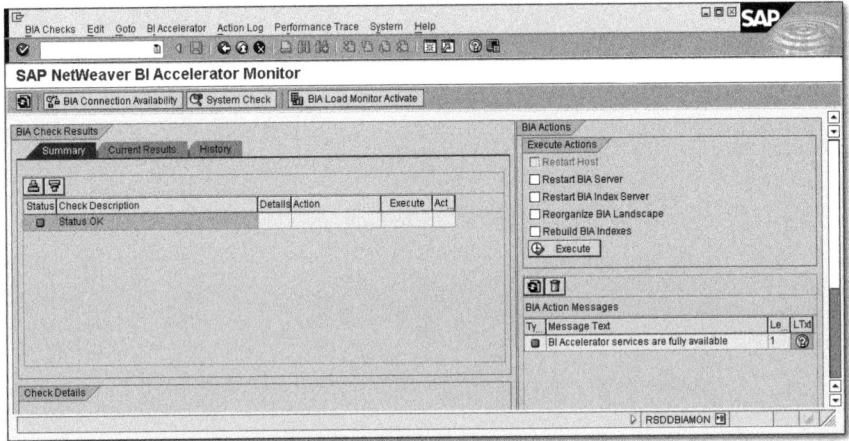

Figure 4.1 BIA Monitor, Initial View

Figure 4.2 shows the monitor with tab Current Results selected.

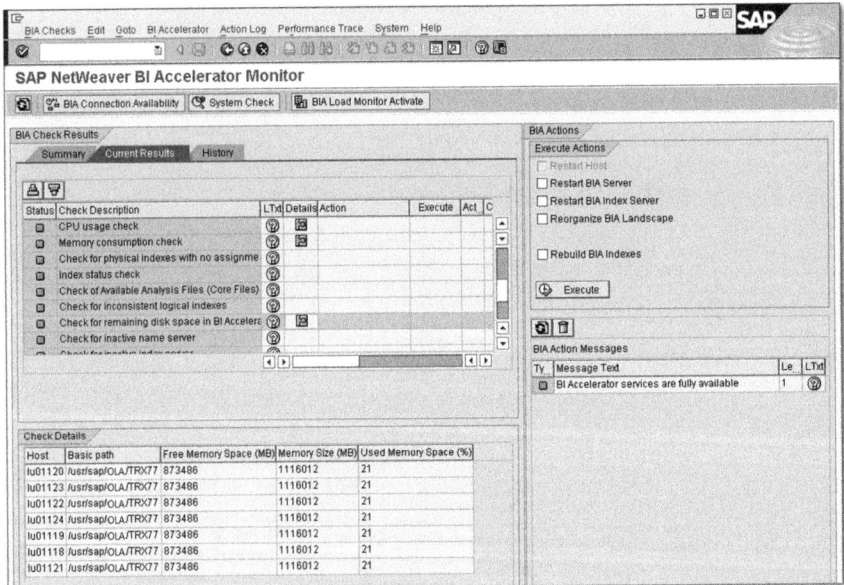

Figure 4.2 BIA Monitor, Current Results Tab

Tab CURRENT RESULTS displays the current results of the consistency checks that were performed. The status of each check is indicated by a green, yellow, or red icon. The system displays general information about each check: the length runtime of the check (in seconds), the date and time at which the check was started, and the check set within which the check was started.

The repair actions proposed in the display invoke BIA functions that can be used to fix the problems. You can start the action from the screen area EXECUTE ACTIONS.

For each action, you can display an explanatory long text by choosing the question icon. If details are available for a check, you can call them by choosing the details icon in the DETAILS column. The system displays the details in the CHECK DETAILS screen area.

For each check, you can display an explanatory long text in the LONG TEXT column by choosing the question icon. If details are available for a check, you can call them by choosing the details icon in the DETAILS column. Again, the system displays the details in the CHECK DETAILS screen area.

The HISTORY tab (see Figure 4.3) shows the results of previous runs for the BIA consistency checks so that you can track developments or changes in the results. You can specify the age of the history displayed when you configure the alert server (see Section 4.2.4).

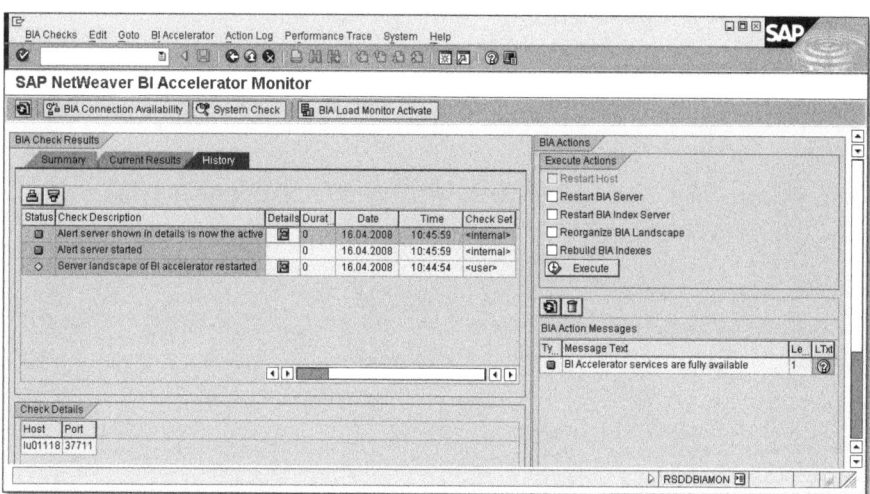

Figure 4.3 BIA Monitor, History Tab

The system displays general information about each check: the length of the check (in seconds), the date and time at which the check was started, and the check set within which the check was started.

For each check, again, you can display an explanatory long text in the LONG TEXT column by choosing the question icon. Because this information is not current, the system does not propose actions.

The lower-left panel CHECK DETAILS can display the details of any check for which a details icon is shown on the tab above. For example, if problems are listed with BIA servers, you can display the names of the affected servers here.

In the BIA ACTIONS screen area, you can execute the most useful actions to resolve problems with the accelerator. Here you can execute actions that can be started from the SAP NetWeaver BI system but not ones that would require direct access to the accelerator. The monitor displays a flag beside any proposed actions.

Recall that on the CURRENT RESULTS tab, the system proposes actions for check results that have status yellow or red. If these are actions that can be executed from the BI system, you can execute them directly from the BIA ACTIONS screen area.

Because some of the actions have potentially disruptive effects, the system performs an additional authorization check for the actions. The check is performed at two levels, one affecting the global settings for the accelerator and the other specific to certain InfoProviders. For further details, see SAP Note 1156093.

In the EXECUTE ACTIONS screen area, the BIA monitor collects all the available actions. It activates the checkbox if the action can be started from the BI system and displays a flag alongside any proposed actions.

Given the appropriate authorizations, the BIA monitor supports the direct execution of the following actions:

▶ RESTART HOST
This action restarts the entire BIA system. Because it can disrupt productive operation, this action is deactivated by default.

▶ RESTART BIA SERVER
This action restarts all the BIA servers and services (including the name server and index server).

► RESTART BIA INDEX SERVER

This action only restarts the index servers (and not the name servers).

► REORGANIZE BIA LANDSCAPE

If the BIA indexes are unevenly distributed over the BIA server landscape, this action redistributes responsibility for indexes more evenly between the BIA servers. The alert server prompts you to trigger reorganization if this is recommended.

► REBUILD BIA INDEXES

This is not a simple action like the others but a substantial program. If a check discovers inconsistencies in the indexes, you can use this action to delete and rebuild all the BIA indexes. This is a drastic action to take and can cause many hours of unavailability for user requests.

The actions RESTART HOST, RESTART BIA SERVER, and RESTART BIA INDEX SERVER are hierarchically related. If the host is restarted, the server is automatically restarted so that this action no longer has to be started explicitly. And if the BIA server is restarted, the BIA index server is automatically restarted. So if you select a higher-level option, the system automatically sets the indicator for the lower-level selection boxes and deactivates them for the selection.

The log display in the BIA ACTION MESSAGES screen area shows information about the processes in the BIA monitor.

If the system reads status information (from check results), it writes this to the log. For example, a log entry might be: STATUS INFORMATION READ FROM BIA.

Where appropriate, the messages are displayed with a status (green, yellow, red). If a question icon is displayed, you can also choose it to display an explanatory long text by choosing the question icon explaining the message. You can refresh the log display with the REFRESH button in the toolbar directly above the message. And you can delete the messages in the log by choosing the trash button beside it in the toolbar.

The toolbar above the BIA CHECK RESULTS panel offers the following functions:

► The BIA CONNECTION AVAILABILITY button activates an RFC availability test to check the availability of the BIA servers via RFC from all the application servers in the BI system (recall that each BIA blade hosts its own RFC server). If you click it, you (should) instantly get a result like that shown in the lower-right panel in Figure 4.3. In the case shown, the BIA services are fully available.

▶ The SYSTEM CHECK button can be used to trigger an extensive system check that you can run if you have any reason to doubt that everything is okay (see Section 4.2.1).

BIA Monitor Menus

The menus at the top of the BIA Monitor screen offer a wide range of useful actions.

The BIA CHECKS menu offers the following options:

▶ BIA AVAILABILITY
Same action as the toolbar button.

▶ SYSTEM CHECK
Same action as the toolbar button.

▶ SCHEDULE E-MAIL NOTIFICATION
Schedules an e-mail broadcasting an overview of the summary and current results of the BIA alert server checks (see Section 4.2.4).

The GOTO menu offers the following options:

▶ ANALYSIS OF BI OBJECTS
Shows screen for analysis and repair of BI objects (Transaction RSRV, see Section 5.2.6).

▶ BIA INDEX MAINTENANCE
Shows screen for maintaining aggregates and BIA indexes (Transaction RSDDV, see Section 4.2.3).

▶ TREX ADMINISTRATION TOOL
Starts Transaction TREXADMIN, tab SERVICES, skipping the initial RFC connection screen.

▶ CONSISTENCY CHECKS
Opens the BI Accelerator Data Consistency Check Center (see Section 5.2.2).

The BI ACCELERATOR menu offers the following options:

▶ EXECUTE ACTION
Same action as the screen button.

▶ BIA LOAD MONITOR ACTIVATE
Same action as the toolbar button.

▶ INDEX CHECKS
  See Section 5.2.2.

▶ INDEX SETTING
  See Section 5.3.5.

▶ INDEX INFORMATION
  See Section 4.2.3.

▶ MAINTENANCE FUNCTIONS

  Offers the following further options:

  ▶ DELETE ALL DATA FOR BI ACCELERATOR: Deletes all BIA indexes and other data and returns the accelerator to its initial configuration. This is an extremely drastic action. An information box warns you of the consequences and asks you to confirm.

  ▶ BACKUP AND RECOVERY: Shows the BIA backup and recovery screen with all relevant information and options (see Section 4.3.3).

The ACTION LOG menu offers the options of refreshing and deleting the action messages shown in the lower-left part of the monitor screen. These options are the same as those offered by the buttons directly above the action messages.

The BIA Monitor offers more, but we shall describe the rest as we describe the relevant tasks and topics.

BIA Monitor Access

You can access the BIA monitor either directly, by running Transaction RSDDBI-AMON, or indirectly. You can access it indirectly either from the Data Warehousing Workbench (DW Workbench, Transaction RSA1) or from Transaction RSDDV.

Alternatively, you can monitor the accelerator using the central alert monitor (CCMS monitoring, Transaction RZ20). This enables you to monitor an entire SAP NetWeaver BI landscape centrally, with the accelerator alongside other systems (see Figure 4.4).

The information and the results that you can find in the BIA CHECK RESULTS screen area of the BIA monitor are displayed in the CHECK RESULTS area on the SUMMARY and CURRENT RESULTS tabs.

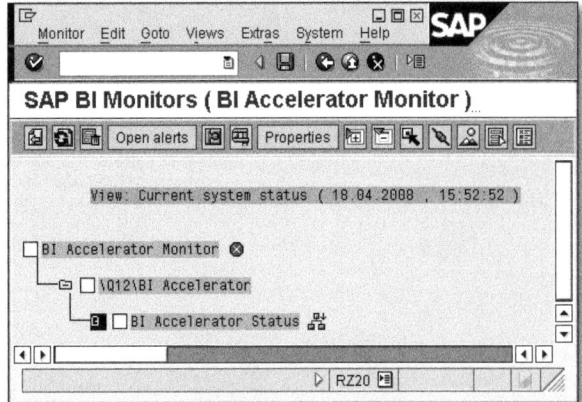

Figure 4.4 Transaction RZ20, BI Monitors

For more information about connecting the BIA monitor into the CCMS monitoring framework, see SAP Note 970771.

4.1.2 Data Warehousing Workbench

You can access the BIA monitor from the DW Workbench (Transaction RSA1). To display the BIA monitor from functional area ADMINISTRATION, in the navigation pane, choose MONITORS • BI ACCELERATOR (see Figure 4.5).

4.1.3 BIA Index Maintenance Transaction

SAP NetWeaver BI Transaction RSDDV is the standard transaction for the maintenance of BI aggregates and BIA indexes. Figure 4.6 shows the initial screen.

If you click the BIA INDEXES button, a list of all the BIA indexes in the system is displayed. If you select an InfoCube and then click BIA INDEX, the BIA Index Maintenance Wizard is started. The wizard is described in Section 4.2.3.

4.1.4 BIA Index Check and Repair Transaction

SAP NetWeaver BI Transaction RSRV is designed for the analysis and repair of BI objects (see Figure 4.7). Among the tests listed are both elementary and combined checks for the BI accelerator. You can select and run the checks in this transaction, as described in Section 5.2.2.

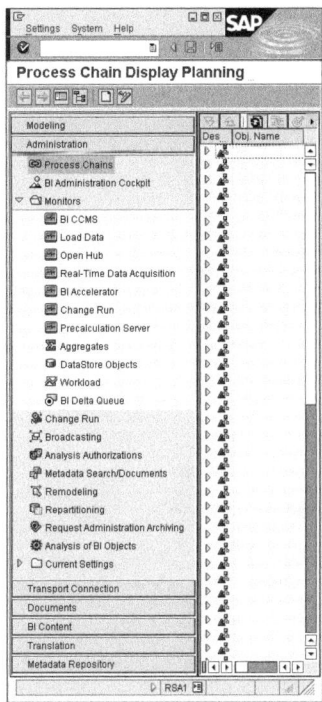

Figure 4.5 Transaction RSA1, Monitors

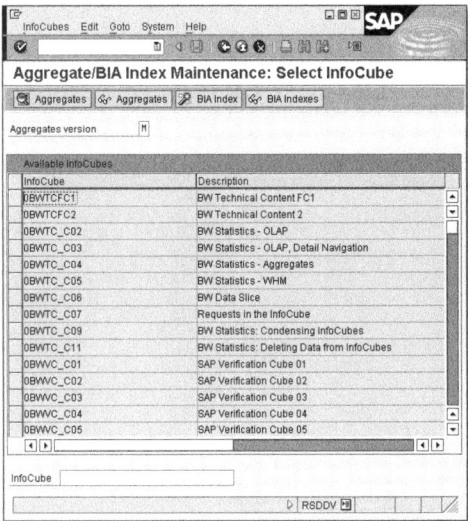

Figure 4.6 Transaction RSDDV, Initial View

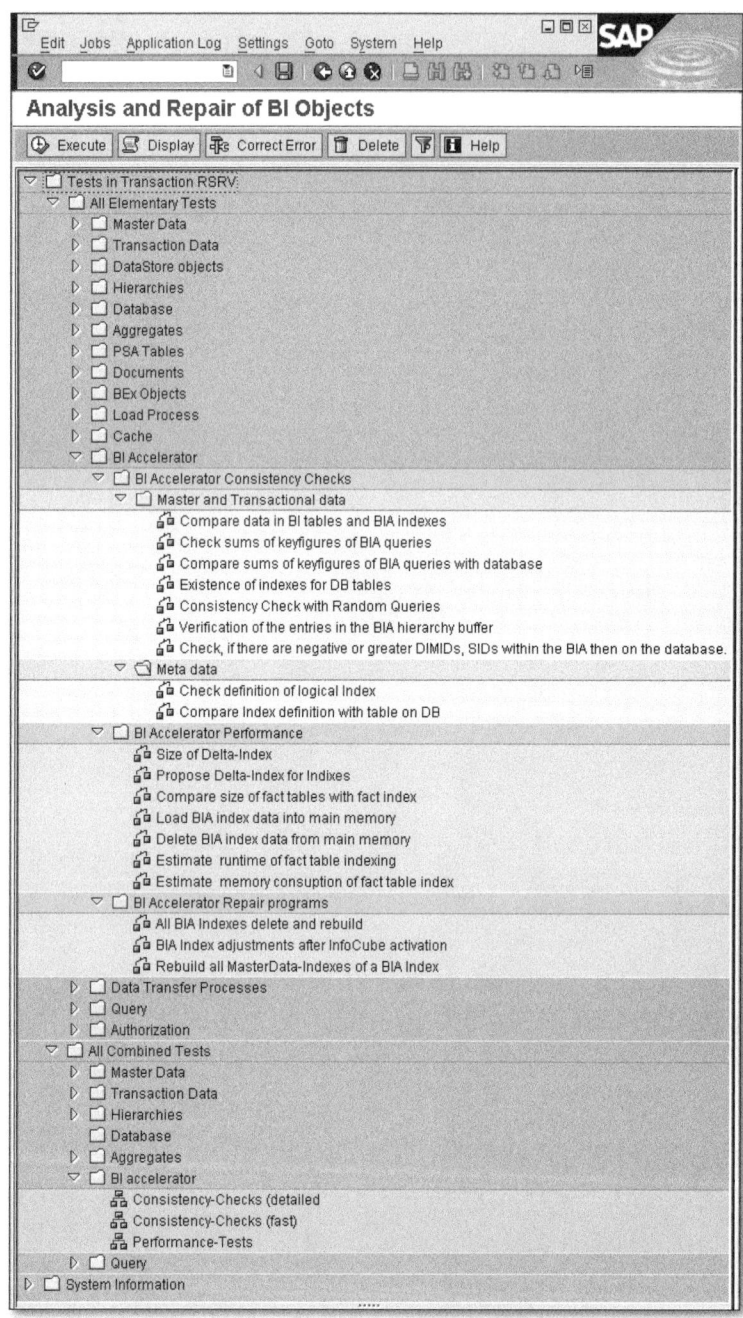

Figure 4.7 Transaction RSRV, BI Accelerator Checks

4.1.5 TREX Administration Transaction

The primary transaction for all dealings with the TREX engine at the heart of the accelerator is TREXADMIN.

If you start Transaction TREXADMIN directly, before you can see the details, you first need to enter or select the RFC connection to the accelerator and execute. Figure 4.8 shows the tool once a connection has been entered. Here the SUMMARY tab is displayed.

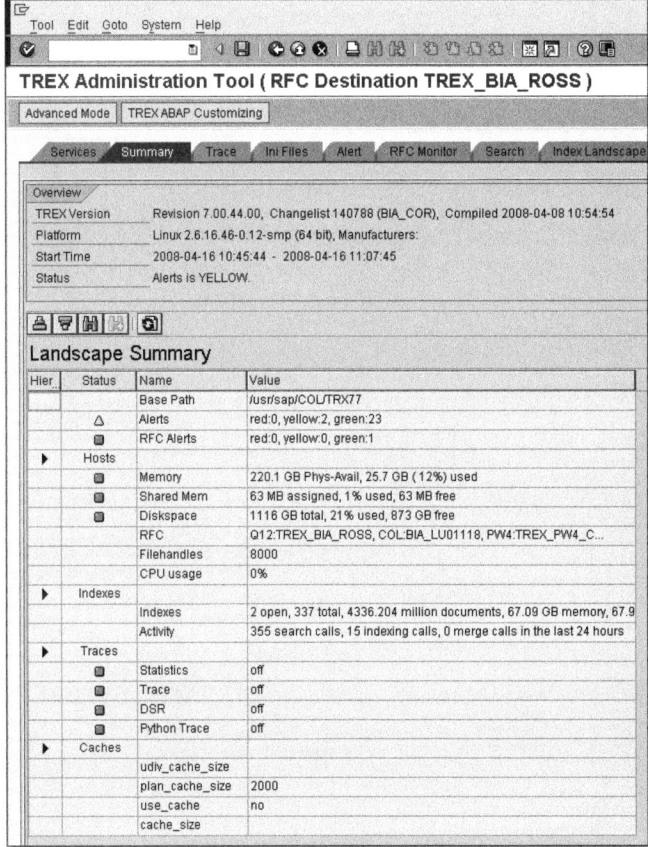

Figure 4.8 Transaction TREXADMIN, Summary Tab

You can also start Transaction TREXADMIN from the BIA monitor. To do so, in the BIA monitor, choose GOTO • TREX ADMINISTRATION TOOL. This displays the SERVICES tab (see Figure 4.9).

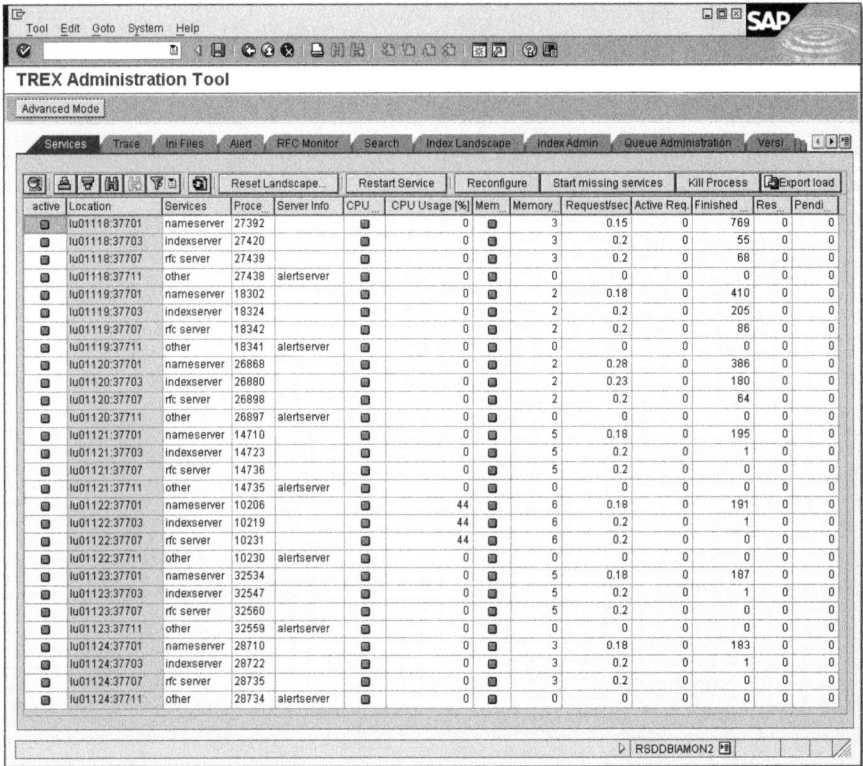

Figure 4.9 Transaction TREXADMIN, Services Tab

4.2 Initial Tasks

The SAP NetWeaver BI Accelerator appliance is preconfigured by the hardware partner, who installs the BIA software and connects it to the SAP NetWeaver BI system.

When the hardware partner installs the appliance at the customer site, a separate subnet of the company's local area network (LAN) must be available to connect the appliance physically to the SAP NetWeaver BI system. The connection must have a bandwidth of at least 1 Gbps (gigabit per second) and must be configured for the exclusive use of the BI accelerator (see Figure 4.10).

An additional management LAN may be used to administer the accelerator appliance, and this LAN may be connected to the main company LAN because any bandwidth limitations on the management LAN are unlikely to affect the performance of the accelerator.

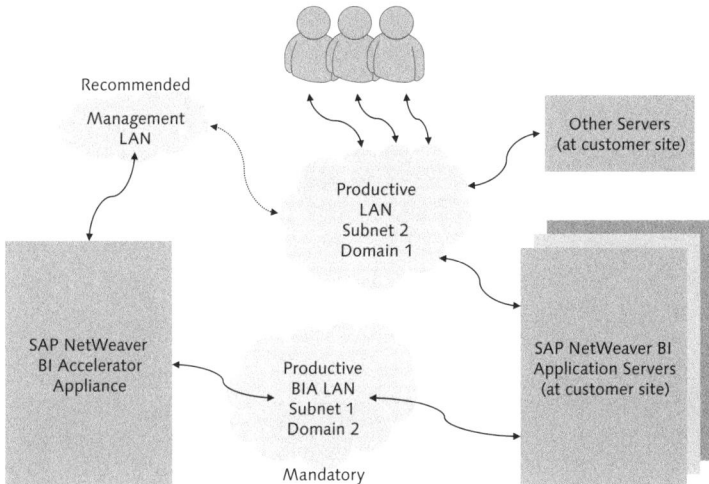

Figure 4.10 Dedicated BIA Subnet

4.2.1 Delivery and Installation

If you are the receiving company's BI administrator, we recommend that you use the following information as guidance during the handover of the accelerator appliance from the hardware partner.

The hardware partner is responsible for installing the accelerator on your company site, connecting it to the network, and running a system check.

BIA System Check

The BIA system check is an extensive and fully automated check designed to ensure that the basic hardware and software prerequisites for successful BIA operation are met. You can start the BIA system check from the BIA monitor (Transaction RSDDBIAMON). To do so, click the SYSTEM CHECK button or choose BIA CHECKS • SYSTEM CHECK.

The hardware partners who deliver your BIA appliance should run this system check both on the bare box before they install the BIA software and on the preconfigured box after they have installed the BIA software. For the bare box, the check is available as a Python script, `checkBIA.py`, which runs in a command shell under Linux. In both cases, the check ensures that the basics are right from the outset.

As a useful troubleshooting option, you can deploy the BIA system check independently of SAP NetWeaver BI. To do so, simply download and run the Python script `checkBIA.py` as explained in SAP Note 992064.

As the receiving company's BI administrator responsible for the accelerator, you should run the check at handover to convince yourself that all is well. The check can take several minutes to run and produces an extensive log display as output (see Figure 4.11), so be prepared to wait awhile and then read the output carefully. If the check results are good, you are ready to go.

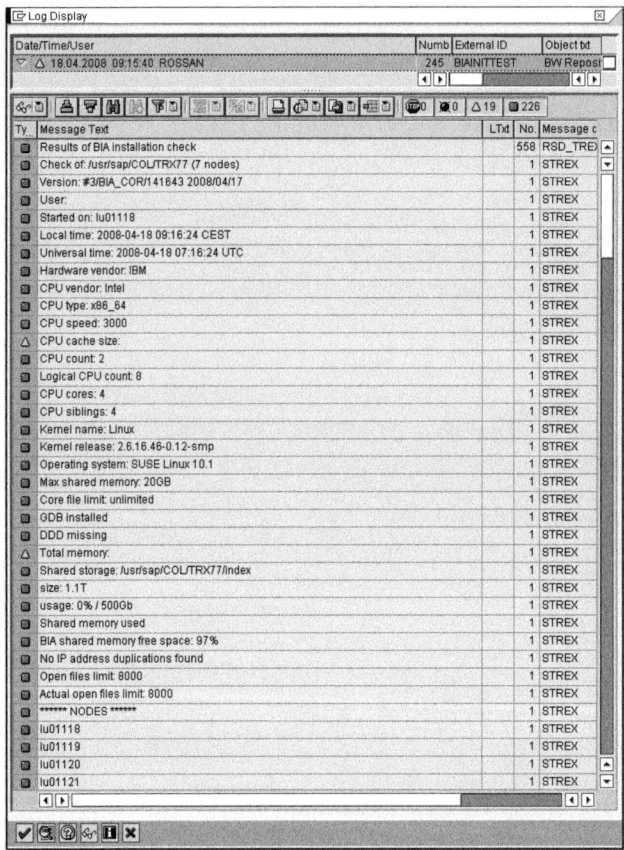

Figure 4.11 BIA Monitor, System Check Results

Starting and Stopping the BI Accelerator

You can start and stop the BI accelerator either via the TREX standalone administration tool or using the shell scripts `startsap` and `stopsap`.

To start or stop the BI accelerator with the TREX administration tool on an BIA blade, you need an X server for the GUI. First, log on as user `<sapsid>adm`. To start the TREX administration tool, go to the *BIA* directory and enter:

`./TREXAdmin.sh`

In the TREX administration tool, select view LANDSCAPE SERVICES, MMC tab.

▸ To start the accelerator, choose SAP SYSTEM: START.

▸ To stop the accelerator, choose SAP SYSTEM: STOP.

Alternatively, start or stop the accelerator from the MMC tab by selecting the TREX host and choosing the appropriate option from its context menu. The options enable you to stop selected hosts or all hosts for a landscape.

To start or stop the accelerator with a shell script, first log on locally to the relevant BIA blade host as user `<sapsid>adm`.

You can execute the script in any directory. If you want to start or stop a single BIA instance `BIA<instance_number>`:

▸ To start it, enter: `startsap BIA<instance_number>`.

▸ To stop it, enter: `stopsap BIA<instance_number>`.

To start or stop all SAP instances on a blade host, including all BIA instances, just enter: `startsap` or `stopsap`.

You can also use the BIA monitor to restart BIA hosts and servers (from screen area BIA ACTIONS). The Technical Operations Manual gives further details about all this.

4.2.2 Maintaining the RFC Connection

You need to set up the RFC connection between the SAP NetWeaver BI system and the BI accelerator. You can do so in Transactions RSCUSTA and SM59. Once the RFC connection is established, you can quickly check the availability of the BI accelerator from the BI system via the BIA monitor.

The accelerator runs an automatic check of all the RFC connections between the individual servers. The results are displayed in the BIA monitor.

You can reconfigure the RFC connection, or check that it is configured correctly, as follows. From your SAP NetWeaver BI system, start Transaction RSCUSTA to display the maintenance view shown in Figure 4.12. If the destination was either entered during installation of the BI accelerator or created on the BIA side later, you will find the RFC destination in the last line as the entry for HPA BI ACCELERATOR. If it was not, you can create an entry using the standalone TREX administration tool (see Section 5.2.1).

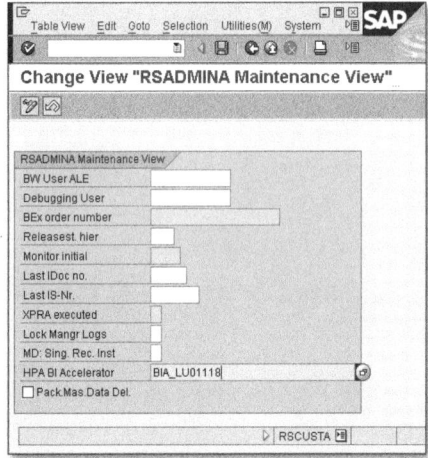

Figure 4.12 Transaction RSCUSTA, Initial Screen

You can test the performance of the RFC connection as follows. Again from your BI system, start Transaction SM59, open the subtree for TCP/IP CONNECTIONS as shown in Figure 4.13, and double-click on the line for the RFC connection to the accelerator. The RFC destination details for the selected destination are displayed as shown in Figure 4.14. On the TECHNICAL SETTINGS tab, you can see that TREX is entered as a REGISTERED SERVER PROGRAM. The program ID was generated automatically when the connection was created. The usual format is:

`Trex_<BI_SID>_<timestamp>`

Here `<BI_SID>` is the BI system ID, and the `timestamp` is a 14-digit number (year-month-day-hour-minute-second) recording the time the connection was created.

To test the RFC connection, choose CONNECTION TEST.

If the connection test is successful, the results will look similar to those shown in Figure 4.15, with short transmission times for packets of various sizes. In fact, the times shown in the figure are near the upper bound of what is acceptable in a productive BIA installation. If the transmissions do not succeed within the preset timeout, a clearly identifiable and color-coded error message will appear here. In that case, follow the troubleshooting advice given in Section 5.2.1.

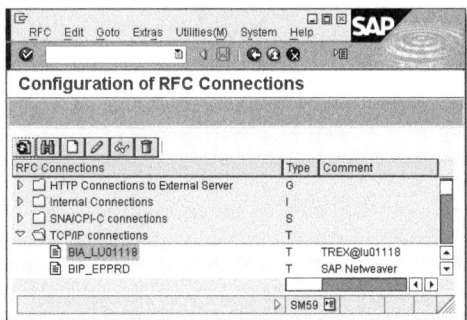

Figure 4.13 Transaction SM59, Initial Screen

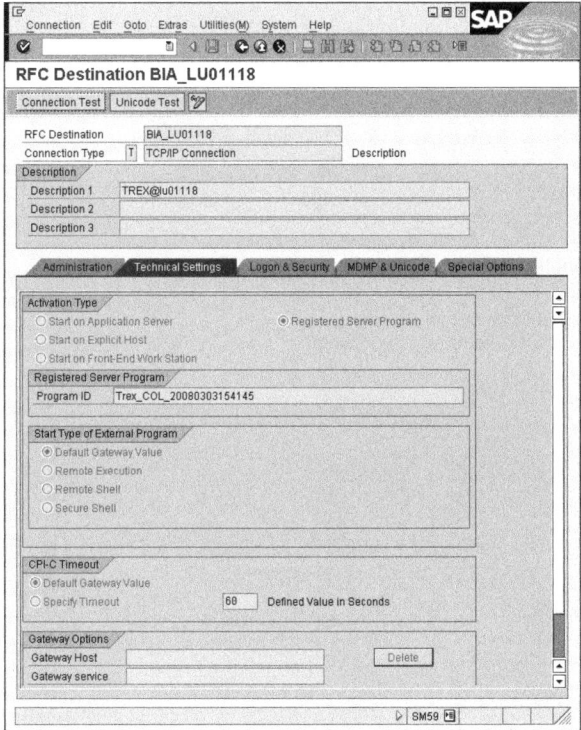

Figure 4.14 Transaction SM59, RFC Destination Details

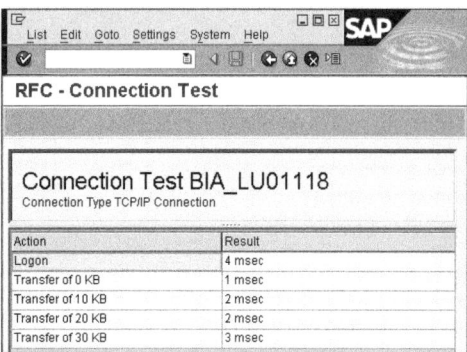

Figure 4.15 Transaction SM59, Connection test Results

Once you have established an RFC connection, you can also test it in Transaction TREXADMIN, tab RFC MONITOR (see Figure 4.16). Simply choose the TEST CONNECTION button and read the result.

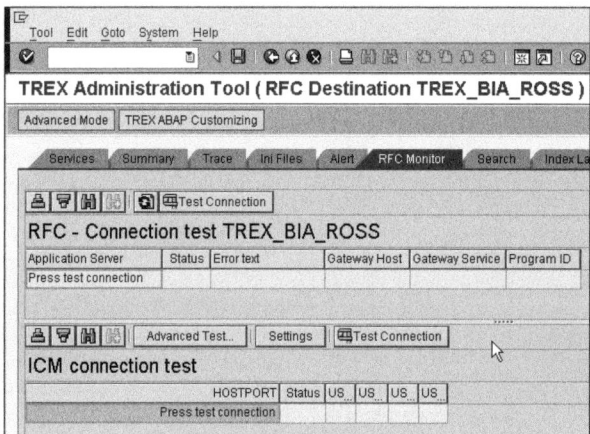

Figure 4.16 Transaction TREXADMIN, RFC Monitor Tab

Only one BI accelerator can be attached to an SAP NetWeaver BI system. This is because master data tables are stored once in the BIA file hierarchy and shared by any BIA indexes that need them, but this sharing does not work if the master data is distributed across multiple appliances. Because a BIA appliance can be scaled to handle the load from the BI system, and a fast failover solution is available for disaster recovery, the limit of one appliance per system sets no limit on the capacity or the availability of the system.

A BI accelerator may only be connected to a single productive SAP NetWeaver BI system. That is, each BI system requires its own dedicated BIA system. Similarly, development or test BI systems also require their own dedicated BIA systems. Depending on the landscape, development and test BI systems can be attached to the same BIA system, but this is not recommended because the behavior of the connected systems may not correctly reflect that of the productive system.

Activating Internet Connection Manager

The Internet Connection Manager (ICM) offers a direct communication path between the SAP NetWeaver BI system and the TREX index server that does not go through an SAP gateway (see Section 5.2.1). You do not need to do anything to activate the ICM with the default settings.

In some customer scenarios, it may be hard to decide whether RFC or ICM is the better means of communication. In any case, you should not change the default settings except on the advice of an SAP expert.

For indexing calls, the ICM is used by default. You can override the default in Table RSDDTREXADMIN. You can define which index call is used separately for S, F, D, X, and Y tables.

For aggregation, the RFC server is the default setting. You can override this in Transaction TREXADMIN on the ABAP CLIENT CUSTOMIZING tab by deactivating the USE RFC FOR AGGREGATION CALL flag. Also, you can activate compression for ICM calls by setting the USE DATA COMPRESSION flag.

In both cases, see the Technical Operations Manual for further details.

4.2.3   Creating BIA Indexes

Although the procedure for creating BIA indexes is easy, the technical process it triggers is complicated. Several aspects are worth describing in some detail here.

From InfoCubes to BIA indexes

The initial sizing for the BI accelerator will have foreseen BIA indexes for all or most of the InfoCubes in the attached SAP NetWeaver BI system. However, you can stage the rollout of the accelerator in your company by first indexing the most important InfoCubes to offer a performance benefit immediately and then indexing the rest over a longer period, without the pressure to show immediate results.

To find out which InfoCubes can benefit most from acceleration, you can measure the performance of query execution in Transaction RSRT. In the transaction, select the query and choose EXECUTE + DEBUG. When the list of options appears, select DISPLAY STATISTICS DATA and DO NOT USE CACHE. After the results are returned, choose the green BACK button. This takes you to the STATISTICS DATA FOR QUERY RUNTIME page. The DATA MANAGER event gives the time spent in the database. The accelerator brings the most benefit for queries that consume a lot of time in the database. On the AGGREGATION LAYER tab, you can see which InfoCubes and aggregates are used to execute the query.

When you create a BIA index for an InfoCube, all the data from the InfoCube that is relevant for reporting is replicated to the BIA server and stored in the BIA index on the accelerator's own storage. When you execute reports using the BIA index, the accelerator does not access the InfoCube data on the database.

The design of a BIA index includes the structure, properties, and status of the BIA index and its table indexes. Tables that are part of the enhanced star schema of the selected InfoCube and are required in the corresponding BIA index form part of the description of the BIA index.

All the dimension tables of the InfoCube are required for the star schema of the BIA index. The E and F fact tables of the InfoCube form one fact index. Of the master data tables, only the X and Y tables (which contain the SIDs) are required; the P and Q tables (which contain the key values) are not required. The SID tables (S tables) are required if the InfoObject has a non-numeric key.

In some special cases, it can be advantageous to create "flat" BIA indexes. These indexes arise from InfoCubes for which the inner part of the star schema is de-normalized. When dimension tables and fact tables are de-normalized, the data in the BIA index looks as if it came from an InfoCube that has only line items. Cases in which such a structure can be better are "bad" InfoCube designs where two or more dimension tables are large. De-normalizing the fact data prevents the accelerator from having to perform expensive join calculations between large indexes. For a flat BIA index, these joins are calculated only once, when the index is loaded into memory. The system decides automatically whether such a flat structure is better for the BIA index and is completely transparent with regard to administration. The only difference you will notice is that for a flat BIA index, only one dimension table is listed (the package dimension table is still used).

BIA index-specific information can be displayed in BIA index maintenance (Transaction RSDDV) and in the BIA monitor (Transaction RSDDBIAMON).

In the BIA monitor, if you choose BI ACCELERATOR • INDEX INFORMATION • DISPLAY ALL BIA INDEXES, an information box appears listing details of all the BIA indexes in the system (see Figure 4.17).

InfoCube	Version	Status	Table Name	Table Size	Index
Information about BIA Indexes					
0BWVC_001	☐	☐	/BI0/SFISCYEAR	490	☐
			/BI0/SUNIT	273	☐
			/BI0/SVC_COL	20	☐
			/BI0/SVC_EVAL	7	☐
			/BI0/SVC_GROU	6	☐
			/BI0/SVC_HOME	209	☐
			/BI0/SVC_LOC	5.960	☐
			/BI0/SVC_MARK	139	☐
			/BI0/SVC_MAT	27	☐
			/BI0/SVC_PAYM	50	☐
			/BI0/SVC_PERS1	1.826	☐
			/BI0/SVC_PROD1	937	☐
			/BI0/SVC_REDU	18	☐
			/BI0/SVC_UNIT1	154	☐
			/BI0/XVC_PERS1	1.826	☐
			/BI0/XVC_PROD1	937	☐
			/BI0/XVC_UNIT1	154	☐
			/BI0/YVC_PROD1	2.807	☐
0BWVC_003			/BI0/D0BWVC_0032	101	☐

Figure 4.17 BIA Monitor, Information About BIA Indexes

The BIA monitor shows more information than you can find in the BIA index maintenance screen, as follows.

▶ INFOCUBE
Here you see the system names or technical names of the InfoCubes for which BIA indexes have been created.

▶ VERSION
If the status icon is green, the BIA index is active. If the status icon is red, the BIA index is not active.

▶ STATUS
If the status icon is green, the BIA index is filled. If the status icon is red, the BIA index is not filled. If the status icon is gray, the BIA index is inactive, which means it is disabled for query usage.

▶ TABLE NAME
Here you see the system or technical name of the relevant table index in the BIA file storage.

▶ TABLE SIZE
This number specifies the approximate current size of the individual tables (number of data records), as calculated from the database statistics.

▶ INDEX STATUS
The status of the index is indicated by a colored icon.

▶ WITH DELTA INDEX
Here a check mark indicates that a delta index is being used for the BIA index. You would expect to see this check mark only for very large table indexes.

▶ MULTIPLE USAGE
With S, X, and Y tables, a "multiple usage" check mark beside a table indicates that it is being shared by another BIA index. Such shared tables contain master data that need only be indexed once for all the BIA indexes that share them. This also simplifies change runs because the accelerator only needs to update the shared table index to update all the BIA indexes that share it.

▶ LAST CHANGED BY
Here you see name of user who made the last change.

▶ LAST CHANGED/TIME STAMP
This gives the date and time of the last change by that user.

The BIA Index Maintenance Wizard

One of the first tasks of a BIA administrator is to create or maintain the required BIA indexes. Transaction RSDDV is the main transaction for dealing with BIA indexes. The initial view was shown earlier in Figure 4.6. To display an interactive list of all BIA indexes, choose BIA INDEXES, which displays the view shown in Figure 4.18. Here you can drill down in the InfoCube tree on the left to display dimensions and view attributes, or you can drill down in the BIA index tree on the right to display the individual table indexes and their properties, such as how many objects they contain and whether they are master data tables that are shared with other BIA indexes (shown by the checkbox to the right of the object totals beside the square green icons).

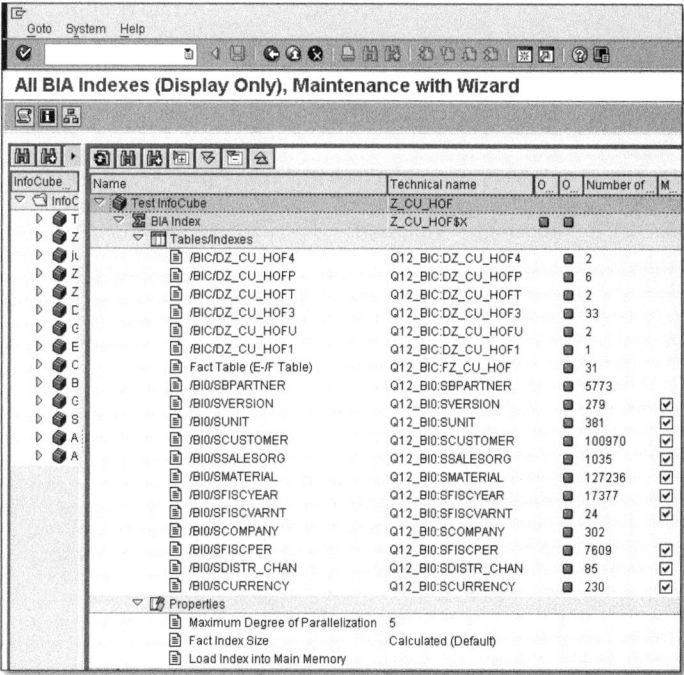

Figure 4.18 Transaction RSDDV, BIA Indexes

To start the wizard for creating a new BIA index from an InfoCube, select the InfoCube from the initial list in Transaction RSDDV, and choose the BIA INDEX button. The wizard is easy to operate. Depending on the situation it finds when it starts, the wizard does one of three things:

▶ If no BIA index for the InfoCube exists, it asks whether you want to create one.

▶ If a BIA index for the InfoCube already exists but is not yet filled, it asks whether you want to delete it or fill it.

▶ If a BIA index for the InfoCube already exists, the wizard asks whether you want to delete it.

The wizard creates a BIA index in two stages. First it creates an empty index, which is a fast operation. Then it fills the index, which can take a long time, from a few seconds to several hours, depending on how much data the InfoCube contains. The wizard offers a button you can choose to view the application logs for the indexing process, in case you want to check on progress during a long job or check that no errors occurred.

You can create only one BIA index for each InfoCube. This BIA index contains a set of table indexes, which in turn contain all the data from the InfoCube. In contrast to the procedure with aggregates, you do not need to make specific selections and restrictions to define the BIA index.

Let us now look at the BIA Index Maintenance Wizard in detail.

The upper area of the wizard screen displays a text field with a question about the current step and three buttons:

▸ INFORMATION (shown as the "!" button in Figure 4.19)

▸ END MAINTENANCE

▸ CONTINUE

If you choose INFORMATION, then three tabs are displayed in the middle of the screen, as shown in the following three figures.

If the selected BIA index is both created and filled, you display the screen shown in Figure 4.19.

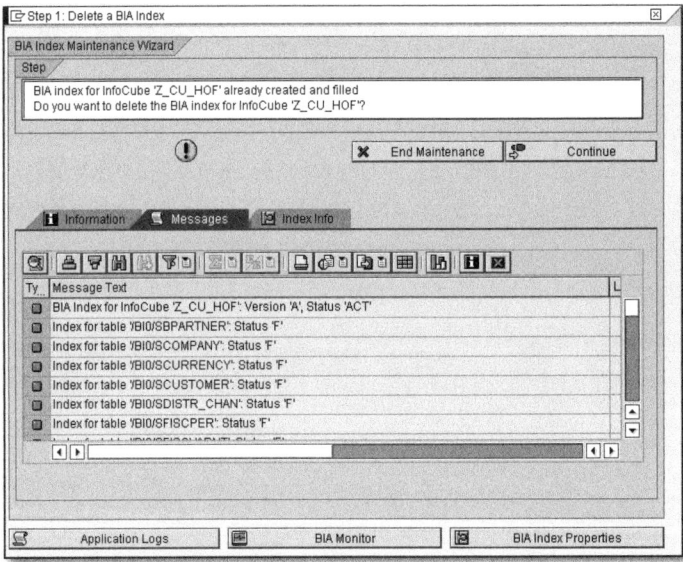

Figure 4.19 BIA Index Maintenance Wizard, Delete Index

If the selected BIA index has not yet been created or filled, you display the screen shown in Figure 4.20.

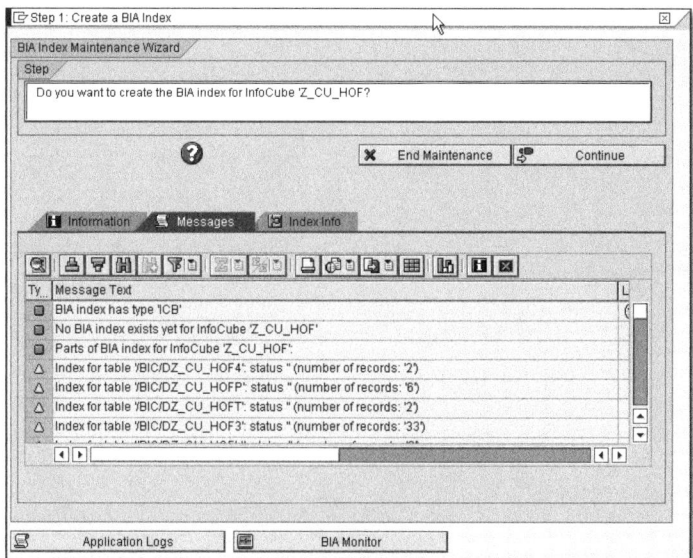

Figure 4.20 BIA Index Maintenance Wizard, Create Index

If the selected BIA index is created but not yet filled, you display the screen shown in Figure 4.21.

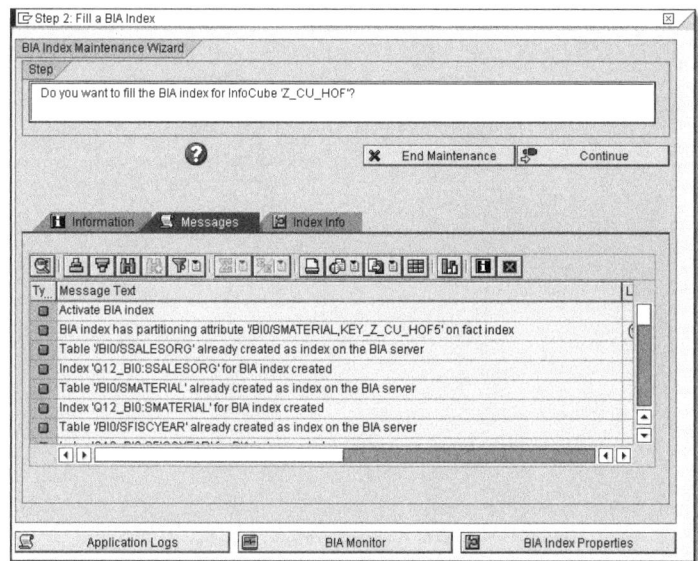

Figure 4.21 BIA Index Maintenance Wizard, Fill Index

At the bottom of the wizard screen are the following function keys:

▶ APPLICATION LOGS

▶ BIA MONITOR

▶ BIA INDEX PROPERTIES

If you choose APPLICATION LOGS, the LOG SELECTION dialog box appears. Here you can select process logs for display. You can select any one of the following processes:

▶ INITIAL FILLING

▶ ROLL UP

▶ COMPRESS INFOCUBE

▶ DELETE REQUEST

▶ CHANGE RUN

▶ CHECK

If you execute your selection, the ANALYZE APPLICATION LOG screen appears, and you can analyze the log.

If instead you choose BIA MONITOR, the BIA monitor screen appears.

If the BIA index has been created, the BIA INDEX PROPERTIES button is displayed. If you click it, the MAINTAIN BIA INDEX PROPERTIES dialog box opens (see Figure 4.22).

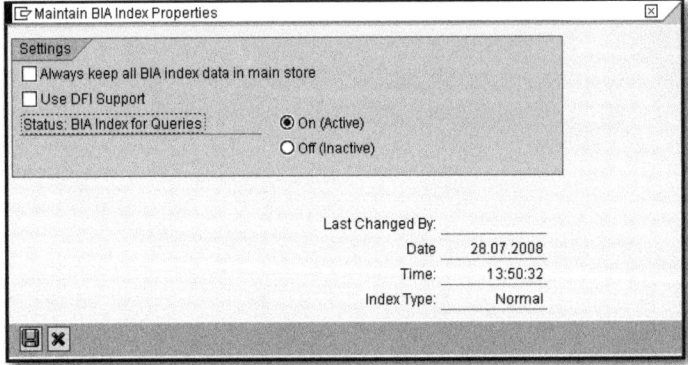

Figure 4.22 BIA Index Maintenance Wizard, Maintain BIA Index Properties

In this dialog box, you can specify the following settings:

▶ ALWAYS KEEP ALL BIA INDEX DATA IN MAIN STORE
This setting ensures that the index is always loaded into memory on startup. It is advisable if the index is used frequently, and you want to ensure the best possible response times against this index. Indexes for which this flag is not set are only loaded when they are needed to answer a query.

▶ USE DFI SUPPORT
This property is for specialists only.

▶ STATUS: BIA INDEX FOR QUERIES
The two radio buttons, ON (ACTIVE) and OFF (INACTIVE), enable you to toggle the index on or off.

The dialog box also provides further information about the BIA index.

You can also access the BIA Index Maintenance Wizard from the DW Workbench screen (Transaction RSA1) shown earlier in Figure 4.5. In the MODELING area on the left, choose INFOPROVIDER. In the InfoProvider tree, navigate to the InfoCube for which you want to create a BIA index. Then from the context menu of the InfoCube, choose MAINTAIN BI ACCELERATOR INDEX. This starts the wizard.

To access the wizard from the BIA index maintenance screen (Transaction RSDDV) shown earlier in Figure 4.6, select the InfoCube you want to index, and then choose BIA INDEX. Again, this starts the wizard.

Once you have started the BIA Index Maintenance Wizard for a selected Info-Cube, three scenarios are possible:

1. The InfoCube does not yet have a BIA index.

2. The InfoCube has a BIA index that has not yet been filled.

3. The InfoCube already has a filled BIA index.

With the background in place, we can now consider these scenarios in turn.

Scenario 1

You call the BIA Index Maintenance Wizard for an InfoCube that does not yet have a BIA index.

The first step is to create a BIA index for the InfoCube. The accelerator creates a table index for each of the tables in the InfoCube for which there is not already a table index in the system. In any case, the BIA engine creates a fact table index and dimension table indexes (F and D indexes), but because the other tables contain master data that is shared with other InfoCubes, that master data may have been indexed already (as S, X, and Y indexes) in the BIA file hierarchy (see Figure 4.20).

When you execute this step, the BIA engine also creates a logical index, which contains the metadata required to enable the engine to work with the BIA index and use it for query execution. Finally, the system activates the BIA index.

The next step is to fill the BIA index because what was created in the first step was an empty logical structure. The wizard treats filling the index as a step that requires additional user confirmation because creating an empty index takes very little time but filling it often takes much longer (see Figure 4.21 shown previously).

To schedule a background job to fill the BIA index, choose CONTINUE. This opens a dialog box for specifying the start time. Specify when you want the fill job to run, and choose the save icon. Running the job immediately is only appropriate if the InfoCube is exceptionally small or if the BIA system is not under load. Otherwise, the fill job should run in background. Once you have scheduled the job, the wizard displays the screen shown in Figure 4.23.

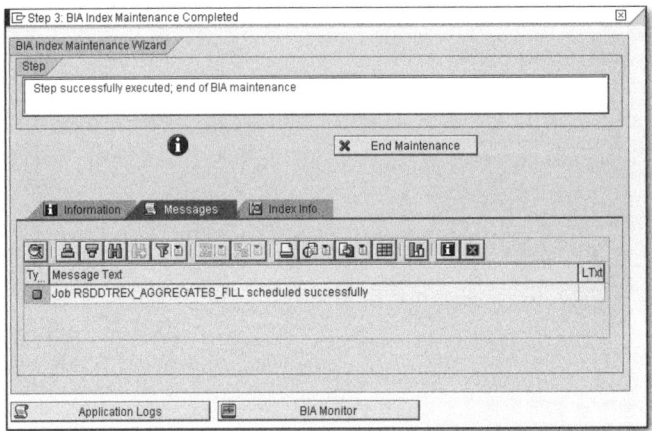

Figure 4.23 BIA Index Maintenance Wizard, Success

Filling may take a long time if the InfoCube tables are large enough to trigger the BIA engine to split the indexes for those tables into parts. Recall that the accelerator has an automatic threshold for splitting an index into parts, and the number of parts is given automatically by the number of hosts in the BIA landscape. The duration of the filling step increases with the number of parts into which the index is split.

When you execute this step, the system starts a process in the background that reads the data in the tables of the InfoCube star schema from the database and writes them to the corresponding indexes on the BIA server. If the index of a master data table (S/X/Y tables) has already been created and filled by another BIA index, the BIA engine only needs to add any records that are additional to those already indexed (this is called mode D in the indexing logs).

Once the BIA index has been filled successfully, the status in the OBJECT STATUS column on the INDEX INFO wizard tab switches to green.

The process of reading the data from the database and writing the data to the BIA server can be performed in parallel in the SAP NetWeaver BI system in different ways. If you are expert enough to fine-tune this parallelization process, you can reset the global indexing parameters described in Section 5.3.5.

The third step completes the index maintenance. After you have triggered the fill process, you can cancel it if necessary and return to the original transaction, or you can continue and complete the BIA index maintenance. The new BIA index is then available and can be used for queries.

Scenario 2

You call the BIA Index Maintenance Wizard for an InfoCube that already has an active BIA index, but the index has not yet been filled or completely filled with data.

In this scenario, the fill process may either have been terminated or not have been started. Because an active BIA index is already available, you can at this point continue to fill it with data or delete it.

You need to decide to fill the BIA index, to continue to fill it, or to delete it. You can see the status of the individual table indexes within the BIA index in the screen area MESSAGES FROM PREVIOUS STEP. To fill the BIA index, choose CONTINUE FILLING. To delete the BIA index, choose DELETE.

Once you have created a BIA index, whenever you have loaded new data packages (requests) into the InfoCube, you need to roll up these data packages into the BIA index before the data is available in reporting.

Scenario 3

You call the BIA Index Maintenance Wizard for an InfoCube that has a BIA index that is already filled with data.

In this scenario, because an active and filled BIA index that can be used for reporting is already available, you can at this point either temporarily deactivate it or delete it. These options can be useful, for example, if you are running performance tests or data consistency checks and you want to ensure that the system is not using a BIA index.

To delete the BIA index, choose CONTINUE. The wizard deletes the definition and the settings of the BIA index in the BI system and also the logical index (metadata) and all the table indexes for the InfoCube in the BIA storage. The only exceptions are the indexes for the master data tables that are still being used by other BIA indexes.

To deactivate the BIA index temporarily, choose BIA INDEX PROPERTIES. A dialog box appears. Select INACTIVE as the status of the BIA index.

A BIA index that is switched off is not used when a query is executed. Because even BIA indexes that are switched off are maintained in a consistent state, you do not have to activate the BIA index again or fill it when you switch it back on.

If the BIA Server Becomes Unavailable ...

If the BIA server becomes unavailable for any reason (for example due to a hardware problem), you can delete all references to the BIA indexes in the BI system and continue work with the InfoCubes on the database. If you then repair the BIA system and recreate the BIA indexes, any old versions of the BIA indexes are first deleted automatically. The BI process chains will continue to work.

If you are interested, the rest of this subsection provides more technical details about how the BIA Maintenance Indexing Wizard works. The wizard performs a series of steps to create a BIA index for a selected InfoCube, persist it on the BIA local storage, and make the new index visible to the SAP NetWeaver BI system.

The name of the BIA index is generated automatically from the system ID and the InfoCube name:

```
<system ID>_<InfoCube name>
```

The name of a table index is generated from the system ID and table name:

```
_<table name>
```

The system deletes the first forward slash from the table name and replaces the second with a colon. For example, the table named `/BIO/SCUSTOMER` from system BWP corresponds to the table index `BWP_BIO:SCUSTOMER`.

The wizard performs the following steps:

▶ CREATE
For a table, the system creates the index on the BIA server in accordance with the table properties. If the (current) size of the table exceeds a preset threshold, the system also splits the index into a predetermined number of parts. Both the threshold and the number of split parts have default values that are normally appropriate but can be overwritten in exceptional circumstances.

▶ INDEX
The data is transferred and written to a temporary file on the BIA server.

▶ PREPARE OPTIMIZE
The data in the temporary file is formatted as required for search and aggregation. Depending on how the index is distributed, this step can take longer than the indexing step.

▶ COMMIT OPTIMIZE
The previously optimized data is made visible. If you perform a rollback for an index, the system rolls back the data to the last commit optimize.

The logs for the initial filling and indexing of a BIA index are in the application log under object RSDDTREX, subobject TAGGRFILL.

You can activate and fill BIA indexes for different InfoCubes at the same time.

However, overlaps may occur if several indexing jobs try to index the same master data tables simultaneously. In this case, the first job locks the table and performs indexing. The other jobs see the lock and schedule the indexing run to take place later. If no new data is loaded in the meantime, the system simply checks that indexing was performed successfully by the competing job. This step is necessary to avoid the system setting a BIA index to active when the index is not actually available on the BIA server because the job was terminated.

The subsequent jobs try a total of five times to start the indexing process or determine the status of the index. If this is not possible due to a long-running process or termination, the system terminates the entire indexing process for the BIA index and notes the InfoCube affected by the lock process. You have to wait until the current program has finished or the error has been fixed before restarting the indexing process.

If a process is terminated by the user or the system during the initial data fill, you can restart the process by choosing the CONTINUE FILLING option during the operation of the BIA Index Maintenance Wizard.

You can also activate and fill a BIA index independently of the wizard.

Enhanced BIA Indexes for Polestar

As part of Enhancement Pack 1 for SAP NetWeaver BI 7.0, the BIA Index Maintenance Wizard has been extended to enable you to create enhanced BIA indexes for accelerating your work in BusinessObjects Polestar.

Before you can create an enhanced BIA index, you need to maintain external key information and a text for any relevant InfoObjects in SAP NetWeaver BI. When you create an enhanced BIA index with the wizard, the wizard deletes the old BIA index, if any, and replaces it with an enhanced one.

To create a Polestar-enabled BIA index in Transaction RSDDV:

1. Select an InfoCube, and click the POLESTAR button (see Figure 4.24). This starts the wizard.

2. Select the user or users to be authorized for Polestar. This creates an authorization index.

3. Select a target unit or currency for each key figure, and activate conversion as required.

4. Choose CONTINUE. This creates a new logical index with enhanced master data indexes and enhanced index metadata.

Once the new BIA index is activated, it is available to accelerate your work in Polestar.

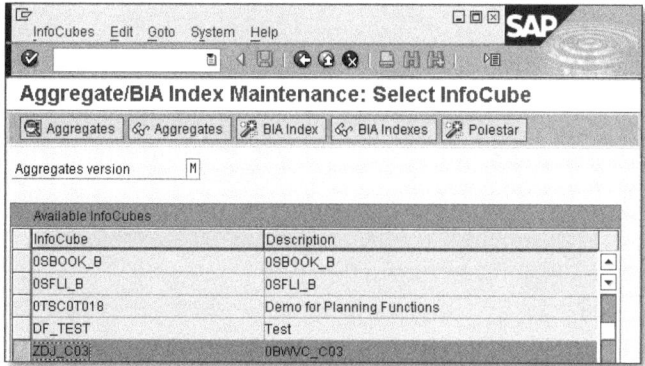

Figure 4.24 Transaction RSDDV, Polestar Enabled

BIA Delta Indexes

You can create a delta index for a table index within a BIA index. If a delta index exists, the system does not write to the main index during each delta indexing or each indexing activity (except during initial creation and filling), and the main index is not optimized. Instead, the system writes data to a second index, which is normally much smaller. The smaller the delta index, the faster the subsequent optimize procedure and the faster the whole process of rolling up data or making modifications after a hierarchy or attribute change run.

You should switch on the delta index only for indexes that are either very large or are updated frequently or both, such as F table indexes and some X or Y table indexes. Otherwise, the runtime overhead imposed by merging the results has a negative rather than positive impact on performance. There is a check you can run in Transaction RSRV that uses index size and change statistics to propose candidates for delta indexing.

If you have created any delta indexes, a BIA monitor check advises you when to merge them with the main index to ensure that reads remain as fast as possible. Alternatively, you can handle delta indexing manually as follows.

1. In Transaction RSRV, ANALYSIS AND REPAIR OF BI OBJECTS, area BI ACCELERATOR • BI ACCELERATOR PERFORMANCE, select the elementary test SIZE OF DELTA INDEX.

2. Choose CORRECT ERROR to access repair mode, and then execute an index merge.

Alternatively, you can schedule program RSDDTREX_DELTAINDEX_MERGE.

To set the delta index for a BIA index:

1. From the BIA monitor screen, choose BI ACCELERATOR • INDEX INFORMATION • SET DELTA INDEX. A dialog box appears.

2. To switch on delta indexing for a table, find the row for the table in the DELTA INDEX column, and set a flag. The new setting takes effect with the next index update.

You can switch off the delta index for the table in the same way by deselecting the flag. Before the next index update, the system merges the delta index and the main index. If the delta index has become very large, the merge may take a while.

In the BIA monitor, the BI ACCELERATOR menu offers the following index-related options:

▶ INDEX CHECKS
From here you can quickly check the size of delta indexes for BIA indexes, the relative size of InfoCube fact tables and their fact indexes, and the relation between tables and indexes (see Section 5.3.2).

▶ INDEX SETTING
The INDEX SETTINGS option offers the following further options:

▷ CHANGE GLOBAL PARAMETERS: Opens a dialog box for changing the global indexing parameters BATCHPARA, NUMPROC, PKGSIZE, SUBPKGSIZE, and FLOAT (see Section 5.3.5).

▷ SET DELTA INDEX: Opens a dialog box listing table indexes with checkboxes that you can flag to set a delta index.

▷ SWITCH ON/OFF BIA INDEXES FOR QUERIES: Opens a dialog box listing Info-Cubes with checkboxes that you can flag to switch off their BIA indexes (see Figure 4.25).

▷ BIA INDEX PROPERTIES: Opens a dialog box listing BIA indexes with check-boxes that you can flag to ensure that the indexes are loaded into memory when the accelerator is started.

▶ INDEX INFORMATION
The INDEX INFORMATION option offers the following further option:

▷ DISPLAY ALL BIA INDEXES: Opens a window with a list of all the BIA indexes and information about them.

InfoCube	Switched Off for Q...	Last Chan	Time St...
0AFMM_C02	☐	USER	20.080.3'
CUBECB	☐	USER	20.080.2:
EPERFTEST	☐	USER	20.080.3l
GR01CUBE1	☐	USER	20.080.3'
ZBWVC_SB1	☐	USER	20.080.2l
ZBWVC_SB2	☐	USER	20.080.2:
ZJCUBE	☐	USER	20.080.3l
Z_CU_HOF	☐	USER	20.080.4l

(Switch On/Off BIA Indexes for Queries)

Figure 4.25 BIA Monitor, Switch On/Off BIA Indexes for Queries

Under the INDEX SETTINGS option, the CHANGE GLOBAL PARAMETERS option enables you to reset the global indexing parameters (see Figure 4.26). For detailed descriptions of the indexing parameters and how to set them, see Section 5.3.5.

Name	Description	Value (Chang...
BATCHPARA	Number of Processes for Batch Parallel Processing of Initial Indexing	4
NUMPROC	Number of Processes for Parallel Processing Using aRFC Dialog Processes During Ir	5
PKGSIZE	Package Size in Bytes for Internal Tables During Indexing Using aRFCs	10000000
SUBPKGSIZE	Package Size (Rows) for EXPORT TO BUFFER During Indexing Using aRFCs	20000
FLOAT	Save FLOAT Key Figure as FLOAT (Any Value) or DOUBLE (Any Value)	FLOAT

(Change Global Indexing Parameters)

Figure 4.26 Global Indexing Parameters

4.2.4 Configuring Alerts

The alert options in the accelerator are extensive and it is well worth getting to know them.

TREX Alert Server

As an administrator, your main source of status information about the BI accelerator is the TREX alert server that forms part of the TREX engine within the accelerator.

The alert server on each TREX host cycles through a list of preset checks at regular intervals and generates an alert if a service becomes unavailable or some other error condition arises. The alert server can be configured to send e-mail notifications of any alerts above a preset threshold to standard SAP monitoring tools. The alert server is installed with a set of default checks activated, but administrators can configure the check sets, by selecting or deselecting checks from a displayed list, or even add their own custom checks. Administrators can also change the default settings for how frequently the check sets are run. In any case, whether additional e-mail alerts are configured or not, the alert server sends alerts to the attached BI system, where they are displayed by the appropriate monitoring tools.

An administrator who does not wish to devote more time than necessary to monitoring the accelerator can therefore configure the alert server to send an e-mail alert notification in any situation where the administrator wishes to be alerted, and then simply wait for mail.

Figure 4.27 shows a sample alert mail in HTML format. In most cases, an administrator would wish to be alerted, for example, if a blade host failed, if more storage capacity were needed, if reorganization of the indexes in the landscape were recommended, or if a consistency check returned an error. Apart from that, the administrator would be well advised to check the monitoring transaction from time to time, and be aware of such things as index sizes and load levels.

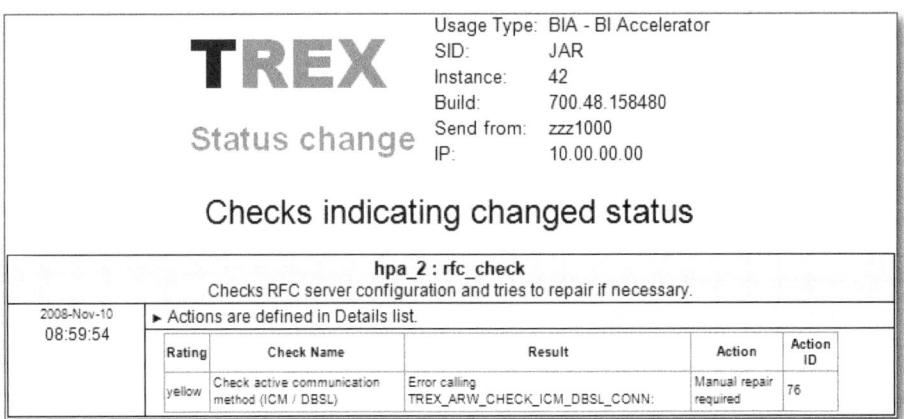

Figure 4.27 A Typical TREX E-mail Alert Message

In Transaction TREXADMIN, the view ALERT shows the same alert check information as displayed in the BIA monitoring Transaction RSDDBIAMON. The information is shown on the same three tabs: SUMMARY, CURRENT, and HISTORY. Additionally, this view enables you to configure the alert server by choosing ALERT SERVER CONFIGURATION, which displays the dialog box shown in Figure 4.28.

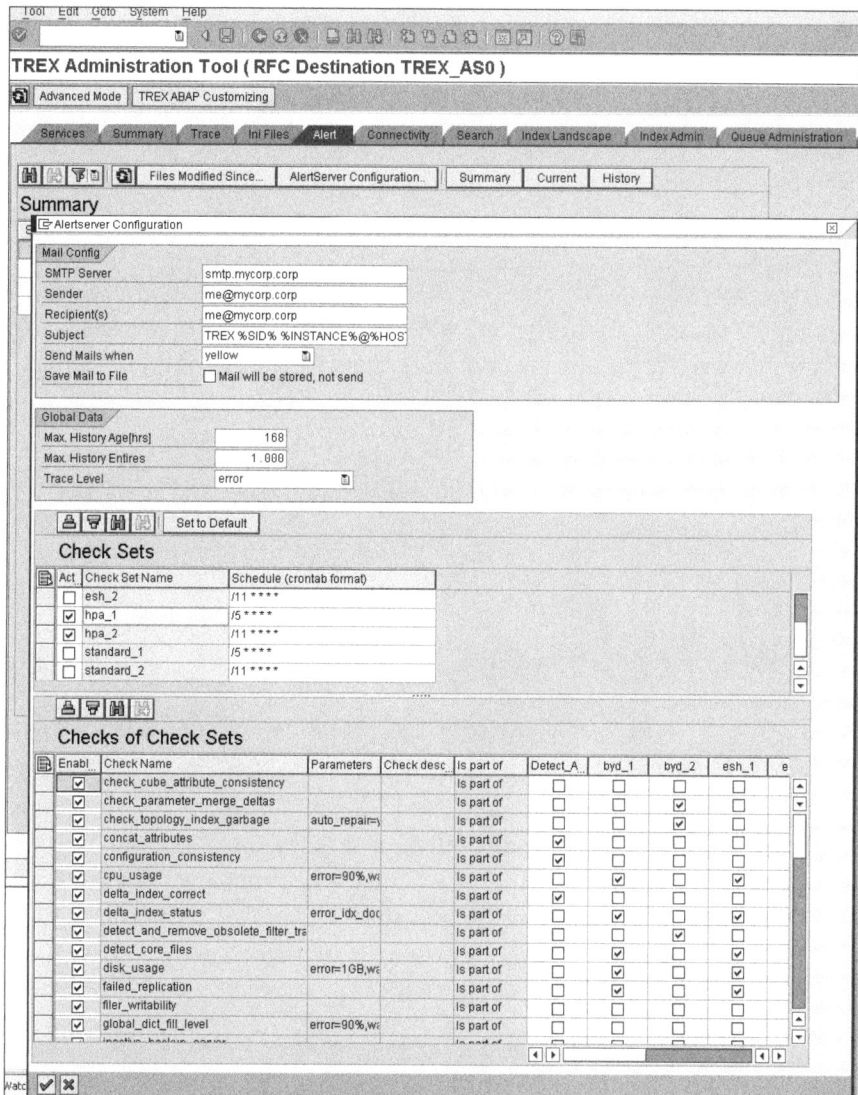

Figure 4.28 TREXADMIN, Alert Server Configuration

For the BI accelerator, three sets of checks, called hpa_1, hpa_2, and Detect_And_Repair, are defined. These check sets are activated by default to cycle through their checks once every 5 minutes (hpa_1), once every 11 minutes (hpa_2), and once a day (Detect_And_Repair). These default settings are good for all normal purposes, but you can reset the frequencies using the TREX standalone administration tool.

You can also make changes to the subset of checks that are activated in all three check sets `hpa_1`, `hpa_2`, and `Detect_And_Repair`, although again in normal operation, there is no good reason for you to do so.

The checks available for activation in the accelerator are as follows:

▶ `check_cube_attribute_consistency`
Returns a list of cubes for which the physical indexes include attributes that have different numbers of items. Within a physical cube index, all attributes must have the same number of items.

▶ `check_topology_index_garbage`
Returns a list of indexes for which the information in *topology.ini* is incorrect.

▶ `configuration_consistency`
Performs several checks of the configuration consistency of the system.

▶ `cpu_usage`
Returns the CPU usage level (warning = 70 %, error = 90 %).

▶ `delta_index_status`
Returns a list of all indexes whose delta index is too big. If the number of documents in a main index exceeds <`error_num_docs` * 10>, then the relative parameters are valid (more than `error_idx_mem_size_pct` = <`error_idx_mem_size_pct`>% of the main index memory size or more than `error_idx_num_docs_pct` = <`error_idx_num_docs_pct`>% of the number of documents in the main index). If not, the absolute parameters are valid (more than `error_num_docs` = <`error_num_docs`> documents or `error_mem` = <`error_mem`> MB memory usage). If MEMWATCHER AUTOMERGE is switched on, this check always returns OK (`error_idx_mem_size_pct` = 10 %, `error_idx_num_docs_pct` = 10 %, `error_mem` = 200, `error_num_docs` = 50000).

▶ `detect_core_files`
Returns a list of core files.

▶ `disk_usage`
Returns any host for which the available disk space is less than a limit (warning = 50 GB, error = 10 GB).

▶ `global_dict_fill_level`
Checks the fill level of the global dictionary (warning = 80 %, error = 90 %).

- `inactive_backup_server`
  Returns the host and port of any BIA backup server that is set up but not running.

- `inactive_index_servers`
  Returns a list of inactive index servers.

- `inactive_name_servers`
  Returns a list of inactive name servers.

- `inconsistent_logical_indexes`
  Returns a list of inconsistent logical indexes.

- `index_data_inconsistencies`
  Checks the internal consistency and housekeeping data structures of the indexes in TREX and returns a list of indexes with inconsistent data. Unlike the consistency checks in Transaction RSRV, this check does not compare the data in TREX for consistency with the application data held in the SAP NetWeaver BI system's primary storage. Although it checks only for internal inconsistencies, this check may cause heavy load on the system and you should only run it if recommended to do so by an SAP service engineer.

- `index_status`
  Returns any indexes that are in an error state.

- `inodes_usage`
  Returns a list of mounted drives and their current inodes status.

- `lonesome_index`
  Checks whether there are physical indexes that are no longer part of a logical index.

- `memory_usage`
  Returns memory usage (`warning` = 75 %, `error` = 90 %).

- `multiple_sysids_at_bia`
  Checks whether there are multiple SAP SIDs connected to an accelerator.

- `network`
  Returns a list of hosts that do not have a network connection.

- `no_master_index_server`
  Returns a list of indexes without active master or backup

- `open_handles`
  Returns the number of open handles (`warning` = 1000, `error` = 1500).

- ▶ `pending_index_server_requests`
  Returns all index servers with `<threshold_value>` or more pending requests.

- ▶ `reorg`
  Returns "yes" if an index reorganization is recommended.

- ▶ `restarted_services`
  Returns all restarted services.

- ▶ `rfc_check`
  Checks the RFC server configuration and tries to repair it if necessary.

- ▶ `shared_memory`
  Returns the level of shared memory usage (`warning` = 75 %, `error` = 85 %).

- ▶ `shared_memory_use`
  Returns a list of hosts that are not using shared memory.

- ▶ `trace_entries`
  Returns critical trace file entries.

- ▶ `trace_file_size`
  Returns a list of any huge trace files (`warning_alertfiles` = 10, `warning` = 50, `error_alertfiles` = 20, `error` = 2000). Because large alert files can impact performance, they have lower thresholds (measured in MB).

- ▶ `unassigned_master_indexes`
  Returns a list of unassigned master indexes.

- ▶ `unloads`
  Returns any attributes of indexes that were unloaded from memory (`warning` = 200, `error` = 300).

- ▶ `version_info`
  Returns the version information about each host.

If necessary, you can activate or deactivate these checks individually, either in Transaction TREXADMIN (see Figure 4.28 shown earlier) or in the TREX standalone administration tool, ALERT SERVER view, ALERT SERVER CONFIGURATION dialog box (see Section 5.1). The alert check lists include more checks than listed earlier, but the additional checks are irrelevant for accelerator administration.

You can also schedule e-mails broadcasting an overview of the summary and current results of the BIA alert server checks from the BIA monitor. To do so, from the BIA monitor choose BIA CHECKS • SCHEDULE E-MAIL NOTIFICATION. This opens the dialog box shown in Figure 4.29. The e-mail is broadcast to all addresses that you may have entered in Table RSDDTREXEMAIL (see the next section).

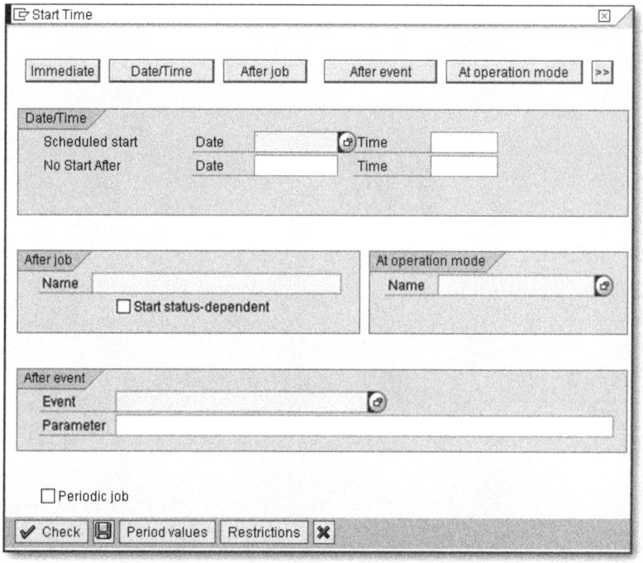

Figure 4.29 Schedule E-mail Start Time Dialog Box

Database Failover Alerts

You can set the BI system to perform an automatic failover to the database if the BIA server becomes unavailable for any reason (for example due to a hardware problem). The failover is triggered only by loss of communication and not by error messages from the accelerator. Any error messages from the accelerator require manual intervention.

To activate the failover and to ensure that you are informed promptly if an automatic failover to the database is triggered, you only need to configure the SAP NetWeaver BI system to send you an e-mail informing you whenever a failover has occurred.

To do so, start Transaction SE16, and enter TABLE NAME RSDDTREXEMAIL (see Figure 4.30). Then choose CREATE ENTRIES, enter your e-mail address in the following screen, and save (see Figure 4.31). To check at any time for e-mail alerts, in Transaction SE16 enter TABLE NAME RSDDTREXEMAIL, choose TABLE CONTENTS, enter your e-mail address, and execute (see Figure 4.32).

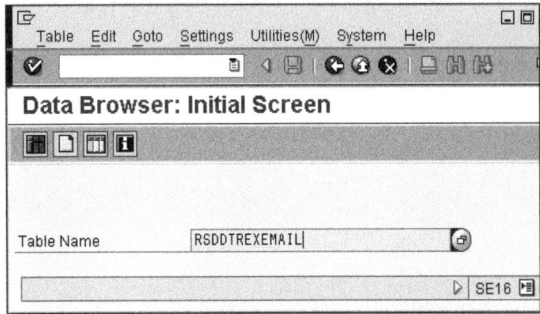

Figure 4.30 Transaction SE16, Table RSDDTREXEMAIL

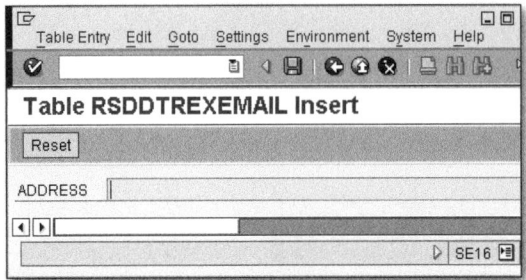

Figure 4.31 Table RSDDTREXEMAIL, Insert Address

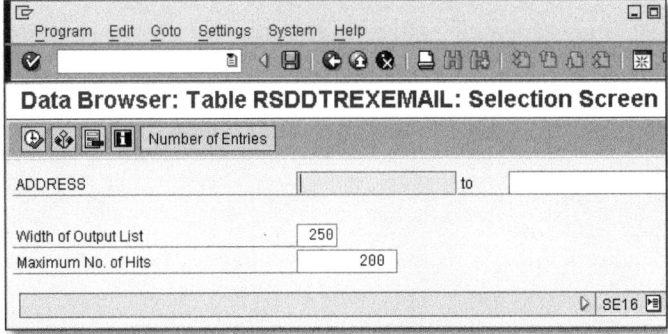

Figure 4.32 Table RSDDTREXEMAIL, Select Messages

Whether you have configured an e-mail address or not, to display a list of any alerts triggered by an automatic failover to the database, in Transaction SE16, enter TABLE NAME RSDDTREXHPAFAIL, choose TABLE CONTENTS, and enter your filter conditions on the selection screen (see Figure 4.33).

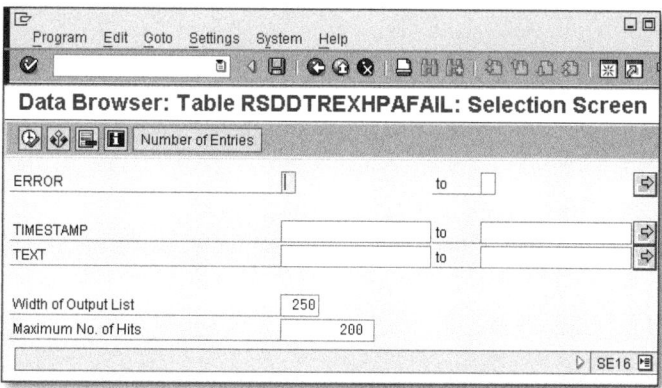

Figure 4.33 Table RSDDTREXHPAFAIL, Select Messages

There may be circumstances where you wish to make the BIA server unavailable, for example, in the case of a communication problem. If those circumstances arise, you may need to switch on a fallback solution manually. To be sure that you are informed in time to do this, you should enter at least one e-mail address in Table RSDDTREXEMAIL.

The SAP NetWeaver BI system saves the time of any error in Table RSDDTREXH-PAFAIL and sends an alert message containing this information to the e-mail address entered in Table RSDDTREXEMAIL.

If and when you receive the e-mail, you can trigger measures to remove the cause of the problem and delete the entry in Table RSDDTREXHPAFAIL. When the entry has been deleted, queries are automatically directed to the accelerator again and not to the database.

For 30 minutes after the BIA server goes down, or until the entry in Table RSD-DTREXHPAFAIL has been deleted, the system directs all query requests for an InfoCube with a BIA index to the database. If aggregates for this InfoCube are still available, the system will use them as appropriate. See SAP Note 940635.

After 30 minutes, if the problem is not resolved, or if the table entry is not deleted or its timestamp changed, the system directs query requests to the BIA server again. If the problem still exists, the system writes a new timestamp and redirects queries to the database again for the next 30 minutes.

Once the problem is resolved or the 30 minutes has passed, the system automatically sends all queries to the BIA index of the affected InfoCube.

4.2.5 Going Live

To ensure user satisfaction, you need a good strategy for going live with the BI accelerator. Best practice for the go-live is to involve the business users actively in the process. Because the accelerator delivers instantly visible performance improvements, many users will react with enthusiasm, and this goes a long way toward a successful implementation. However, expectation management is still required. The biggest performance improvements come from queries that previously consumed long stretches of runtime in the database. The accelerator cannot do much to speed up queries that spend long times in the BI analytic processor or that generate very large result sets (which need to be transported through the network).

Once you have decided which InfoCubes to index, you need a strategy for activating the BIA indexes in your production environment. After successful completion of testing in your development and quality assurance systems, you can either activate all the indexes at once or use a phased approach. Activating all at once provides a more dramatic demonstration of the benefits. If you find you have problems for certain InfoCubes, you can easily and instantly deactivate their BIA indexes. Because there is no great risk, the all-at-once approach is appealing.

If, as we recommend, you phase the roll-out of the accelerator for multiple Info-Cubes, you need to ensure that the business users know where and when they can expect to see performance improvements. If they don't know, they may start calling your help desk. Because you can activate or deactivate BIA indexes for specific users or queries, you have the technical freedom to manage user expectations precisely during the roll-out. You can also activate or deactivate BIA indexes for specific users (see SAP Note 988989).

Next, you need a strategy for deactivating (but not deleting) aggregates and ceasing to compress fact tables. A conservative strategy is to go live with BIA indexes but also continue to maintain the aggregates until IT and the business users are comfortable, which may take a few weeks. Then you can begin to delete the aggregates, to free up database disk space, and reduce your administration workload.

> **Caution!**
>
> A caution needs to be emphasized here. Once you have stopped maintaining the aggregates, you become dependent on the accelerator. If it becomes unavailable for any reason, the BI system will direct queries to the database, and response times may become unacceptably slow.

4.3   Regular Tasks

The BIA indexes require regular maintenance to keep them up to date. Because the BI system sees the BIA indexes logically as aggregates, the previous BI change run and roll-up routines for keeping aggregates up to date apply also to BIA indexes. If the consistency of your data is of critical importance, you may wish to check your BIA indexes regularly for consistency with the InfoCubes on the database. Also, if your BIA indexes are so large and critical that you cannot afford downtime to rebuild them, you may wish to back up the BIA indexes regularly, in preparation for the unlikely eventuality that you need to perform a recovery.

4.3.1   Index Maintenance

Roll-Ups

To ensure that delta data loads to the InfoCubes in the BI system become visible in the BIA indexes for reporting, you need to include a roll-up in the process chain. As soon as you know which InfoCubes will be indexed, you should check that the delta load process chain has a roll-up step at the end or the InfoCube is marked for automatic roll-up. You can do this before you go live with the accelerator.

The compression of data packages after roll-up, as performed with aggregates to improve efficiency, does not apply to BIA indexes because the data on the BIA server already exists in a read-optimized format. However, if the InfoCube is compressed heavily and becomes much smaller, you may be able to improve accelerator performance by rebuilding its BIA index from time to time. In the BIA monitor, one of the performance checks compares the number of records in the fact indexes with the number of records in the corresponding fact tables (see Section 5.3.2). If the numbers differ significantly for a BIA index, the check issues a message saying you may want to rebuild the index to reduce its memory footprint and improve read performance.

When you roll up data for an InfoCube, the system first loads the new data into any aggregates that exist in the InfoCube, and then determines the delta of the new records for all the tables that have an index in the BIA index for the InfoCube and indexes that delta. If new SIDs are generated when transaction data is loaded, the system also writes new records to the indexes of the S, X, and Y tables. When the system has indexed all the indexes successfully, the data of the most recent request is released for reporting.

In InfoCube administration, where you can see whether a roll-up is missing, running, or successful, the system does not distinguish between whether the Info-Cube has aggregates or a BIA index. For most cubes, you will either have aggregates or a BIA index but not both. However, you may well decide to maintain aggregates alongside a BIA index for a transitional period, as a fallback option for the possibility that you decide not to use the accelerator for that cube.

Change Runs

Because the SAP NetWeaver BI Accelerator stores data from master data tables (X and Y tables) in table indexes within BIA indexes, it is affected by changes to master data.

However, in contrast to aggregates, BIA fact table indexes do not contain the current data for the master data. So administrators do not need to run the delta calculations they need to run for aggregates. Instead, they only transfer the changed records from the master data tables and change them in the X and Y table indexes in the BIA index.

Because the hierarchy tables are not in the BIA index either, there is no preaggregation on specific hierarchy levels, as is the case with aggregates, so again recalculation is unnecessary. The accelerator stores some views of hierarchies that occur in queries as temporary indexes in case they can be reused, but if the hierarchy is changed, it deletes these temporary indexes. During a change run, the accelerator changes the master data.

Deleting Data

In SAP NetWeaver BI, if you delete data selectively from an InfoCube, you need to rebuild the BIA index. When you execute selective deletion, the BI system automatically deletes the affected BIA index.

When you delete a data package from an InfoCube, the entry in the package dimension index for the package dimension table is invalidated. The facts in the fact index remain, but they are no longer referenced by an entry in the package dimension table. Therefore, more entries exist in the index than in the table of the InfoCube. If you regularly delete data packages, the number of unused records increases, increasing memory consumption. This can have a negative effect on performance. In this case, it is a good idea to schedule time for rebuilding the BIA index. You can run a performance check to detect such excessively large indexes (see Section 5.3.2).

Delta Index Merges

Without delta indexing, any changes to the data in a BIA index are written directly into the index, which may consume more time than is acceptable during periods of heavy system load. With delta indexing, any changes to the data in a BIA index are first written to the delta index, and the delta index is accessed in parallel to the main index during query processing. If the delta index is not allowed to become too large, it can improve query performance. If you have activated delta indexing for any indexes, you should run the index check SIZE OF DELTA INDEX (see Section 5.3.2) regularly to check whether one or more delta indexes have grown too large. If necessary, the accelerator merges them in repair mode.

Index Reorganization

If a host in the BIA landscape fails or if new hardware becomes available, index reorganization is needed to maintain good performance; but in other situations, for example, when indexes gradually become larger or smaller through updates and would benefit from being redistributed, reorganization can be scheduled for a quiet period when users will be least disturbed. Section 4.4.3 describes how to perform index reorganization.

During reorganization, only the assignment of indexes to TREX index server processes is changed. This is done in accordance with the chosen distribution algorithm. The physical representation of the indexes as flat files is unaffected, and their location on the storage remains unchanged.

4.3.2 Monitoring Load

The load on your BI accelerator will vary. Monitoring the load variations will enable you to schedule jobs that should run during periods of low system load. Alternatively, you may discover a steady rise in load that suggests the need to install additional capacity. To monitor load, the BIA monitor offers a convenient button on the main screen.

The BIA Load Monitor Activate button calls the BIA load monitor in a separate window that refreshes itself independently (see Figure 4.34).

Host:Port	Memory Process	Total Memory	Memory Available	CPU All Proc.	CPU per Proc.	Resp. Time	Requests	Requests	Req.(+Internal)	Active Req	Req. Pending
lu01118:37703	356.120 kB	2.854.604 kB	100.076.152 kB	0 %	0 %	0.000 s	0.083 /s	58	33.540	0	0
lu01119:37703	357.224 kB	1.604.272 kB	100.076.152 kB	0 %	0 %	0.000 s	0.083 /s	286	33.741	0	0
lu01120:37703	355.572 kB	1.953.416 kB	100.076.152 kB	0 %	0 %	0.000 s	0.083 /s	183	33.640	0	0
lu01121:37703	303.952 kB	5.651.152 kB	100.076.152 kB	0 %	0 %	0.000 s	0.083 /s	4	33.208	0	0
lu01122:37703	303.960 kB	6.620.332 kB	100.076.152 kB	0 %	0 %	0.000 s	0.083 /s	4	33.200	0	0
lu01123:37703	303.432 kB	5.043.624 kB	100.076.152 kB	0 %	0 %	0.000 s	0.083 /s	4	33.191	0	0
lu01124:37703	303.960 kB	3.110.080 kB	100.076.152 kB	0 %	0 %	0.000 s	0.041 /s	4	33.183	0	0

Figure 4.34 BIA Monitor, Load Monitor

In this window, you can see the following BIA key numbers:

▶ HOST:PORT
The host and port where the BIA index server is attached.

▶ MEMORY PROCESS
Memory usage of TREX index server process.

▶ TOTAL MEMORY
Memory usage of all processes.

▶ MEMORY AVAILABLE
Total memory available on the host.

▶ CPU ALL PROC.
CPU usage of all running processes.

▶ CPU PER PROC.
CPU usage of TREX index server processes.

▶ RESP. TIME
Average response time for the past few queries.

▶ QUERIES
Number of queries requests handled per second.

▶ REQUESTS
Number of external requests.

▶ REQUESTS (+ INTERNAL)
Number of external and internal requests.

- ACTIVE REQ.
  Number of currently active requests.

- REQ. PENDING
  Number of waiting or pending requests.

You can only start one load monitor at a time. Because the load monitor is started in a new window, it uses a new SAP mode, so before you activate the load monitor, you may wish to check that a mode is available.

For technical reasons, the load monitor window is kept open. You can continue to work in this window or close it.

You can end the load monitor from the BIA monitor. As soon as you start the load monitor, the button function is reset to BIA LOAD MONITOR DEACTIVATE. After you have stopped the load monitor, the button is reset again to BIA LOAD MONITOR ACTIVATE.

4.3.3 Creating Backups

Because BIA indexes contain data that was read from the BI database, and the data in the database is backed up independently of the accelerator, it may seem unnecessary to create backups of the BIA indexes. However, if the BIA indexes on the accelerator storage become unavailable for any reason, it may be faster to restore them from backups than to rebuild them anew. For this reason, it is worth considering a backup strategy for your BIA indexes.

The main task here is to schedule the regular creation of backups for the BIA indexes in your system. Periods of low system load (with few or no business users) are the best times to create backups.

You should take locking into account when planning a backup. During a backup run, all indexing processes are automatically put on hold and wait until the backup is completed. The locks of these waiting processes remain in place.

An BIA backup involves exporting all committed data in the BIA system at a given time. The data includes all BIA indexes with status created, whether or not they have been filled, but does not include the TREX installation binaries. The backups are executed as full and not as incremental backups. Any data loads to the accelerator are automatically put on hold during the exports.

The SAP NetWeaver BI system assigns each exported dataset an ID and a times-tamp. The backups are called snapshots. So a snapshot is an export of all indexes. The BI system triggers the TREX backup server to take a snapshot of the current status in the accelerator.

The BIA monitor displays only the last 20 snapshots. Performing a recovery with an old snapshot brings little benefit, and a complete re-indexing may be faster. So you do not need to archive snapshots, and you can delete old snapshots on a regular basis.

You can create a snapshot from the BIA monitor as follows:

1. Choose BI ACCELERATOR • MAINTENANCE FUNCTIONS • BACKUP AND RECOVERY (see Figure 4.35).

2. Schedule a BIA snapshot, and give it a name.

3. Check the logs to ensure that the snapshot was generated without errors.

4. View the snapshot details to ensure that it contains data.

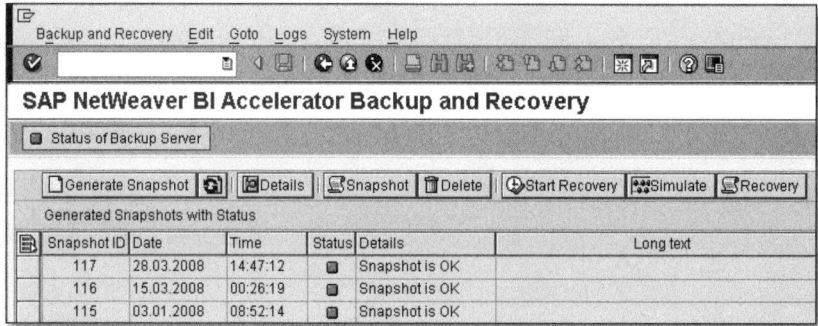

Figure 4.35 BIA Monitor, Backup and Recovery

Best Practice for BIA Backups

If you decide it is worth making backups of your BIA indexes:

▶ Schedule a daily backup in a load-free time window.

▶ Perform additional backups manually after major changes to the data.

▶ Decide how many backups you wish to keep and for how long.

▶ Delete the oldest backup after each successful backup creation.

▶ Check the success of backup creation periodically.

4.4 Occasional Tasks

The blade server hardware for the SAP NetWeaver BI Accelerator is extremely reliable, but occasionally a blade will require maintenance. The TREX standalone administration tool (see Section 5.1) enables you to stop the services running on a blade (by stopping the daemon) so that the blade can be serviced or replaced. The servicing at blade level may include updating or patching the Linux operating system or installing more memory capacity. Such tasks are independent of the BIA software, but other tasks that need to be performed at blade level involve the BIA software itself. These include cloning an existing BIA instance from the BIA file server to a newly installed blade or a newly maintained blade and updating the BIA software on the BIA file server to update the BIA installation as a whole. Another occasional task is to trigger index reorganization, as prompted by alerts in the BIA monitor.

4.4.1 Cloning a BIA Instance

When a new blade server is added to the enclosure and connected to the blades on which the accelerator is running, you first need to check that the correct Linux build is installed and that the file system mount point exists on the new host.

Cloning a BIA instance is the process of installing the instance from the file server onto the new blade and making the new instance available to the BIA landscape. The most convenient way to do this is to run the installer script on the new blade and simply follow its instructions.

The installer script is likely to be among the files on the storage, where it was left by the hardware partner who did the initial setup. Alternatively, if the original installation script is no longer available, you can run the shell script for cloning directly. It is called `cloner.sh` and should be found in the global directory for the system.

If the mount point is called, say, `/filer`, to clone a BIA instance <SAPSID> from an existing blade in the enclosure to the blade, proceed as follows:

1. Open a command shell on the new host and check that the file server mount point exists on it. In a default installation, the mount point is called `/filer`.
2. Execute `/filer/<SAPSID>/SYS/global/cloner.sh` where <SAPSID> is the SAP system ID for the BIA instance. There is also a link to the mount point called `/usr/sap/`, which can also be used for navigation.

3. To check that cloning was successful, start Transaction TREXADMIN, choose ADVANCED MODE, and click the HOSTS tab. You should see the new host listed with the others, as shown in Figure 4.36.

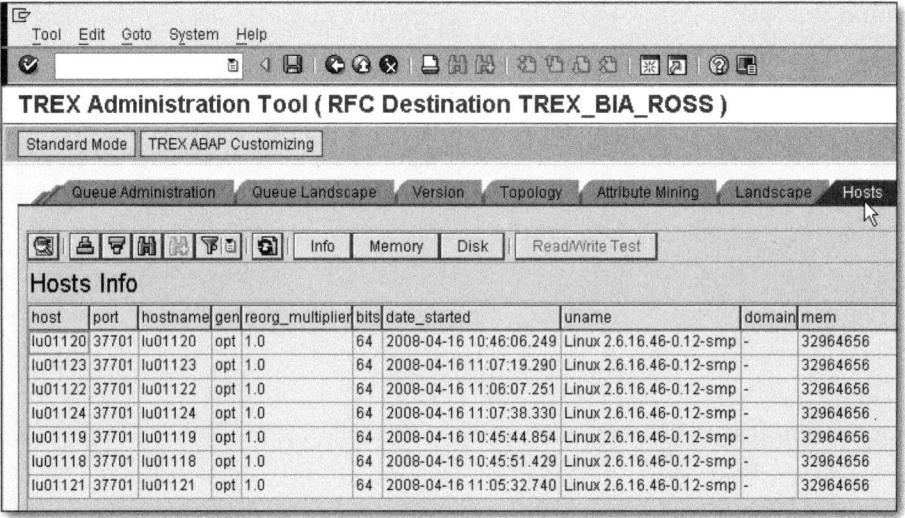

Figure 4.36 TREXADMIN, Advanced Mode, Hosts Tab

The cloner script executes several steps:

▶ It creates user `<sid>adm` in the group `sapsys` at operating system level on the new blade.

▶ It installs the start scripts to run the BIA instance automatically after a reboot of the system.

▶ It adds a new directory to the path `/usr/sap/<SAPSID>/TRX<NN>/` (where `NN` is the instance number) with the name of the new blade and copies the BIA configuration files into the directory.

▶ It adds the new instance to the existing landscape by updating the topology file.

Once this script has run, the new instance should be recognized and displayed in Transaction TREXADMIN (see Figure 4.9 shown earlier). To take full advantage of the new host, you should trigger an index reorganization to redistribute the BIA indexes evenly over all the available hosts.

4.4.2 Updating a BIA Instance

As an administrator, you should always keep the revision level of their BIA installation to the latest published in SAP Service Marketplace. Before an update, you should stop all BIA services on the BIA hosts.

To update a BIA instance from the installed revision to a new revision, proceed as follows.

1. Download the latest BIA revision from SAP Service Marketplace. Download it to the BIA blade with the lowest number because this blade hosts the default master name server for the BIA landscape.

2. Log on as root, and execute `install.sh -u`. If you execute `install.sh` instead, you will be prompted to confirm that you wish to perform an upgrade.

3. Follow the script, and enter any requested information. If you are prompted for a password, enter the root password.

After the update, start Transaction TREXADMIN, and check that all BIA services are up and running and that the latest BIA version information is displayed (see Figure 4.37).

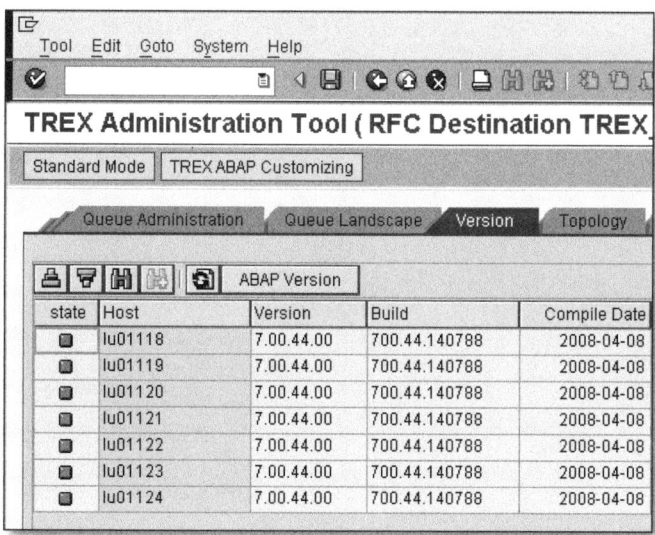

Figure 4.37 TREXADMIN, Advanced Mode, Version Tab

4.4.3   Reorganizing the BIA Indexes

As existing BIA indexes are updated and new indexes are added, the distribution of indexes over the available hosts in the BIA landscape can become suboptimal. Although TREX automatically estimates an optimal index distribution over the BIA landscape and allocates any new indexes in accordance with its estimation, the existing indexes stay where they are until they are reorganized.

An alert server check, which is activated by default, regularly checks the index distribution and generates an alert message if the actual index distribution deviates too much from the estimated optimum. The message recommends a reorganization of the indexes.

The reason for recommending reorganization rather than simply performing it automatically whenever it becomes advantageous is that there is a brief interruption of service caused by the reorganization. As the BIA indexes are reallocated between the BIA hosts, they are reloaded into memory from the attached storage, and this takes a few seconds, depending on how much data needs to be read from storage. Because users may be inconvenienced by this interruption, the exact timing of the reorganization is left as a manual task for the administrator.

The BIA monitor enables you to trigger index reorganization with minimal effort. In the EXECUTE ACTIONS screen area, you simply flag the checkbox for REORGANIZE BIA LANDSCAPE and execute.

Transaction TREXADMIN also enables you to trigger index reorganization easily. Switch to advanced mode (by clicking the toggle for advanced and standard modes), select the REORG tab, and then click START REORG (see Figure 4.38).

The advantage of working via Transaction TREXADMIN to reorganize the BIA indexes is that the lower part of the Reorg tab shows exactly why TREX recommends reorganization and how much improvement you can expect.

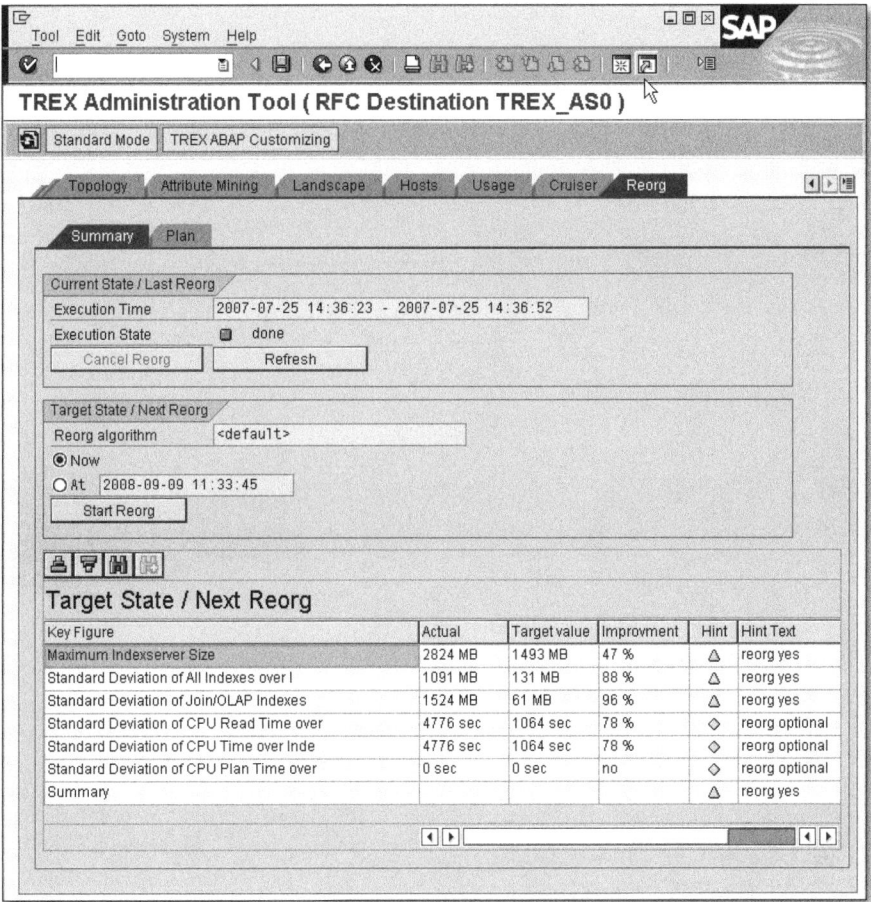

Figure 4.38 TREX Administration, Advanced Mode, Reorg Tab

4.5 Summary

The administration tools available for the SAP NetWeaver BI Accelerator are sufficient to ensure that all routine tasks can be accomplished smoothly, and most tasks can be performed within SAP transactions. The main transactions for this purpose are the BIA monitor, the Data Warehousing Workbench, the BIA index maintenance transaction, the BIA index check and repair transaction, and the TREX administration transaction.

The tasks that can be accomplished with these tools can be classified as initial, regular, and occasional tasks. Initial tasks include setting up the RFC connection, creating BIA indexes, and configuring alerts. Regular tasks include maintaining BIA indexes, monitoring load, and possibly creating backups. Occasional tasks include cloning and updating BIA instances and reorganizing the indexes.

5 Advanced Administration

The administration tasks described so far have been part of the required skill set for any administrator of an SAP NetWeaver BI system with a BI accelerator attached. The tasks described in this section are more advanced and require additional skill to perform safely.

For users with sufficient experience, the TREX standalone administration tool offers a wealth of opportunities for deeper technical interaction with the TREX software within the accelerator. If a company requires SAP help to manage issues with its accelerator installation, an administrator can grant SAP service engineers remote access through the company firewall to the accelerator blades and thus allow them to use the TREX standalone administration tool over the Internet.

Section 5.1 introduces the TREX standalone administration tool. Section 5.2 describes some exceptional tasks such as repairing the connection to the BI system, checking and repairing the indexes, and performing a recovery. Section 5.3 describes some optimization tasks, including landscape reorganization, performance checks, and adjusting indexing parameters. Section 5.4 describes some tasks related to any necessary collaboration with SAP service experts, such as setting up a service connection, checking the BIA landscape, and creating trace files. Section 5.5 summarizes the chapter.

5.1 The TREX Standalone Administration Tool

For fully detailed interaction with the TREX engine at the heart of the SAP NetWeaver BI Accelerator, there is no better tool than the TREX standalone administration tool. This is a graphical tool supporting point-and-click and drag-and-drop interaction. Most administrative tasks can be handled through the SAP Transactions RSDDBIAMON and TREXADMIN, but some more advanced tasks require use of the TREX standalone administration tool. This tool was built by and for TREX developers, to enable them to work more easily with their own growing creation, and for this reason it offers powerful features that can be dangerous in the hands of a beginner. The tool does not include the safeguards that a beginner might expect, and therefore it should not be made accessible to anyone who is not qualified to use it safely.

The TREX standalone administration tool supports a huge range of interactions and can display enough system information to enable technical experts to do whatever may be necessary to resolve any TREX issues that can arise in a productive BIA installation. If remote access to the tool is granted, SAP service engineers can use it to perform any troubleshooting task in TREX.

To start the TREX standalone administration tool:

1. Open a command-line window on one of the BIA hosts.
2. Change to user `<sid>adm`.
3. Go to directory `/usr/sap/<SAPSID>/TRX<NN>/`.
4. Execute command `TREXAdmin.sh`.

The default host on which to start the tool is the BIA blade hosting the active master name server. This is normally the first blade numerically in the set of BIA blades because the installation automatically assigns consecutive numbers to the blades, and the default master starts on the first blade. However, the tool can be started from any blade in the landscape and display the same information.

The TREX standalone administration tool opens at the view displayed when it was last closed. However, the natural view to display first is the SUMMARY view (see Figure 5.1). The STATUS line above the STATUS DETAILS panel tells you what you need to know first. In this case, all the alert icons are green (square). Above the STATUS line are some version and platform details, and the STATUS DETAILS panel displays the more major check results such as memory consumption, number and total size of indexes, and whether traces are on or off.

After the SUMMARY view, the first view to check in the TREX administration tool is perhaps the SERVICES view (see Figure 5.2). All the main services on all the hosts in the landscape are listed. In this case, there are four blades in the landscape, and on each blade, there are name server, index server, RFC server, and "other" (alert server) services running. The green (square) icons down the left side show that all the services have status OK. The bars toward the center show that at the time of this screen capture, there is very little CPU activity or memory consumption on the blades.

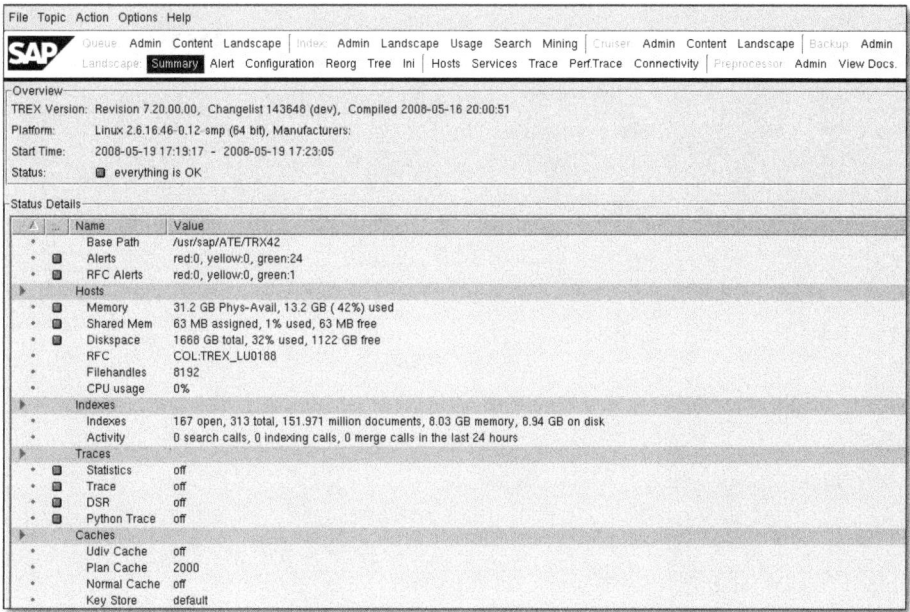

Figure 5.1 TREX Admin Tool, Summary

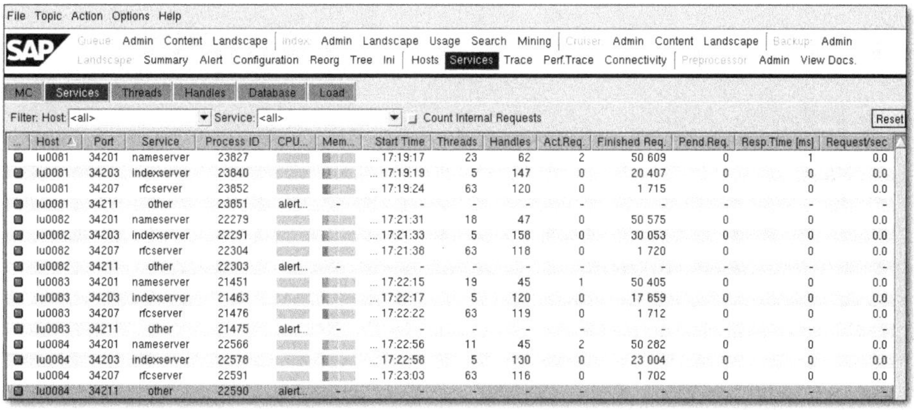

Figure 5.2 TREX Admin Tool, Services

To configure the BIA landscape, choose the CONFIGURATION view (see Figure 5.3).

The SCENARIO panel at the upper left enables you to select usage of backup index servers (the other options are inapplicable for the accelerator).

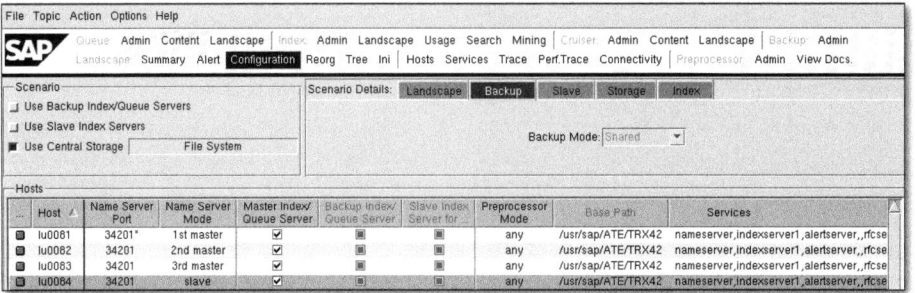

Figure 5.3 TREX Admin Tool, Configuration

In the SCENARIO DETAILS panel toward the right, the BACKUP tab offers a drop-down menu for selecting a backup mode. The available modes are:

▶ SHARED (one backup for all masters)

▶ DEDICATED (one backup for each master)

▶ MULTIPLEXED (one backup for several masters)

▶ MUTUAL (each master is backup for another master)

The INDEX tab enables you to change the size threshold for splitting a large BIA index.

Below the tabs, the HOSTS panel includes more detailed information and indicates with an asterisk which blade hosts the currently active master name server. Use of the word "slave" is an inheritance from the text search world and has no meaning for the accelerator.

Instead of configuring the alert server via Transaction TREXADMIN, you can do so from the TREX standalone administration tool by selecting the ALERTS view, and then choosing ALERT SERVER CONFIGURATION (see Figure 5.4). Both these alternatives offer the same functional capabilities.

In the top panel of the configuration dialog box, you can enter an e-mail address to which alerts above the given threshold (trace level) should be sent. In the middle panel, you can override the default set of checks that run regularly, at times specified by the code in the middle column, and you can change how often they run by editing the displayed cron job specification (for which there is a nearby CRONTAB HELP button in case you forget the format). In the bottom panel, you can change the selection of individual checks that run in the selected check set.

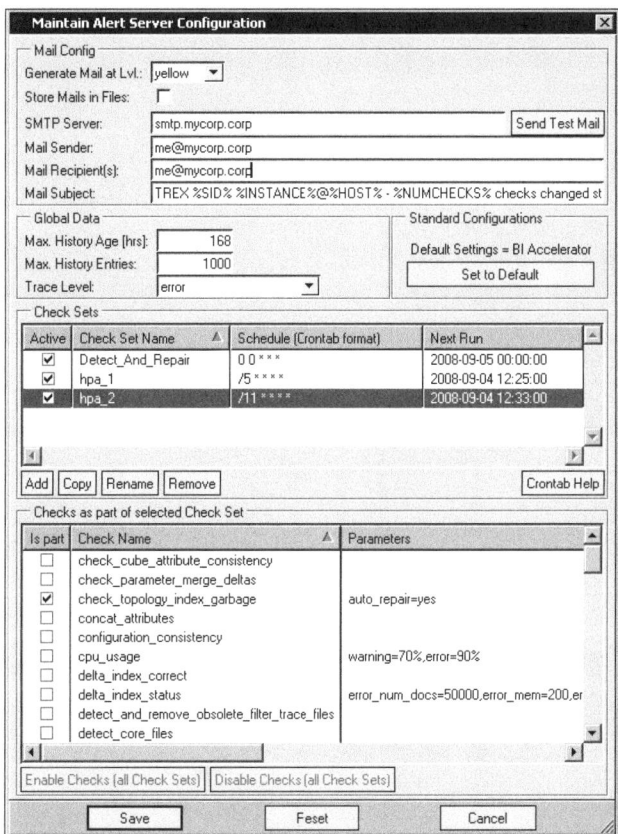

Figure 5.4 TREX Admin Tool, Alert Server Configuration

You should ensure that the BIA blades can reach the SMTP server you specify as the destination for e-mail alert messages. Each TREX installation runs its own alert server, and the results from the checks run by each of the alert server processes are consolidated on the blade that hosts the active master name server so the active master sends the alert messages, but this can only succeed if TREX can access the SMTP server.

5.2 Exceptional Tasks

As an administrator, you should be able to handle not only the tasks that arise during routine operation of the SAP NetWeaver BI Accelerator, but also certain tasks you would need to perform only in exceptional circumstances. Here we review some of these tasks.

5.2.1 Repairing the RFC Connection

If the RFC connection between the BIA blades and the SAP NetWeaver BI system is broken for any reason, the situation can be diagnosed and in most cases repaired using the TREX administration tool. The tool offers full support for creating and editing RFC destinations, pinging hosts to locate network problems, reporting in detail on any issues that arise, and automatically repairing broken connections.

Alerts are color-coded to highlight any that require manual intervention. In general, red alerts indicate an error status that the tool cannot repair by itself, while yellow alerts indicate issues that the tool can resolve automatically. The red alerts indicate situations that require human action. The yellow alerts will be repaired in the next check run if the RFC check in the alert server is activated (where the check runs by default every 5 minutes).

You can create a new RFC destination in the SAP NetWeaver BI system for the accelerator by using Transaction SM59, as described in Section 4.2.2. The connection type is TCP/IP, and TREX runs as a registered server program. The program ID is unimportant because the accelerator overwrites it automatically with a correct ID.

To ensure that you receive sufficient warning of any RFC problems that may arise, you can check that the TREX alert server is configured to perform regular automatic RFC connection checks and to send you an e-mail if a problem is sufficiently serious.

To do so, in the TREX standalone administration tool ALERT view, choose ALERT SERVER CONFIGURATION to display the dialog box shown earlier in Figure 5.4. There you can check that your e-mail contact information is entered correctly, and you can review the checks that have been selected. To receive RFC warnings, you should ensure that in one of the selected check sets, the check rfc_connection has been flagged.

To handle matters related to the RFC communication between the accelerator and the BI system, choose the CONNECTIVITY view in the TREX standalone administration tool, as shown in Figure 5.5.

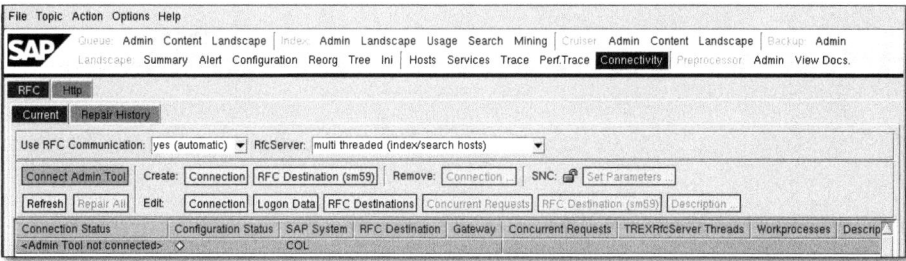

Figure 5.5 TREX Admin Tool, Connectivity View

The view opens to show the RFC tab with its CURRENT tab showing. The tool indicates any recommended next action by highlighting the relevant button with a different color. In the case shown, the administration tool has not yet connected itself to the BI system, as indicated by the gray (diamond) icon, and the recommended next action is to choose the CONNECT ADMIN TOOL button.

If the TREX standalone administration tool attempts to connect itself to the BI system, but the required connection data is missing in the accelerator, the tool will show a message highlighted in yellow as shown in Figure 5.6.

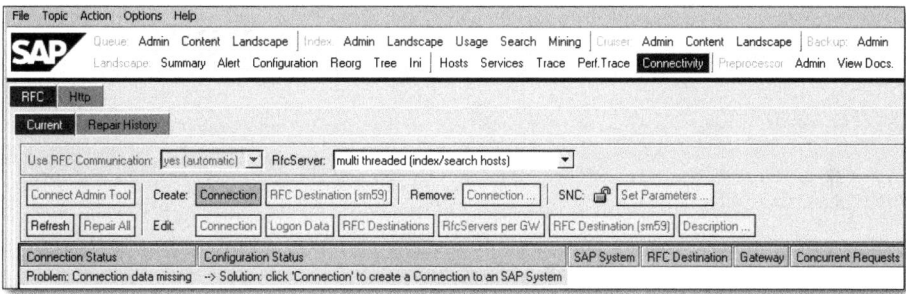

Figure 5.6 TREX Admin Tool, Connection Data Missing

The recommended next action is to create a connection. This is indicated by the highlighting of the button you should choose next to create a connection. When you do so, the dialog box shown in Figure 5.7 appears.

This dialog box enables you to create a connection to the specified SAP system on the assumption that a correctly configured RFC destination exists in that system. Within TREX, the connection data you enter in the dialog box is stored in the *saprfc.ini* file, and the logon data you enter is encrypted and stored in *topology.ini*.

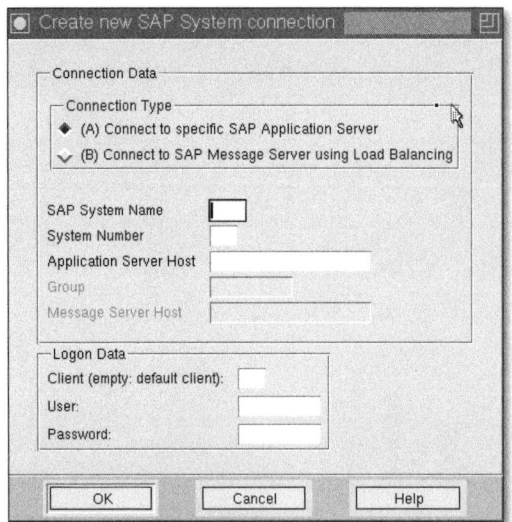

Figure 5.7 TREX Admin Tool, Create New SAP System Connection

When you set up an RFC destination, you need to specify whether your accelerator connects to your SAP NetWeaver BI system landscape via local gateways or a central gateway (see Figure 5.8). Each TREX instance has one RFC server process, which spawns as many threads as required.

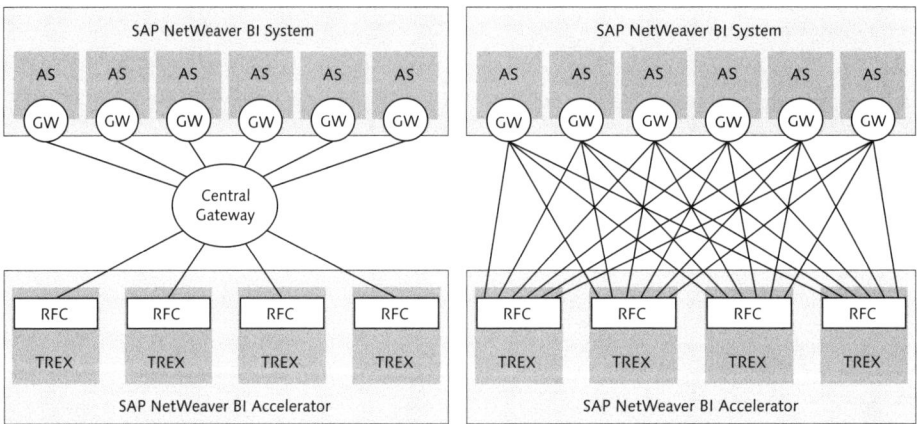

Figure 5.8 Central and Local SAP Gateways

A central gateway between the local gateways on the application servers and the RFC servers in TREX appears to offer simpler traffic flow because each node at either end communicates with only a single node represented by the central gateway but has the disadvantage that this central node is a single point of failure and can be a bottleneck in a heavy load scenario. For this reason, we recommend the use of local gateways for communication with the accelerator.

In the local gateway configuration, each application server communicates directly through an RFC server with every TREX instance in the BIA landscape, and vice versa. As Figure 5.8 shows, this can give rise to a large number of RFC server threads on each BIA host, but no extra administration is required. The administrator simply leaves the gateway option fields blank when setting up the RFC destination. TREX then starts as many RFC server threads as needed.

If a suitable RFC destination does not yet exist in the target SAP system, you can create one, either in Transaction SM59 or in the TREX standalone administration tool.

If TREX does not find a suitable RFC destination in the target SAP system, the tool prompts you (with highlighted buttons) either to enter into TREX the information about an existing RFC destination that is defined in a connected SAP system (see Figure 5.9) and store the information in the TREX *topology.ini* file or to create a new RFC destination in a connected SAP system (see Figure 5.10). If you create a new destination, you do not need to enter a program ID because TREX generates one automatically for use at both ends of the connection. Again, the information is stored locally in the TREX *topology.ini* file. As soon as the destination has been created, a "created successfully" information box appears.

Creating a new RFC destination from TREX as shown in Figure 5.10 is equivalent to doing so in the SAP system using Transaction SM59. Both ways of setting up an RFC destination require the same information.

Connecting the TREX administration tool to the SAP system is just the first step. Once the tool has successfully connected, it determines whether all the BIA blade server hosts can communicate correctly with the SAP system. If not, for example, because an application server has been removed from the landscape or added to it, the tool may display information similar to that shown in Figure 5.11, with error details highlighted in red, other unresolved issues in yellow, and a yellow (warning triangle) status icon for the affected system. The problems highlighted in yellow can be solved by the automatic repair capabilities built into the administration tool. In this case, the tool prompts you with highlighting to choose the REPAIR ALL button. Because the RFC check runs automatically in the background,

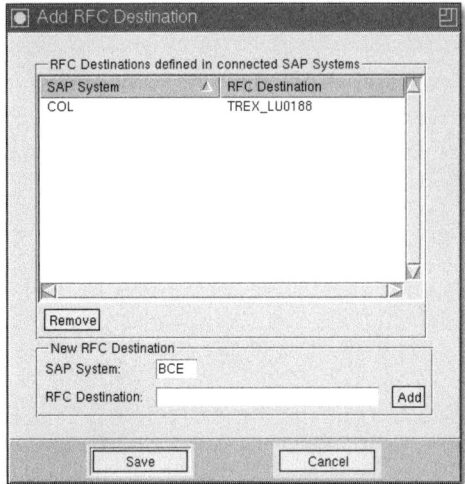

Figure 5.9 TREX Admin Tool, Add RFC Destination

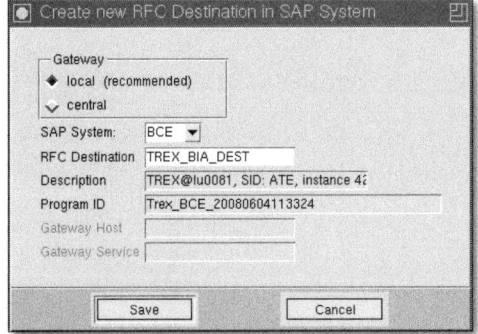

Figure 5.10 TREX Admin Tool, Create New RFC Destination

you can simply wait to let the repair run, and check that it has done by clicking REFRESH as often as necessary, but clicking the highlighted REPAIR ALL button can speed up the repair if you are in a hurry.

Fortunately, the problems shown here were not too serious, and TREX solved them all in seconds, as shown in Figure 5.12. Now the tool shows a green (square) configuration status icon and highlights the connection details in green to indicate that all is well. Generally, the tool offers clear visual feedback in this way to ensure that the administrator knows as exactly as possible what to do next.

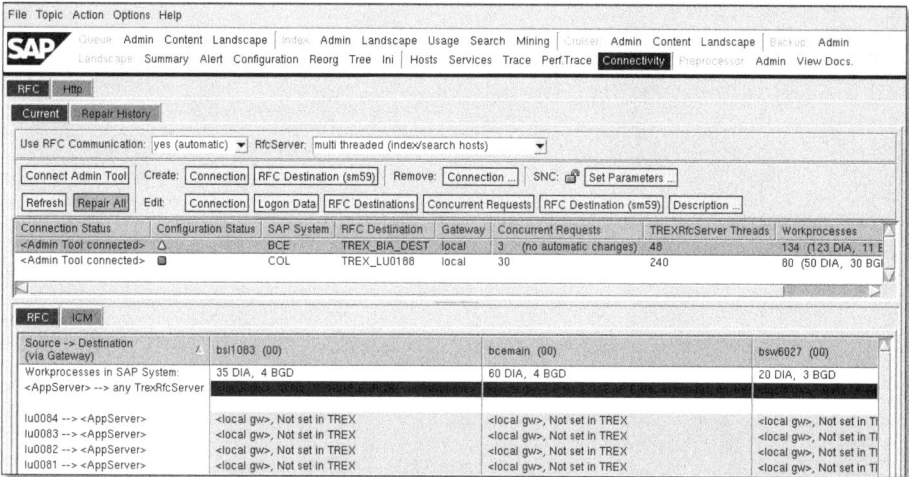

Figure 5.11 TREX Admin Tool, Repair Connectivity

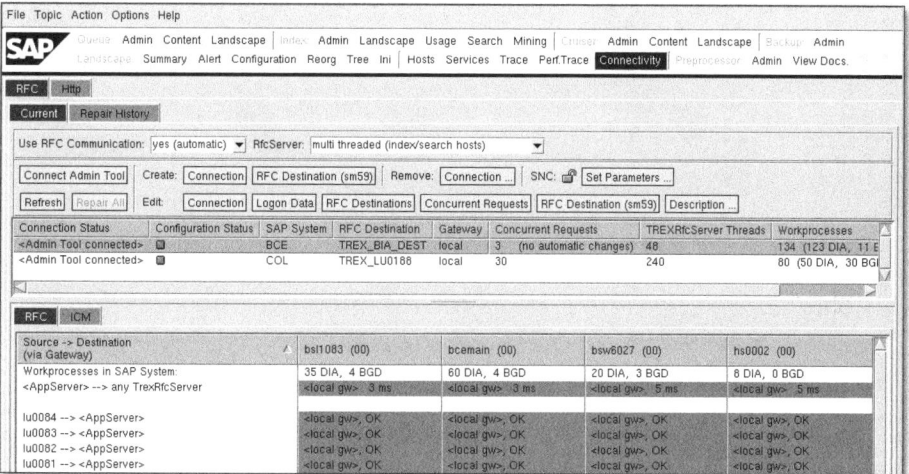

Figure 5.12 TREX Admin Tool, Connectivity Repaired

The TREX administration tool includes a great deal more functionality for the automatic repair of connectivity issues, but the user experience is always similar to that illustrated here, and an experienced administrator should have no difficulty with it.

5.2.2 Consistency Checks

To ensure that the data in your BIA indexes are consistent with the InfoCube data in the BI system, you can run a variety of consistency checks. The main launch point for such checks is the BI Accelerator Data Consistency Check Center.

From the BIA monitor, choose GOTO • CONSISTENCY CHECKS. This opens the BI Accelerator Data Consistency Check Center. From this center, you can execute consistency checks, schedule these checks, and view the logs of checks that have run (see Figure 5.13).

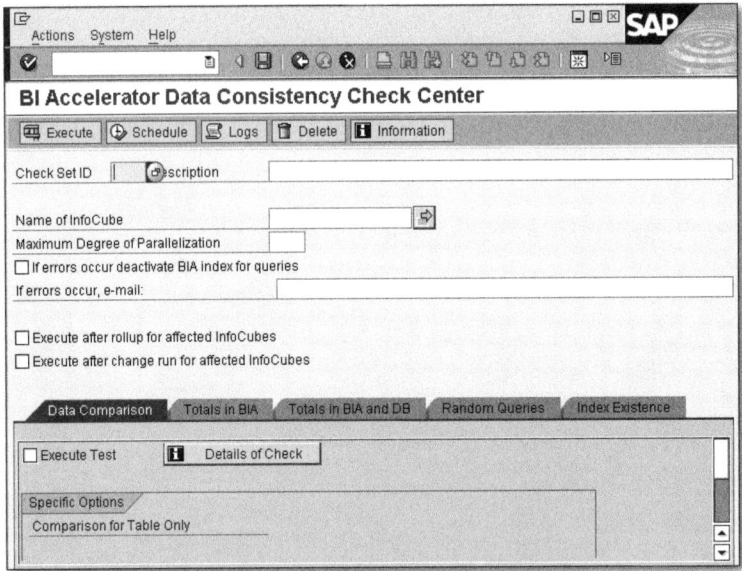

Figure 5.13 BI Accelerator Data Consistency Check Center

The BI Accelerator Data Consistency Check Center offers the following tabs from which you can execute the checks:

▶ DATA COMPARISON
Enables you to compare the contents of each individual table in an InfoCube with the contents of the corresponding index, record by record. This check is only suitable for relatively small tables and indexes.

▶ TOTALS IN BIA
Enables you to check key figure sums internally by executing a query on the BIA index using all key figures. Then the BI system executes a query for each

characteristic and navigation attribute occurring in the InfoCube that aggregates over all key figures. All the characteristics and navigation attributes that exist in the InfoCube are then included individually in the drilldown, and the totals are calculated. The system compares the result with the result of the first query. This test checks the completeness of the join paths to the fact tables. If the test shows that the data is incorrect, you need to rebuild the BIA index and its master data indexes.

▶ TOTALS IN BIA AND DB
Enables you to compare key figure sums on the database against and in the BIA index. The system executes a query for each characteristic and navigation attribute occurring in the InfoCube that aggregates over all key figures on the BIA index and the database. Then it sums individually over all the characteristics and navigation attributes occurring in the InfoCube and compares the results from the database and the accelerator. The runtime of the test can be long. If it shows that the data is incorrect, you need to rebuild the BIA index and its master data indexes.

▶ RANDOM QUERIES
Enables you to checks for consistency by executing random queries, reading the data once from the database and once from the accelerator. The results should be the same. However, they can differ if the InfoCube data has been changed between execution of the query on the database and in the accelerator. You can verify the results as described later in this section. To repair the index, you need to rebuild it.

▶ INDEX EXISTENCE
Enables you to checks whether indexes have been created for all the (relevant) tables in the star schema for the InfoCube. The test is very fast. If an index is missing, the BIA index needs to be rebuilt.

As an alternative to working from the BI Accelerator Data Consistency Check Center, you can run some fast index checks from the BIA monitor. Or you can run the more thorough checks in Transaction RSRV, to check that the indexes are complete and consistent.

To execute one or more sets of automatic BIA index checks in the BIA monitor, choose INDEX CHECKS • BI ACCELERATOR.

This offers the following further options:

▶ INDEX CHECKS SCHEDULE/DESCHEDULE
Toggles the index checks schedule on or off.

▶ EXECUTE/DISPLAY/CHANGE CHECKS
Displays a dialog box inviting you to flag the check set or sets you want to run, and then execute (see Figure 5.14). Once the checks have run, the results are displayed. In the run shown in Figure 5.15, 11 checks ran smoothly, and no red or yellow alerts were generated.

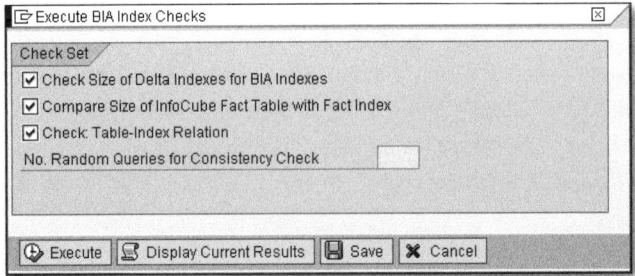

Figure 5.14 BIA Monitor, Execute Index Checks

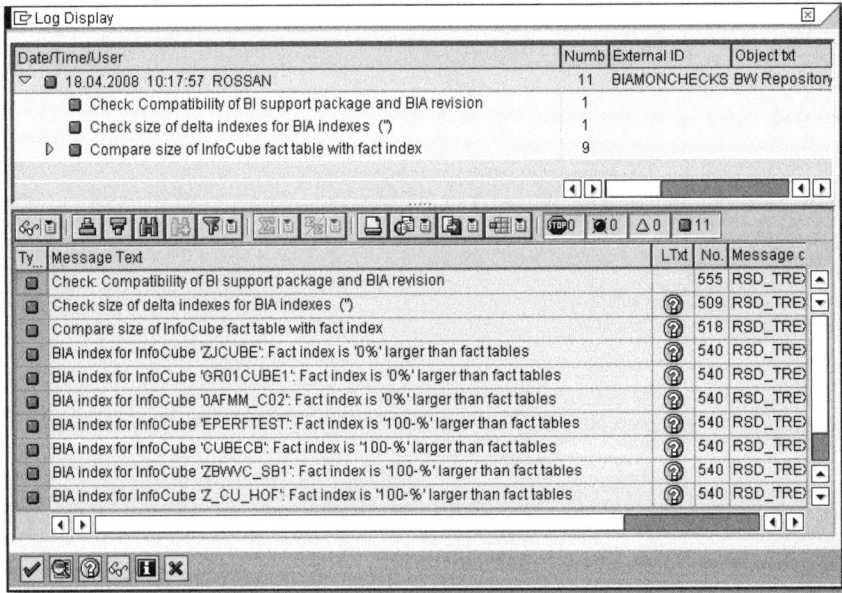

Figure 5.15 BIA Monitor, Index Check Results

The default set of index checks currently includes three checks. Check 1 looks at the size of delta indexes for BIA indexes, check 2 compares the size of InfoCube fact tables with their fact indexes, and check 3 looks at the relation between tables and indexes. The checks run quickly and provide useful information about performance and consistency. They can also be found and run in the analysis and repair environment (Transaction RSRV, see Section 5.2.6).

To execute selected elementary or combined checks in Transaction RSRV, drill down in the check set tree displayed on the left side of the screen to find the accelerator checks that you wish to run and double-click on them. This causes their names to appear on the right side of the screen (see Figure 5.16). Alternatively, you can drag them to the right and drop them there. Then, for each check on the right, you need to set the relevant parameters (this generally means specifying the InfoCube or InfoCubes to be checked). To do this, click on the lines at right to open a dialog box (see Figure 5.17) where you can enter the required values. When you are ready, choose EXECUTE and wait for the results (see Figure 5.18). These are displayed as a detailed list with a colored icon for each line to show at a glance whether all went well.

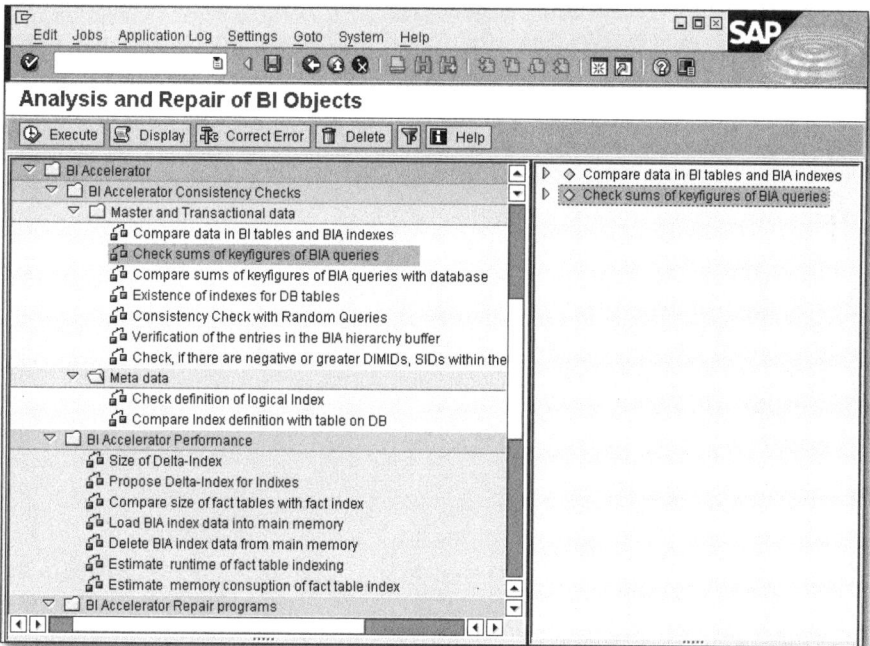

Figure 5.16 Transaction RSRV, Select Checks to Run

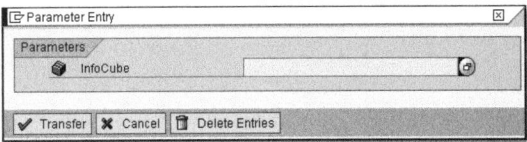

Figure 5.17 Transaction RSRV, Dialog Box for Parameter Entry

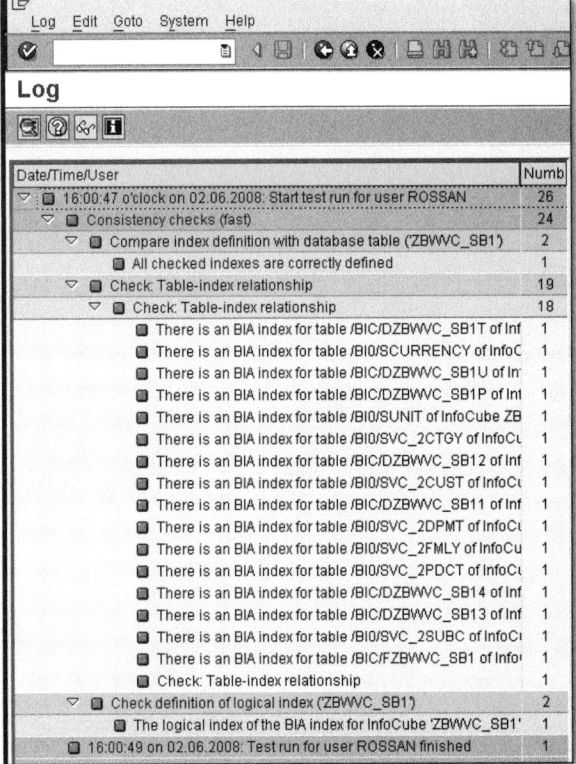

Figure 5.18 Transaction RSRV, Check Results

When to Run Checks: A Matrix

With so many checks, so many indexes to check, and so many possible reasons to run a check, it may seem impossible to follow a regular plan here. However, a little preparation can help. Draw a matrix with checks and reasons to run checks as its columns and rows, and then fill it out for yourself in view of your index landscape and your own priorities.

Table 5.1 shows a possible matrix. Here the 6 consistency checks listed below the matrix are numbered in the column heads and mapped to the 13 reasons to run checks listed in the rows. Check 1 is a query load generated by the RSTT trace tool described in Section 5.4.3, and checks 2–6 are listed with brief descriptions in Section 5.2.2.

As an example of how to read this matrix, the dots in it specify that after a roll-up or a change run, you plan to run the checks 2–6, and after hardware changes or performance shortfalls, you plan to run checks 1, 4, and 5.

The pattern of dots in this matrix is just san example, and as an administrator, you should plot your own matrix. Ideally, you should also insert more detail, for example, by adding a line specifying how often in the routine case you plan to run the check and a line indicating approximately how much time on average the check takes to run.

Consistency Check	1	2	3	4	5	6
Roll-up		•	•	•	•	•
Change run		•	•	•	•	•
Request deletion		•	•	•	•	•
Selective deletion		•	•	•	•	•
Metadata changes				•	•	•
Rebuild all indexes		•	•	•	•	•
Usage of delta index				•	•	•
Repair master data index	•	•	•	•	•	•
SPS/SP update	•	•	•	•	•	•
Revision update	•	•	•	•	•	•
Incorrect data		•	•	•	•	•
Hardware changes	•			•	•	
Performance issues	•			•	•	

1. Transaction RSTT generated query load
2. Compare data in BI tables and accelerator indexes
3. Check sums of key figures of accelerator queries
4. Check for consistency using random queries
5. Check existence of indexes for DB tables
6. Check definition of logical index

Table 5.1 Example of an Index Check Matrix

Recommended best practice is to regularly check the data in your accelerator and compare it with the data in the database. You can do so from the BIA monitor by choosing GOTO • CONSISTENCY CHECKS, which opens the BI Accelerator Data Consistency Check Center (see Figure 5.13 shown earlier).

To minimize the system load and runtime for the consistency checks, use the following hints in a three-step approach:

1. **Check the facts**

   The fact indexes usually contain the most data and therefore take longest to check. To reduce the runtime of the check TOTALS IN BIA AND DB, set the DRILL-DOWN WITH INFOOBJECT ONLY option to a characteristic with few attributes such as CALYEAR (see Figure 5.19).

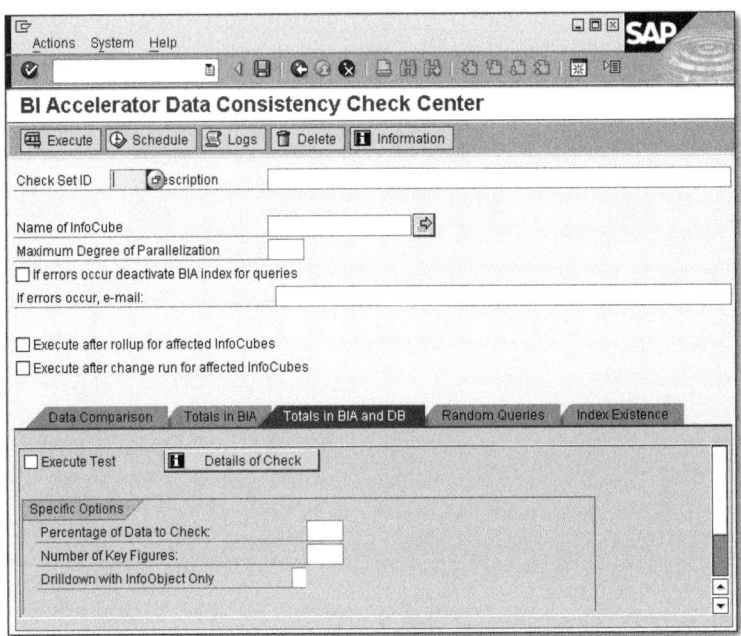

Figure 5.19 Data Consistency Check Center, Totals Tab in BIA and DB

If the InfoCube contains many key figures, you can reduce the load on the accelerator by reducing the number of key figures. If the runtime of this check is still too long, try reducing the percentage of data to be checked. A key figure overflow occurs during the check if the key figure type cannot contain the sum of all values.

2. **Check the completeness of the star schema indexes**

   These indexes can be very large, and we do not recommend a regular completeness check because it is too expensive.

   Instead, use the TOTALS IN BIA check to find incorrect or missing records in the fact tables. Execute all joins of the extended star schema, and compare the results as a complete aggregation on the fact table. This acts like a filter because if there are incorrect or missing records in one of the indexes, the result of the aggregation on the fact table is different from the reference result.

   Again, if the InfoCube contains many key figures, you can reduce the load by reducing the number of key figures, and if a key figure overflow occurs, you can reduce the percentage of data checked.

3. **Check data consistency in complex situations**

   You can check the BIA data using random queries with complex conditions. The performance of this check depends on the performance of the query in the database. If your database still has aggregates for the InfoCube you want to check, then some of the randomly generated queries can be processed efficiently in the database, and in this case the performance of the check will be better.

For the details behind these hints, see SAP Note 1095886.

Master Data and Transaction Data

We now look one by one at the consistency checks available in the analysis and repair Transaction RSRV.

COMPARE DATA IN BI TABLES AND BIA INDEXES

This check compares the contents of each individual table with the contents of the corresponding index, record by record. It is only suitable for tables or indexes that do not contain a large amount of data, such as dimension tables, certain S tables, and X and Y tables. Fact tables are normally too large for this check. If a table contains 10,000 records or more, it is not checked.

In some situations, the content of the indexes of the BIA index may differ from the content of the corresponding database table. This may be the case if requests have been deleted from the InfoCube or if an InfoCube has been compressed.

CHECK SUMS OF KEY FIGURES OF BIA QUERIES

This check first executes a query on the BIA index, which is aggregated using all key figures, then includes all the characteristics and navigation attributes that exist in the InfoCube individually in drilldowns, and calculates the totals. The results are now compared to check the completeness of the join paths to the fact tables.

The runtime of the check depends on the number of characteristics and attributes and on the size of the fact table. If the test shows that the data is incorrect, you need to rebuild the BIA index and the master data indexes.

CHECK SUMS OF KEY FIGURES OF BIA QUERIES WITH DATABASE

This check executes highly aggregated queries and compares the results from the database with those from the BIA index. For large InfoCubes, the runtime may be long.

CHECK EXISTENCE OF INDEXES FOR DATABASE TABLES

This test checks whether all the (relevant) indexes for a given InfoCube have been created on the BIA server. Its runtime is very fast. If the test reveals that an index is missing, the BIA index needs to be rebuilt.

CHECK FOR CONSISTENCY USING RANDOM QUERIES

This check executes random queries without persisting them. The system reads the data once from the database and once from the accelerator, and then compares the results. If the results differ, an error message is output.

The results can be different if the data of the InfoCube is changed between execution of the query on the database and in the accelerator.

To verify the results, execute program RSDRT_INFOPROV_RANDOM_QUERIES with the following parameters:

▶ InfoProvider: Name of the InfoCube

▶ Number of queries: 10

▸ Starting value: Same as used by the random generator

▸ Trace comparison: X

You can leave all other values unchanged. If the results are the same as from the check, you need to rebuild the BIA index.

VERIFY THE ENTRIES IN THE BIA HIERARCHY BUFFER

When queries are executed in hierarchies, the hierarchy nodes are expanded to the relevant leaves and the expansion saved in a temporary index in the accelerator. The hierarchy buffer manages expanded hierarchies according to an LRU (least recently used) algorithm.

This check verifies whether all temporary indexes in the hierarchy buffer contain correct data. If the hierarchy buffer contains incorrect entries, do not delete the hierarchy buffer but send a customer message to SAP Service. If you urgently need to continue work, you can delete the entire hierarchy buffer, but this will make it harder to troubleshoot the error.

Metadata

CHECK DEFINITION OF LOGICAL INDEX

This check compares the definitions of each of the table indexes in a BIA index with the current versions of the database tables. It checks whether the number, name, and type of the table fields in the database match the definition for the index on the BIA server. If you do not specify an InfoCube, the system executes the test for all InfoCubes that have a BIA index.

If a table definition has been changed, the system deletes the old index, creates a new index with the current definition, and fills it. All BIA indexes that use this index are set to inactive and become unavailable for reporting during this time. The period of unavailability depends on the size of the table that needs to be re-indexed.

COMPARE INDEX DEFINITION WITH TABLE ON DATABASE

The system checks the logical index of a BIA index. The logical index contains the metadata for the BIA index, such as the join conditions and the names of the fields, and may change if the InfoCube is changed. If you do not specify an Info-Cube, the system executes the test for all InfoCubes that have a BIA index.

If the logical index has been changed, the system deletes the old index and creates a new index with the correct definition. The system temporarily sets the BIA index to inactive, and the index is unavailable for reporting during this time.

FIND INDEXES WITH STATUS UNKNOWN

The system checks whether BIA indexes contain indexes that have the status unknown. This only occurs in exceptional cases when the Commit Optimize call terminates during indexing. Because in this case it is not clear whether the previously indexed data is available, the affected indexes are rebuilt in repair mode.

5.2.3 Check Sets for BIA Indexes

From the BI Accelerator Data Consistency Check Center, you can create and schedule check sets. To access the center from the BIA monitor, choose GOTO • CONSISTENCY CHECKS. This displays the Data Consistency Check Center (see Figure 5.13 shown earlier). On this screen, you can schedule and run checks of the index data on the BIA server, view the logs of checks that have run, and group certain checks to form check sets.

Procedure for Creating a New Check Set

To create a new check set, follow these steps:

1. Give the check set a description.

2. Specify the InfoCubes corresponding to the accelerator indexes for which the check set is to be executed. Input help is available.

3. Specify the maximum degree N of parallelization for background processing, if the checks are to run in background. The system starts up to N simultaneous dialog processes, with one for each InfoCube.

4. If necessary, set the indicator to deactivate an accelerator index for queries if errors occur. If this indicator is set, the accelerator index is inactivated (so that it cannot be used for queries) as soon as the check set reports incorrect data in the accelerator index. This prevents the accelerator from using incorrect data for reporting. In some circumstances, a check can report incorrect data even

though the data is correct. Then deactivation is unnecessary, but it is still better than using incorrect data for queries.

5. If you want an e-mail to be sent if an error occurs (if incorrect data is reported), enter the address of the recipient in the relevant field.

6. If the check set is to be executed immediately after the roll-up of new requests to an InfoCube, set the relevant indicator. The check set is then still part of the process (this is relevant for integration into a process chain), but the lock on the process is no longer valid so that other processes are not interrupted. The check set is not executed for all InfoCubes, but only for the InfoCube for which the data was rolled up.

7. If the check set is to be executed immediately after the change run, set the relevant indicator. As before, the check set is still part of the process, but the lock on the process is no longer valid. The check set is only executed for the Info-Cubes whose accelerator index was adjusted in the change run.

8. Each tab in the screen controls a test, as described in Section 5.2.2. Select the checks you want for your check set, and select the relevant options.

9. Save the check set. A check set ID is allocated and displayed.

Displaying and Changing a Check Set

To display an existing check set, select it from the input help for the CHECK SET ID field (see Figure 5.20). You can change the parameter values of the selected check set and save it again. The CHECK SET ID stays the same.

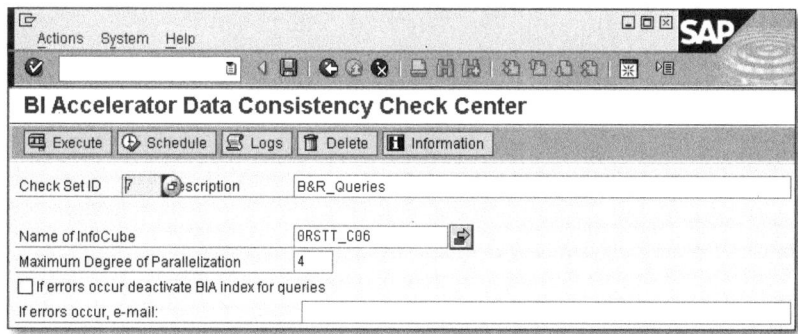

Figure 5.20 Display a Check Set

To delete a check set, select it, choose DELETE, and confirm at the prompt.

Executing a Check Set

To execute a check set, just select it, and choose EXECUTE. The checks are executed in the dialog (and not in parallel). If you have just created the check set, you do not even have to save it. When the check is complete, the system displays the results in the application log.

To schedule a check set, choose SCHEDULE. This opens the START TIME dialog box. Here you can schedule the check set to run once or periodically in the background. You need to save your entries to set the schedule. The name of the scheduled job is BW_TR_RSDDTREX_INDEX_CHECK.

You can also execute a check set by using program RSDDTREX_INDEX_CHECK.

To do this, you need the check set ID, or you can select the check set from the input help. You can also use this program to add a check set to process chains. To call the logs, choose LOGS.

5.2.4 Index Repair Programs

The following are the index repair programs:

▶ DELETE AND REBUILD ALL BIA INDEXES
This repair first deletes and then recreates and fills all the BIA indexes in the accelerator. This is an extremely drastic action that can put your accelerator under full load for many hours and will make it unavailable for user requests during that time. In exceptional circumstances, if a critical error occurs, you may need to execute this action for a successful restart with consistent data, but before you run it you should consider the consequences carefully.

▶ BIA INDEX ADJUSTMENTS AFTER InfoCube ACTIVATION
If an InfoCube is changed, for example, by adding a key figure, the accelerator does not automatically adjust the BIA index because the adjustment may take a long time (see Section 5.2.5). This repair writes information about any changes to the log and makes the required changes in repair mode. If you execute this repair, we recommend that you run it as a background job.

▶ REBUILD ALL MASTER DATA INDEXES OF A BIA INDEX
We strongly recommend that you do not execute this repair. It deletes and rebuilds all master data indexes of a BIA index. These master data indexes are used by other BIA indexes, so the repair may result in terminations or poor performance during query execution. This repair also requires various data

loading processes to be locked. The repair is only for use in cases where there is incorrect data in the master data indexes of a BIA index. Such problems are serious. If you find such a problem, you should open a customer message. SAP service will analyze the problem, determine which index contains incorrect data, and rebuild the index using a program that is not released for general use. As of Support Package 18, this repair is no longer available in Transaction RSRV.

5.2.5 Impact of Metadata Changes on the Accelerator

If you change the metadata for an InfoCube that has a BIA index, the BIA index may need to be adjusted as well. In most cases, this adjustment occurs automatically as soon as the InfoCube is activated. The system compares the current metadata of the BIA index with the metadata from the newly changed InfoCube, and any discrepancies trigger adjustment actions. If the metadata changes for the Info-Cube are transported to a system, the comparison and the adjustment occur in a post-activation step for the transport.

There are rare cases where the adjustment is not automatic. If you change the structural design of the InfoCube by adding or deleting a key figure or a characteristic, this change requires a complete rebuild of the BIA index. The rebuild is not performed automatically because the process may have a long runtime and impose significant load on the system. Instead, the BIA index is simply deleted. In this case, you need to schedule the rebuild manually to run at a convenient time.

For example, if you add a new navigational attribute to an InfoObject, this does not have an immediate impact on any BIA index, so no adjustment is triggered when you activate the InfoObject. The index data and metadata in the BIA index needs to be adjusted only if the navigational attribute is turned on for an Info-Cube. In that case, the logical index of the BIA index, which holds the metadata, is re-created for this InfoCube. Then the master data indexes need to be dropped and re-created with the data for the new navigational attribute.

To ensure consistency, the system rebuilds not just a single index but all the master data indexes for the InfoObject, which means all the S, X, and Y indexes. Rebuilding the master data indexes can be a time-consuming process, too, so if the size of the table exceeds a preset limit (the default value is 50,000 lines), the rebuild runs in a separate background process.

If this adjustment process fails for any reason, you can repair the BIA index in Transaction RSRV by running the repair program BIA INDEX ADJUSTMENTS AFTER INFOCUBE ACTIVATION. This is equivalent to running program RSDDTREX_ INDEX_ADJUST. The program compares the metadata and then triggers any necessary adjustments. For performance reasons, you should run the program as a background job.

5.2.6 Rebuilding Indexes

If you find that a BI query reads data from the BI accelerator and outputs incorrect data or data that is different from the results returned when the database is read, you should do some preliminary troubleshooting before you approach SAP service experts for help.

First, make sure the problem is not caused by the database. You can do this by running the query twice in Transaction RSRT in debug mode, once on the database and once with the accelerator. If the results are different, make sure the latest database patches are applied, and check for SAP Notes on the patches. If you still have a problem, mention this test result in your customer message to SAP.

To enable SAP experts to solve the problem effectively, you need to tell them both which query delivered the wrong data and all information needed to reproduce the problem. You should specify the row and column of at least one cell that contains incorrect data, together with the name of the key figure and the characteristic values. If possible, you should provide a second query that shows the discrepancy when compared with the first. If data disappear during navigation, you should describe this navigation and create an OLAP trace. It is helpful to reduce the queries to the absolute minimum of selected values. For further details, see SAP Notes 995364, 1060387, and 1095886.

In exceptionally rare cases, BIA indexes can become corrupt and require rebuilding. A set of BIA checks can be activated to check the indexes, for example, to compare the index data with the BI table data or to check that the lists of indexes and tables correspond. If there is a problem with an index, the index can be deactivated, and any individual table within an index can be rebuilt as required to render the index fully functional again. All the functionality for checking, rebuilding, and rechecking the indexes is highly automated.

In Transaction RSRV (see Figure 4.7 shown earlier), you can analyze and repair BI objects such as BIA indexes.

Checks are available for:

- Testing for inconsistencies between the data in the InfoCube on the database and the data in the BIA index — node BI Accelerator Consistency Checks

- Testing whether an accelerator index is running with optimal performance — node BI Accelerator Performance Checks

- Completely or partially building or rebuilding all BIA indexes or a specific BIA index — node BI Accelerator Repair Programs

The exactness and duration of each of these checks vary. For most purposes, you would run data consistency checks from the BI Accelerator Data Consistency Check Center (see Section 5.2.2) rather than from Transaction RSRV.

In the BIA monitor, you can specify that the system is to run a small number of tests on a daily basis. You do this by choosing BI Accelerator • Execute/Display Index Checks.

Some of the tests work with statistics data. The statistics have to be switched on for the relevant InfoProvider. You make this setting in the statistics properties maintenance screen. On the Data Warehousing Workbench screen, choose Tools • Settings for BI Statistics.

Transaction RSRV currently includes the following groups of consistency checks, performance checks, and repair programs for the accelerator:

- Consistency checks for master and transactional data
- Consistency checks for metadata
- Performance checks
- Repair programs

These tests can be run separately or combined. There are three predefined combinations of tests:

- Consistency checks (detailed)
- Consistency checks (fast)
- Performance

To run one or more checks, proceed as described in Section 5.2.2. If a check discovers a corrupt or missing index, one option is to start Transaction RSDDV and rebuild the entire BIA index containing that index.

If the option of rebuilding the entire BIA index requires too much runtime, or perhaps fails in execution for any reason, another option is available to an SAP Service engineer. This is to identify which individual table index or indexes need to be rebuilt and rebuild them separately. This option requires deep understanding of the SAP NetWeaver BI system landscape and is not supported for use by anyone except SAP Service engineers.

You can find out which table index is causing a problem by looking at the indexing logs. Running the BIA Index Maintenance Wizard in Transaction RSDDV generates application logs.

To view the logs, choose the APPLICATION LOGS wizard button. A dialog box appears. Select the process logs you wish to see and execute. The screen shown in Figure 5.21 appears, with the OBJECT ("RSDDTREX", BIA index), SUBOBJECT ("TAGGRFILL", fill BIA index), and EXTERNAL ID fields already filled. Enter any further information, and execute. The indexing logs are then displayed, with colored icons to indicate the success of the indexing steps.

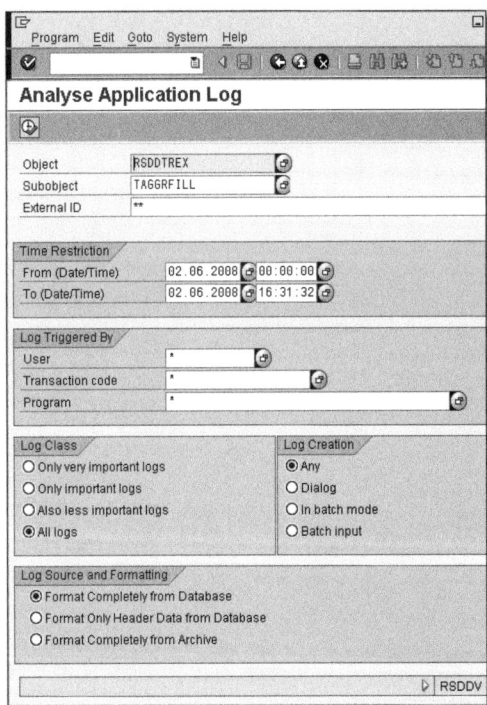

Figure 5.21 Transaction RSDDV, Analyse Application Log

To verify that the BIA indexes now have status green, start Transaction RSDDV, and choose BIA INDEXES. Drilling down on an index displays the details shown in Figure 5.22. In this case, all the table index icons are green, and all is well for this BIA index. The flags on the right indicate that some of the master data tables are shared with other BIA indexes.

Name	Technical name	O	O	Number of	M
▽ 🌐 Test InfoCube	Z_CU_HOF				
▽ 📊 BIA Index	Z_CU_HOF$X	⬜	⬜		
▽ 🔲 Tables/Indexes					
📄 /BIC/DZ_CU_HOF4	Q12_BIC:DZ_CU_HOF4	⬜		2	
📄 /BIC/DZ_CU_HOFP	Q12_BIC:DZ_CU_HOFP	⬜		6	
📄 /BIC/DZ_CU_HOFT	Q12_BIC:DZ_CU_HOFT	⬜		2	
📄 /BIC/DZ_CU_HOF3	Q12_BIC:DZ_CU_HOF3	⬜		33	
📄 /BIC/DZ_CU_HOFU	Q12_BIC:DZ_CU_HOFU	⬜		2	
📄 /BIC/DZ_CU_HOF1	Q12_BIC:DZ_CU_HOF1	⬜		1	
📄 Fact Table (E-/F Table)	Q12_BIC:FZ_CU_HOF	⬜		31	
📄 /BI0/SBPARTNER	Q12_BI0:SBPARTNER	⬜		5773	
📄 /BI0/SVERSION	Q12_BI0:SVERSION	⬜		279	☑
📄 /BI0/SUNIT	Q12_BI0:SUNIT	⬜		381	☑
📄 /BI0/SCUSTOMER	Q12_BI0:SCUSTOMER	⬜		100970	☑
📄 /BI0/SSALESORG	Q12_BI0:SSALESORG	⬜		1035	☑
📄 /BI0/SMATERIAL	Q12_BI0:SMATERIAL	⬜		127236	☑
📄 /BI0/SFISCYEAR	Q12_BI0:SFISCYEAR	⬜		17377	☑
📄 /BI0/SFISCVARNT	Q12_BI0:SFISCVARNT	⬜		24	☑
📄 /BI0/SCOMPANY	Q12_BI0:SCOMPANY	⬜		302	
📄 /BI0/SFISCPER	Q12_BI0:SFISCPER	⬜		7609	☑
📄 /BI0/SDISTR_CHAN	Q12_BI0:SDISTR_CHAN	⬜		85	☑
📄 /BI0/SCURRENCY	Q12_BI0:SCURRENCY	⬜		230	☑

Figure 5.22 Transaction RSDDV, Check Index Status

Finally, to confirm that the indexing was successful, you can check the logs again as follows. Start Transaction SLG1, specify OBJECT "RSDDTREX" and SUBOBJECT "TAGGRFILL", and execute (the screen is as shown earlier in Figure 5.21). This will display a set of logs with colored icons indicating the success of the indexing actions. If there were problems here and you wished to drill deeper, you could start Transaction SM21 and study the system log.

5.2.7 Performing a Recovery

During a recovery, no indexing is possible, and any indexing processes that were running before the event that necessitated the recovery are terminated.

A BIA recovery involves importing a saved snapshot to a BIA system. Any other data loads to the accelerator are automatically put on hold during the imports.

A restore from an import deletes all the BIA indexes that have been backed up and imports all the indexes from the backup. The new BIA indexes are distributed over the BIA servers as before. After the recovery has completed, you may need to trigger a reorganization of the index landscape.

Once the snapshot is imported, the next step is index adjustment. If an index has not been changed because the snapshot was created (which is checked by comparing timestamps), no adjustment is needed. If the index has changed, the adjustment depends on the index type. Fact index requests can be reloaded (if they have not been compressed), dimension indexes are completely rebuilt (except the package dimension index, which is adjusted), and S/X/Y indexes are completely rebuilt.

You can perform a recovery from the BIA monitor as follows:

1. Choose BI ACCELERATOR • MAINTENANCE FUNCTIONS • BACKUP AND RECOVERY.
2. If you wish to estimate how long the recovery process will take, select the relevant snapshot, and choose SIMULATE.
3. Select the snapshot you want to recover, and start the recovery process. The job executes immediately and cannot be scheduled.
4. You can view the job log. A new button is displayed indicating that the recovery process is running. To view the log, click the button.
5. Check the BIA configuration, the initial BIA logs, and the consistency of the BIA indexes.

To ensure that you are prepared to perform a recovery if necessary, you can simulate a recovery. This can also give you an indication of whether it would be faster to re-index all your data from scratch.

If you like, instead of simulating a recovery to decide whether it would be faster than re-indexing, you can evaluate the following factors:

▶ Age of the snapshot and how many updates have occurred since it was made
▶ Degree of parallelism and number of CPU cores of the TREX backup server
▶ Performance of the storage system for the backups
▶ Bandwidth between the TREX backup server and the storage system

Before performing a BIA recovery, it may be a good idea to check anything in SAP NetWeaver BI that can affect the status of the accelerator:

▶ Check the InfoCube data to ensure that the roll-up status is up to date.
▶ Check that all the master data used in BIA have been updated.

▶ Check the BIA configuration by running a system check.

▶ Check the initial BIA logs.

▶ Check the consistency of the BIA indexes.

5.3   Optimization Tasks

In a large system landscape with a changing workload, the opportunities for further optimization are endless. The SAP NetWeaver BI Accelerator offers several tools to help you optimize your operations.

5.3.1   Index Landscape and Reorganization

The BIA monitor offers basic functionality to reorganize indexes over the BIA landscape. The TREX administration tool includes more advanced functionality to monitor the index distribution and reorganize the distribution to balance the load on the hosts. The extra functionality includes graphical displays of the actual and recommended distributions as well as an estimation of the expected improvement.

When one of the BIA reorganization algorithms assigns responsibility for individual BIA indexes to the respective BIA master hosts in the landscape, it does so in a way specific to the algorithm.

The first criterion is the amount of memory space required for a given index. There must be enough space available on the host, and the hosts must all end up with approximately equal loads.

Depending on the algorithm selected, additional considerations may be used, such as how often a given index is used, how many table indexes there are in a given BIA index, how many of those table indexes contain shared master data, or where the other BIA indexes are that must share access to those master data indexes.

In any case, the algorithm fixes an assignment of BIA indexes to the available master hosts. Then, whenever those indexes are loaded into memory in order to execute user requests, they are loaded onto the assigned hosts. In any case where a BIA index contains a split index, the split parts are distributed over the hosts.

More exactly, the logical index for such a split index resides on the assigned host, just as if the index were not split. But the physical parts of the split index are loaded onto the respective hosts so that each host takes an approximately equal share of the load generated by usage of that index. The logical index coordinates the parts and merges the results, so for most purposes the BIA index behaves as if it contained no split indexes. But the splitting is important for the reorganization algorithm, which attempts to optimize the distribution of split parts over the available hosts.

There is a computational overhead associated with splitting an index. During indexing, the rows of the table to be split need to be distributed to the hosts, which is done using a simple round robin algorithm, and this generates extra network traffic between the BIA hosts within the BIA appliance. Then, whenever a query execution plan is generated that touches the split index, the plan must run in parallel over all the master hosts in the landscape. Again, extra network traffic is generated as the partial results are sent back to the master hosting the logical index for the split index for merging into a single result set. However, the exact overhead is hard to calculate, and the size threshold for splitting a large index is inevitably rather arbitrary. The default setting of 100 million (rows times columns) is good enough in most cases, but experienced administrators with time to experiment may be able to fine-tune performance with other settings.

The TREX standalone administration tool offers extensive performance and load measurement functionality to enable administrators to fine-tune the organization of their indexes. Conversely, the tool automates the process so far that for administrators in a hurry, there is nothing to do but respond to an index reorganization alert message by clicking the REORG button.

Views

The TREX standalone administration tool offers a large number of useful views, some of which we now review.

In the SERVICES view, the LOAD tab (see Figure 5.23) offers a graphical representation of the load over time, with a range of options for changing the load details displayed and the time period covered. The lower-left panel shows the hosts and time periods displayed, while the lower-right panel shows which load parameter (key performance indicator, KPI) options have been selected for display. You can change the displayed parameters here, and you can change the timescale displayed via the drop-down menu to the upper left of the graph.

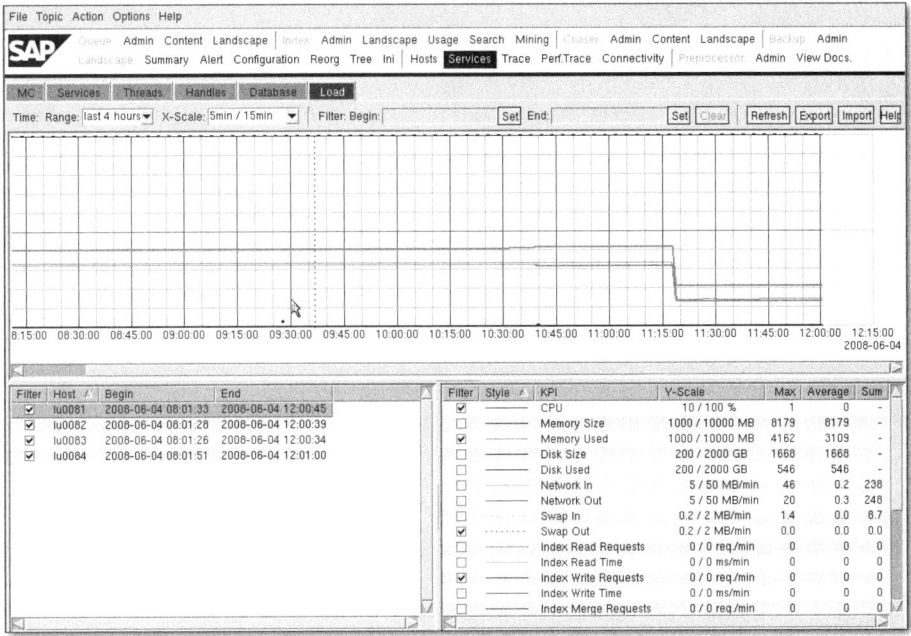

Figure 5.23 TREX Admin Tool, Services View, Load Tab

The INDEX ADMIN view (see Figure 5.24) displays details of all the BIA indexes stored by the accelerator. In the hierarchical list of indexes shown in the left panel, a star icon (gold) indicates a logical index for an entire InfoCube, and a cylinder icon (pink) indicates one of the physical indexes within a logical index, where each such index corresponds to a table within an InfoCube. A multicylinder icon (purple) indicates a split index for a large table, where under it in the node hierarchy are the physical indexes for the split parts.

This view enables you to monitor not only the size but also numerous further details of the indexes, such as the view attributes, key figures, join conditions, and join paths they contain. All these are displayed on the tabs in the lower-right panel.

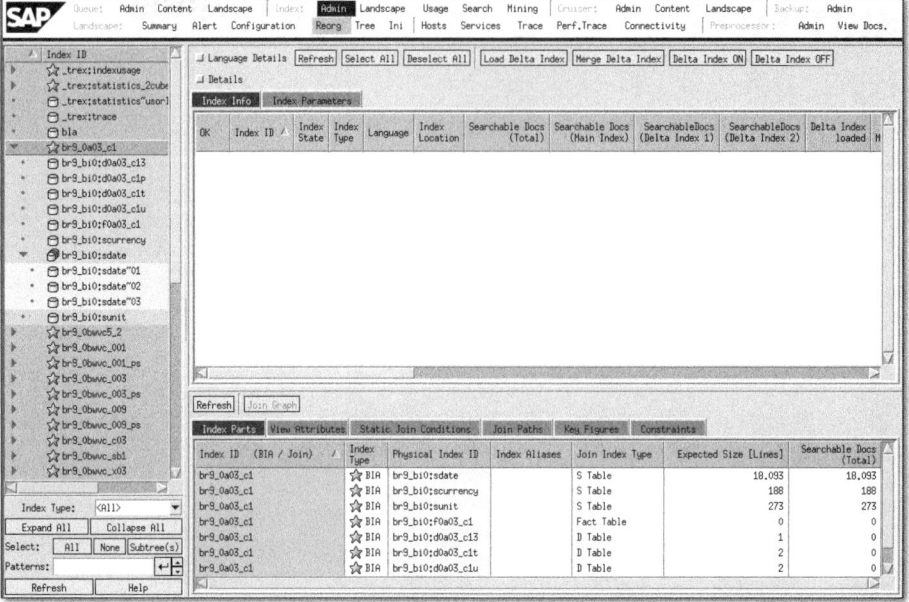

Figure 5.24 TREX Admin Tool, Index Admin View

You can activate the JOIN GRAPH button in the lower panel by selecting a BIA index from the list in the lower panel. If you now choose the button, a window opens that displays the join graph for the selected index (see Figure 5.25).

This join graph is equivalent to the extended star schema for the associated Info-Cube and enables you to see how the tables or table indexes fit together logically in the cube. The different types of table index (F, D, X, Y, S) are shown with color-coded title bars, and their attributes are listed below the title bars, with key attributes starred and join attributes shown bold. You can drag the table index symbols around on the screen to display their joins more clearly.

If you select a join condition in the list below the graph, the corresponding line on the graph is highlighted. If you select a join path, the lines are highlighted and numbered to indicate the sequence of joins along the join path. Moving the cursor over a line displays a tool tip giving its join name. In the case of a 1:n join, moving the cursor over the line also displays labels indicating the direction of the join.

Although this graph tool is intended mainly for data modelers, you can use it to become more familiar with the logical structure of your data.

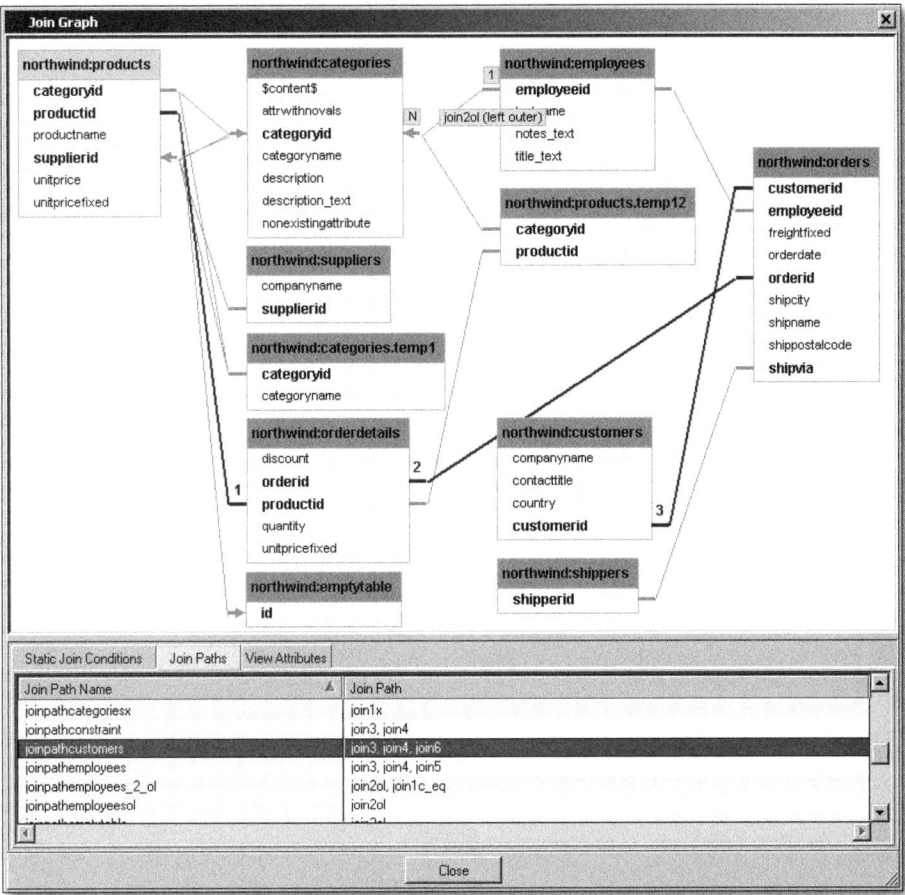

Figure 5.25 TREX Admin Tool, Join Graph

The INDEX LANDSCAPE view (see Figure 5.26) displays the assignment of BIA indexes to blade server hosts. For each index listed at the left of the screen, the host currently assigned as the master for that index is shown toward the right. An expert user can right-click on entries and change the host assignments. But such manual changes are likely to be unhelpful and are anyway unnecessary because the automatic index reorganization capabilities are already highly optimized.

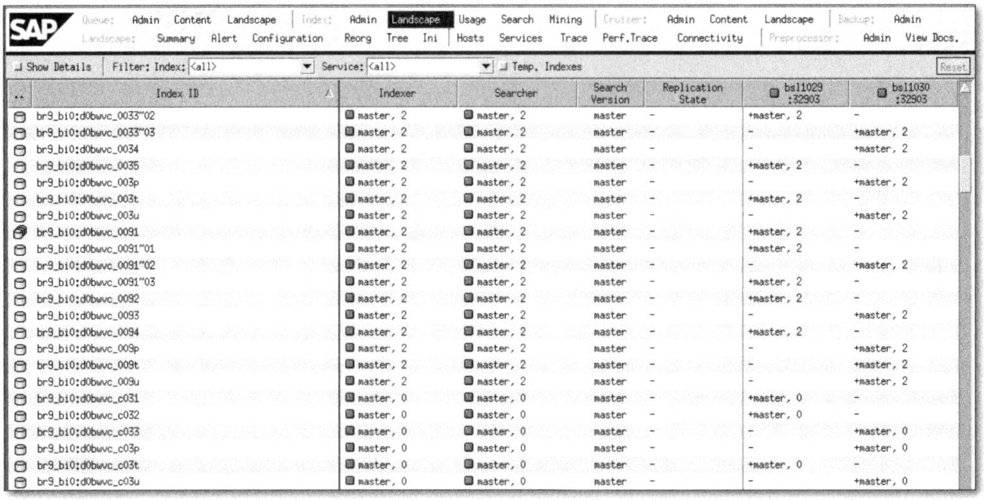

Figure 5.26 TREX Admin Tool, Index Landscape View

The INDEX LANDSCAPE view offers many more features for experts, who only needs to right-click on a line in a specific column to open a context menu with a tailored set of options for that column.

The REORG view opens with the SUMMARY tab, which shows when the last index reorganization was executed and displays an icon to indicate the current status (see Figure 5.27). The status icon is green (square) to indicate that the last reorganization completed successfully. The TARGET STATE panel shows the results of key figure checks indicating whether reorganization is worthwhile. Once the checks have run, the expected improvement (as a percentage) between actual and target states is shown, and a summary recommendation, yes or no, is offered. You can trigger reorganization by clicking the button on the right, or you can schedule a reorganization to start at a later time.

In the REORG view, the USAGE BY SERVICE (I) tab (see Figure 5.28) gives a bar-graph representation of the actual index distribution (upper panel) and the target distribution (lower panel). Each green bar represents one of the hosts in the landscape. If backup hosts are configured, the bar for a backup host is colored blue. Each black-framed green rectangle represents an index, and the distributed parts of a large split index that belong together light up together automatically and display helpful part numbers as you pass the mouse cursor over any one of the parts.

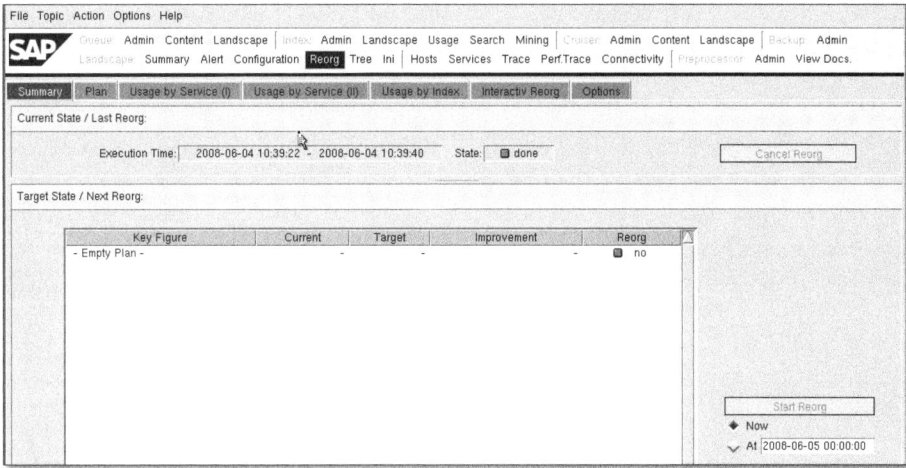

Figure 5.27 TREX Admin Tool, Reorg View, Summary Tab

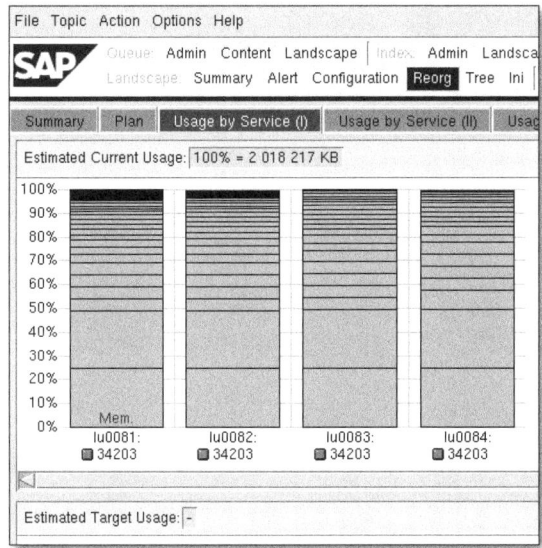

Figure 5.28 TREX Admin Tool, Reorg View, Usage by Service (I) Tab

In the graph, the height of a bar for a host indicates the memory space occupied by indexes as a fraction of the 100 % value indicated in the field at the top of the panel. This 100 % value is the maximum occupancy achieved on any of the hosts (in this case, about 2 GB), although it does not normally equal the entire space available on any host, and would only equal the entire space in the theoretical limiting case that the indexes were packed into memory with no room to spare.

The target bars are not necessarily the same height for the different hosts. This is because some distribution algorithms consider not only space allocation but also CPU usage for loading and reading the indexes. This ensures that "expensive" indexes do not create local hot spots. Also, some algorithms optimize the index distribution with regard to clusters of table indexes that are likely to be read together.

In the REORG view, the USAGE BY SERVICE (II) tab (see Figure 5.29) displays the same information as the graphs in the previous tab but now in tabular form. The table gives exact numerical values for index sizes plus some related information.

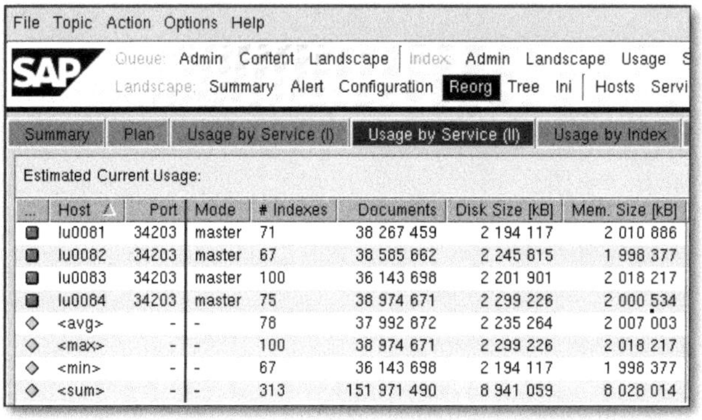

...	Host	Port	Mode	# Indexes	Documents	Disk Size [kB]	Mem. Size [kB]
	lu0081	34203	master	71	38 267 459	2 194 117	2 010 886
	lu0082	34203	master	67	38 585 662	2 245 815	1 998 377
	lu0083	34203	master	100	36 143 698	2 201 901	2 018 217
	lu0084	34203	master	75	38 974 671	2 299 226	2 000 534
	<avg>	-	-	78	37 992 872	2 235 264	2 007 003
	<max>	-	-	100	38 974 671	2 299 226	2 018 217
	<min>	-	-	67	36 143 698	2 194 117	1 998 377
	<sum>	-	-	313	151 971 490	8 941 059	8 028 014

Figure 5.29 TREX Admin Tool, Reorg View, Usage by Service (II) Tab

As an extra feature, both the upper- and lower panels of the view display a JOIN GRAPH button (upper right, not shown). If a Graphviz graph editor is installed, choosing the button opens a window in which you can select a BIA index and display its join graph. If the graph editor is not installed, a popup tells you it can be obtained online as freeware from *www.graphviz.org*. If a graph is displayed, it is color-coded to indicate the hosts on which the respective table indexes reside. The same colors are shown to highlight the host names on the tab. The join graph corresponds to the star schema for the associated BI InfoCube.

In the REORG view, the INTERACTIVE REORG tab is for experts only and offers a graphical view of the index distribution, like that shown in Figure 5.28 earlier, with the extra feature that you can drag and drop the index rectangles from one host bar to another to perform a manual reorganization. It is worth saying again that in most cases the default reorganization algorithm will achieve better results than such a manual reorganization, and this tab is only for performance tuning in extreme cases where an individual query can be optimized by relocating its indexes.

In the REORG view, the OPTIONS tab (see Figure 5.30) enables an expert user to decide which index redistribution algorithm to employ to reorganize the index landscape.

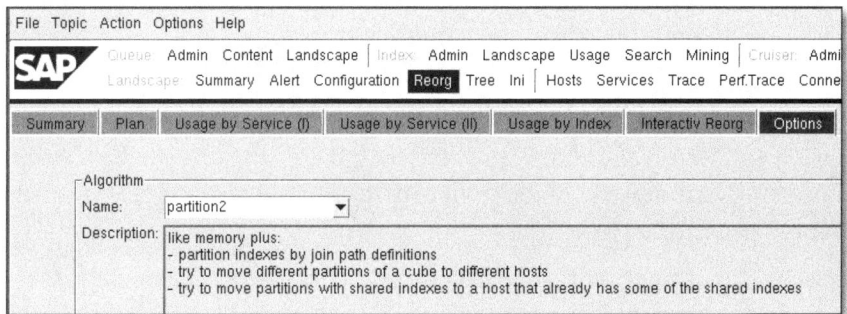

Figure 5.30 TREX Admin Tool, Reorg View, Options Tab

The reorganization algorithms currently available for selection in the tool are as follows:

▶ The memory algorithm distributes the indexes between the available index servers according to their nominal size in memory, where the nominal size is the sum of the sizes of all indexes belonging to the join or OLAP index. If multiple servers are candidates for an index, the algorithm selects the current server. If there are multiple index servers per host, the algorithm uses the next host for the next index if possible. For large indexes, the algorithm fills memory space in the order given by index size, starting with the biggest indexes. If split indexes are similar in size, it uses the size to achieve an even load distribution. The algorithm uses a penalty of 50 % to prevent multiple parts of a split index from being allocated to the same host. Once the big indexes have been distributed, the algorithm fills the remaining memory with small indexes so that there are similar numbers of small indexes on all index servers.

▶ The partition 1 algorithm is like the memory algorithm except that it partitions indexes by join path definitions and tries to move different partitions of a cube to different hosts.

▸ The partition 2 algorithm is like the partition 1 algorithm except that it tries to move partitions with shared indexes to a host that already has some of the shared indexes.

▸ The random algorithm creates a different distribution plan each time.

▸ The round robin algorithm simply goes through the list of indexes sorted by index name and allocates each index to the next host in turn, which equalizes the number of indexes per host independently of index size or usage frequency.

▸ The CPU usage algorithm distributes indexes by the CPU time used to read them. It tries to give every service the same CPU usage and to distribute indexes with very low CPU usage evenly over all the hosts.

▸ The plan CPU usage algorithm is the same as the CPU usage algorithm except that it distributes indexes by the CPU time used to create query execution plans for them.

▸ The plan partition algorithm is like the partition 2 algorithm except that it takes account of plan operation statistics.

The default algorithm for the BI accelerator is partition 2, and in most circumstances, it should work well. It should not be changed except by an expert who can predict that a different algorithm would achieve superior results.

5.3.2   Performance Checks

Here, for reference, are some details about the performance checks available in Transaction RSRV.

Size of Delta Index

It is useful to create a delta index for large indexes that are often updated with new data. Then any new data is not written to the main index but to the delta index. This can significantly improve performance during indexing. The data from the delta index is used at query runtime. If the delta index is large, this can lengthen response times for queries.

This check issues a warning whenever the size of the delta index reaches 10 % of that of the main index. The accelerator merges the delta and main indexes in repair mode. The index settings are retained.

Propose Delta Index for Indexes

This check proposes using a delta index for certain indexes based on their statistics. Delta indexes are proposed for indexes that have received new data more than 10 times during the past 10 days. A prerequisite for these proposals is that the statistics for the InfoCube are switched on.

The check sets the HAS DELTA INDEX property for the proposed indexes. The delta index is created when the data is next loaded for this index.

Compare Size of Fact Tables with Fact Index

This check calculates the number of records in both fact tables (E and F tables) for an InfoCube and compares them with the number of records in the fact index of the BIA index. If the number of records in the BIA index is significantly greater than the number in the InfoCube (more than a 10 % difference), you can improve query performance by rebuilding the BIA index.

Differences in the numbers of records can arise in two ways. If the InfoCube was compressed after the BIA index was built, the BIA index may contain more records than the InfoCube. And if requests were deleted from the InfoCube after the BIA index was built, they are deleted from the BIA index in the package dimension only. The records in the fact index are therefore no longer referenced during query execution, but the rows are not deleted until the index is rebuilt.

The database statistics for calculating the size of the fact table must be up to date because the test uses them without recounting.

Load BIA Index Data into Main Memory

This action loads all the data for a selected BIA index from the file server into the memory of the accelerator, if the data is not there already.

The action enables you to ensure that queries using that BIA index achieve optimal performance the first time they are executed and do not have to wait for the data to be read into memory from the file server.

Whenever new data is added to an index (during a roll-up or a change run), the index data in memory (if any) is deleted. If you want to ensure that the accelerator reloads the new data into memory immediately, you can set the BIA index properties to ensure that as soon as the index is updated, the new data is automatically loaded into memory.

If you do not specify an InfoCube, the accelerator loads all BIA indexes that are active and filled.

Delete BIA Index Data from Main Memory

This action deletes all the data for a selected BIA index from the memory of the accelerator. Master data indexes that are still required by other InfoCubes are not deleted from memory. The index data on the file server is not deleted, and the BIA index is still set as active.

The action enables you to clear some free space in memory on the BIA server. It is useful when the data you delete from memory is no longer used or is used only rarely, or if the space is needed for another purpose (perhaps only for a short time).

If you do not specify an InfoCube, the accelerator clears from memory all BIA indexes that are active and filled.

Estimate Runtime of Fact Table Indexing

This check estimates the time required to fill the fact index for a selected Info-Cube. The calculation uses the current parameter values for background and dialog parallel processing, and takes account of the processes available and the estimated maximal throughput of data records in the database, the application server, and the BIA server.

The calculated duration is only an estimate. The load on the system, the distribution of data across blocks, and other factors can all affect the actual time taken.

Estimate Memory Consumption of Fact Table Index

This check estimates the size of the fact table index of a BIA index. In doing so, the system analyzes the data in the fact table and provides a projection.

If data distribution is poor, the actual memory consumption can deviate from the projected value. A more exact analysis would demand more time than that required to rebuild the index because it would involve counting the number of distinct values in each column of the fact table.

5.3.3 Delta Indexing

You can improve overall system performance by activating delta indexing for any indexes that meet either or both of the following conditions:

▶ They are very large, with several million rows for each CPU core in your BIA landscape.

▶ They are updated frequently, for example, several times per day.

To set delta indexing for a BIA index, in Transaction RSDDBIAMON, choose BI ACCELERATOR • INDEX INFORMATION • SET DELTA INDEX to display the dialog box shown in Figure 5.31. In this dialog box, scroll to the table name for the BIA index, set the DELTA INDEX flag, and click SAVE.

Table Name	Table Size	Delta In
/BIC/FZBWVC_SB1	171.554	☐
/BIC/FZBWVC_SB2	171.540	☐
/BI0/XMATERIAL	135.268	☐
/BI0/SMATERIAL	127.236	☐
/BI0/SCUSTOMER	100.970	☐
/BIC/FEPERFTEST	53.570	☐
/BI0/SCOORDER	46.171	☐
/BI0/SFISCYEAR	17.377	☐
/BIC/DEPERFTEST	16.861	☐
/BI0/SDATE	10.206	☐
/BI0/SPROFIT_CTR	10.055	☐
/BIC/DZBWVC_SB1	7.856	☐
/BI0/SVC_2CUST	7.855	☐
/BIC/DZBWVC_SB2	7.854	☐
/BI0/SFISCPER	7.609	☐
/BI0/SBPARTNER	5.773	☐
/BI0/YCOSTCENTE	5.722	☐
/BI0/SCOSTELMNT	5.435	☐
/BI0/SCOSTCENTE	5.337	☐
/BIC/DZBWVC_SB2	1.563	☐
/BI0/SVC_2PDCT	1.561	☐
/BI0/XVC_2PDCT	1.560	☐
/BIC/DZBWVC_SB1	1.560	☐
/BI0/SCALWEEK	1.080	☐
/BI0/SSALESORG	1.035	☐
/BI0/SCOMP_CODE	912	☐
/BI0/SCO_AREA	875	☐
/BIC/DEPERFTEST	807	☐
/BI0/SPLANT	634	☐

Figure 5.31 Accelerator Monitor, Delta Index Settings

5.3.4 Statistics for BIA Index Maintenance

As an advanced exercise in performance tuning, or perhaps in the course of troubleshooting, you may wish to study query runtimes in detail. To get an overview of the runtimes of specific subprocesses in BIA index maintenance, you can display the statistics Table RSDDSTATTREX (see Figure 5.32). This table stores the runtimes of the specific TREX subprocesses involved in initial indexing, roll-up, and modifications after change runs.

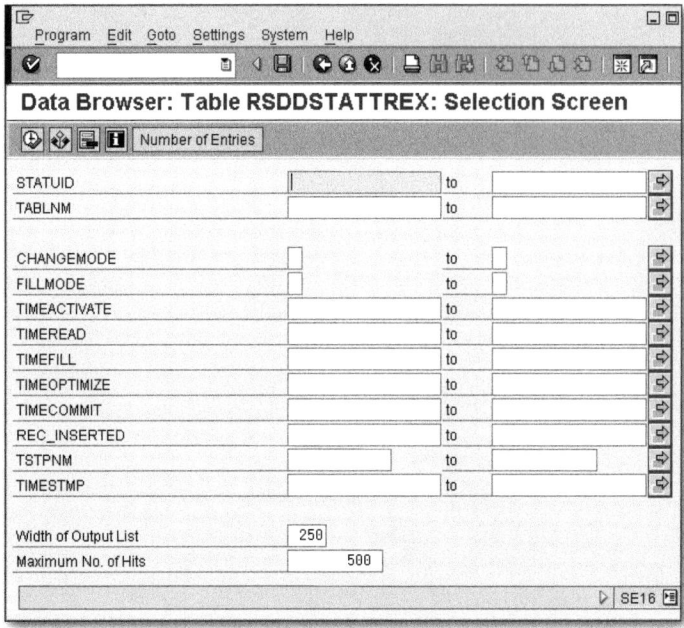

Figure 5.32 Display Table RSDDSTATTREX

Some BIA tests in the analysis and repair environment work with statistics data. The statistics need to be switched on for the relevant InfoProviders. You make this setting in the statistics properties maintenance screen. In the Data Warehousing Workbench screen, choose TOOLS • SETTINGS FOR BI STATISTICS.

To study the TREX times for indexing a cube, in Transaction RSDDV, select the cube, call the BIA Index Maintenance Wizard, choose the APPLICATION LOGS button, select the ROLL UP button, press ENTER, modify the time restriction if necessary, and execute. Expand the log and note the indexing statistics UID.

To study the overall TREX time statistics for the various tables, in Transaction SE16, select Table RSDDSTATTREX, and enter the statistics UID in the selection screen.

Table RSDDSTATTREX (see Figure 5.33) contains the following information for each table that is indexed:

▶ **STATUID**
Unique identification key.

▶ **TABLNM**
Table name.

▶ **CHANGEMODE**
Specifies whether the process is for a new or rebuilt BIA index (N), a roll-up (R), or a modification after a change run (C).

▶ **FILLMODE**
Full (F), delta (D), or change run (C).

▶ **TIMEACTIVATE**
Time of activation.

▶ **TIMEREAD**
Time required to read data from the database.

▶ **TIMEFILL**
Time to fill the index with the table data.

▶ **TIMEOPTIMIZE**
Time to prepare the optimize call.

▶ **TIMECOMMIT**
Time to commit the optimize call.

▶ **REC_INSERTED**
Number of indexed records.

▶ **TSTPNM**
User (test person name).

▶ **TIMESTMP**
Timestamp for start of indexing job.

The fill process for BIA indexes is executed in parallel background jobs. Each background job creates a series of packages. A set of packages is indexed in parallel via asynchronous RFC calls. Figure 5.34 depicts the process flow and indicates the meaning of the parameters that govern the fill process.

To see the TREX times subdivided into server time, client time, RFC time, and ABAP time, instead of Table RSDDSTATTREX, select Table RSDDSTATTREXSERV.

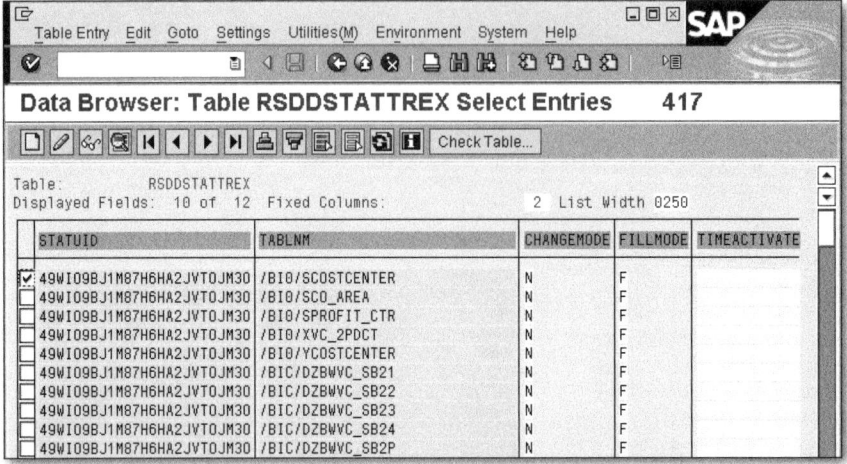

Figure 5.33 Table RSDDSTATTREX

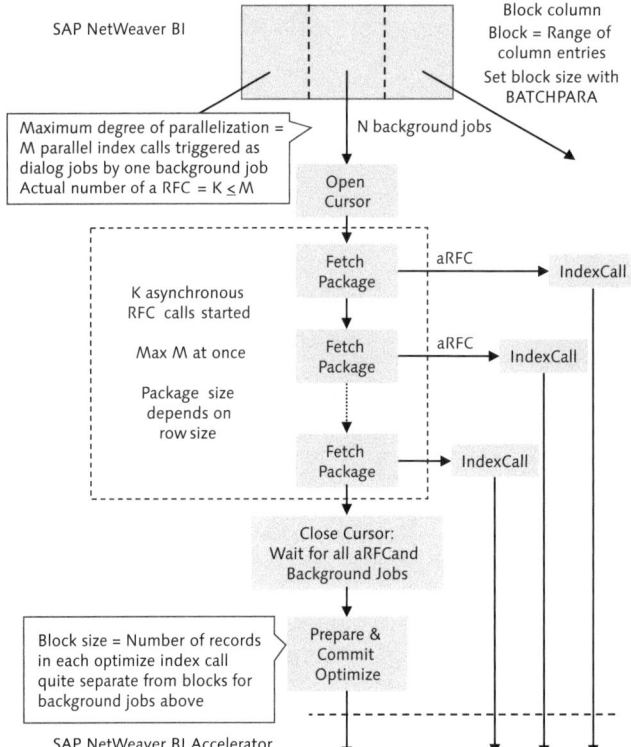

Figure 5.34 Parallel Fill of BIA Index

Table RSDDSTATTREXSERV contains the following query runtime information:

▶ **ABAP_RFC_TIME**

Round trip time (a) from the SAP NetWeaver BI side of the TREX ABAP API through the SAP gateway, RFC server, and TREX index server and back.

▶ **RFC_SERVER_TIME**

Round trip time (b) from the SAP gateway side of the RFC server through the TREX index server and back.

▶ **TREX_CLIENT_TIME**

Round trip time (c) from the RFC server side of the TREX client through the TREX index server and back.

▶ **TREX_KERNEL_TIME**

Round trip time (d) from the TREX client side of the TREX index server and back.

For a closer analysis, the intervals between these times are of interest. The difference between times (a) and (b) is the time spent (in both directions) in the TREX ABAP API and the SAP gateway. The difference between times (b) and (c) is the time spent (in both directions) in the RFC server, excluding time in the TREX client. And the difference between times (c) and (d) is the time spent (in both directions) in the TREX client.

5.3.5 Indexing and Index Parameters

You can change the indexing settings in the BIA monitor. Choose BI ACCELERATOR • INDEX SETTINGS. The INDEX SETTINGS option offers the CHANGE GLOBAL PARAMETERS option. THIS OPTION OPENS a dialog box for changing the global indexing parameters BATCHPARA, NUMPROC, PKGSIZE, SUBPKGSIZE, and FLOAT (see Figure 4.26 in Chapter 4).

The parameters currently displayed by default are BATCHPARA, NUMPROC, PKGSIZE, SUBPKGSIZE, and FLOAT.

They have the following significance:

▶ BATCHPARA

This parameter specifies the number of parallel background processes for initial indexing (not for roll-up). The default value is 4.

The F and E fact tables of the InfoCube are split into a number of blocks, and the `BATCHPARA` parameter specifies the number of blocks. The E table is split using the partitioning characteristic or another time characteristic; the F table is split using the request. These blocks are then read from the database and written to the accelerator separately.

▶ `NUMPROC`
This parameter specifies the number of processes for parallel processing using asynchronous RFC dialog processes during indexing. The default value is 5.

The data is read from the database table on a package-by-package basis. The system calculates the package size from the width of the table and the default value for the package size (in bytes) in the system.

If you set a degree of parallelization greater than one, each of these packages is indexed in a new asynchronous job in dialog mode. When the indexing job for the package is started, the system reads a new package immediately. Ideally, you should reduce the indexing time to the time that is required to read the data and pack it for the RFC module.

If you set the degree of parallelization to one, the system performs serial processing.

The optimization of the BIA index cannot be parallelized on the SAP NetWeaver BI side. However, optimization automatically runs in parallel on the accelerator server if the index is split.

▶ `PKGSIZE`
This parameter specifies the package size in bytes for internal tables during indexing using asynchronous RFC calls. The default value is 10,000,000.

▶ `SUBPKGSIZE`
This parameter specifies the package size (in rows) for export to the buffer during indexing using asynchronous RFC calls. The default value is 20,000.

During dialog parallel processing with the `NUMPROC` parameter, packages with size `PKGSIZE` are read and indexed using asynchronous RFC calls. To do this, the data packages are transferred by exporting them to a data buffer. This is done on a package-by-package basis because it requires a large amount of CPU and memory resources. The `SUBPKGSIZE` parameter specifies the number of rows for the package. We recommend a value between 10,000 and 20,000.

▶ `FLOAT`
This parameter specifies whether `FLOAT` key figures are saved as `FLOAT` (which

occurs for any parameter value except DOUBLE) or as DOUBLE (which you can specify by entering value DOUBLE) as described later in this section.

All these global indexing parameters have defaults that are good for normal operation. They should only be changed by an expert as part of a well understood tuning or troubleshooting strategy.

For mathematical reasons, operations with numbers of type FLOAT always generate rounding errors. Because InfoCubes in the BI system may be compressed or aggregated, the numbers in the BIA indexes and on the database are not always identical, and the rounding is also performed differently. If the numbers are large but your query calculates relatively small increments, the rounding differences in the final result may be significant.

For this reason, we recommend that you use FLOAT only if you can accept such rounding differences and not in cases where you require results accurate to many decimal places. If you require more than three decimal places in a key figure of type DEC, see SAP Note 460652.

You can specify in the BI system whether you want to save key figures of type FLOAT in the BIA server as FLOAT numbers or as DOUBLE numbers. Saving the key figures as DOUBLE numbers increases memory consumption and slightly decreases performance.

You can make this setting only for all BIA indexes together. If you change this setting, you need to delete BIA indexes for InfoCubes with FLOAT key figures first, and then recreate them after you have changed the setting. The setting is displayed in the BIA monitor and you can only change it there. To change the setting, enter the value DOUBLE, and save your entry.

Even after you have changed to 8-byte FLOAT numbers, there may still be small rounding differences between query results from the database and from the accelerator. Again, the reasons for this are mathematical.

5.3.6 Tips and Tricks for High Performance

This subsection presents answers to a few frequently asked questions. The accelerator is pretuned for high performance out of the box, and additional tuning measures are not required. However, there are some tips and tricks you can use to get the best performance from your accelerator in various scenarios. We briefly review some of them.

As you will see, in most cases there are detailed SAP Notes with exact advice on how to proceed. These notes generally require some care and patience to understand and apply, but they are an invaluable resource for experts.

You Want To Find Out Which Queries Will Benefit Most from Acceleration

The queries that will benefit most feature high data read or data manager (DM) times and/or involve a high aggregation ratio (such that even when many records are selected, only small sets are transferred back to the BI system). The best way to find these queries is to study your BI statistics. There are various ways to do this. You can identify queries with a high aggregation ratio by studying Table RSDDSTAT_OLAP in Transaction SE16. Or you can execute queries on a statistics cube to measure the query performance for specific cubes. Or, as explained in Section 5.4.3, you can execute queries in debug mode in Transaction RSRT, read the statistics and identify queries with a high DM time.

A Query Transfers a Large Number of Records in Result Sets.

In this case, we recommend first that you limit the query to just those key figures and characteristics that you really need. Further, you can:

▸ For multiqueries, activate FEMS compression to remove duplicates from results (Technical Operations Manual).

▸ With non-cumulative key figures, limit the size of the validity table, compress the InfoCube, and re-index it (SAP Note 1160520).

▸ For large data volumes, activate package-wise read (SAP Notes 1157582, 1002839, 1018798).

▸ For queries that dump large data volumes and require no further drill-down, consider using a DataStore object and not an InfoCube.

A Query Involves Sophisticated Analytic Operations That Cause Long Times for the BI Analytic Engine.

Have patience. The accelerator does not boost query performance in every case. Boosting analytic performance by letting the accelerator take over jobs currently done by the BI analytic engine is on the BIA roadmap.

A Query Contains Virtual Characteristics and/or Virtual Key Figures.

In this case, make sure the virtual characteristics or key figures are well defined (SAP Note 1143411). If you want to deactivate the BI accelerator for queries with virtual key figures, see SAP Note 1149760.

Master Data Tables Are Very Large, So Joins of SIDs and DIMIDs Are Expensive.

To minimize the expense, you should use filters and avoid unselective joins. If possible, you should redesign your data model (SAP Notes 1047527, 1169640, 1074559). In some very unusual cases, the accelerator transfers a large amount of data between the blades.

You Execute Multiple Loads Simultaneously and Want to Take Advantage of Parallelism for BIA Indexing.

To do so, you need to focus on parallelization for BIA indexing (SAP Notes 1161395, 1023843, 1158597).

After an Initial Sizing, You Start Indexing More and More InfoCubes.

Make sure you do not overload the BIA system (SAP Notes 1093719, 1132572, 1163149).

Data Is Transported from the Data Manager to the Analytic Processor in a Structure with Too Many Fields.

Here you need to reduce the BIA query size for complex cases (SAP Note 1085745). Also, you can enhance the interface between the data manager and analytic processor (SAP Note 1091714).

5.4 Collaborative Tasks

In some error scenarios, you may have to perform a more detailed analysis of the problem. In such cases, it is quite normal to get help from SAP. This section can help you work more smoothly with SAP experts.

5.4.1 Setting Up the Service Connection

If you send SAP a customer message requesting help in investigating problems with your BIA landscape, you need to assign the SAP service engineers a user with password for remote access to the accelerator hardware. You are requested to set up a Windows Terminal Server (WTS) connection to a host in the company intranet from which the accelerator blades can be reached and on which PuTTY is installed. PuTTY is a freeware tool for building secure Telnet connections via SSH to hardware such as BIA blades. Ideally, the WTS machine should also have Virtual Network Computing (VNC) or at least a Java Runtime Environment (JRE) installed, so that the SAP team can work using the TREX standalone administration tool. The SAP team observes all reasonable security precautions for the assigned user and strictly respects the privacy of company data.

The technical details for setting up a service connection to the BIA blades are as follows. Before you start, you need to have the following:

▶ An SAProuter connection to SAP (SAPservX)

▶ Executable `trxrss.x` on your BIA server

If the process does not work correctly, check that environment variables `DIR_INSTANCE` and `SAPSYSTEM` are set. Before starting the `trxrss` binary, in the shell environment set:

```
export SAPSYSTEM=NN
export DIR_INSTANCE=<sapsid>
```

Here `NN` is the TREX instance number, and `<sapsid>` is the first part of the BIA administration user name `<sapsid>adm`.

Now you are ready to set up the service connection. There are three main steps, as follows.

Step 1: Set Up the SAProuter

1. Find out which route permission Table SAPROUTTAB is used by the SAProuter.
2. Add an entry in the following format:
   ```
   P <IP address SAP-SR> <IP Server> 3NN09
   ```
3. Here `NN` is again the TREX instance number.

4. Save the changed file, and restart the SAProuter.

5. Check that the SAProuter can reach the target host (IP address or host name).

Step 2: Start the TREX/BIA Executables

The standard installation includes the TREX/BIA executables for the service connection.

1. Log on to your BIA system with the user `<sapsid>adm`.

2. Navigate to the `<TREX_DIR>` directory:

   `/usr/sap/<sapsid>/ TRX<NN>`

3. Execute the file `trxrss.x` by entering the following command in a command prompt:

   `./TREXSettings.sh trxrss.x`

Step 3: Maintain the Connection and System Data, and Open the Service Connection

1. Log on to SAP Support Portal using alias `/serviceconnection`.

2. Choose MAINTAIN CONNECTIONS.

3. Choose the required system by clicking the system ID.

4. The SERVICE CONNECTION screen appears.

5. Choose SET UP CONNECTION TYPES.

6. Select the TREX/BIA connection in the list.

7. In the next screen, in the INDIVIDUAL PORT field, specify port number `3NN09`, and choose the contact name from the list.

8. Save your entries.

9. At the top or bottom of the screen, choose SYSTEM DATA.

10. A new window opens. Select the OTHER SERVER tab.

11. If necessary, choose CREATE SERVER.

12. A new window opens. In the SERVER DATA screen area, from the list under USED AS, choose TREX SERVER and specify:

    ▸ Host name

    ▸ IP address

185

- ▹ Operating system
- ▹ OS version
- ▹ Additional SAProuters (only if you want to use two SAP routers, one after the other)

13. Save your entries, and close the window.
14. Display the list of active service connections by choosing OPEN/CLOSE CONNECTIONS.
15. Choose the name of the service connection.
16. Specify how long the connection should be open.
17. Choose OPEN CONNECTION.

Now the BIA service connection is established and open. For any recent changes here, see SAP Note 1058533.

5.4.2 Landscape Overview

In many troubleshooting scenarios, one of the first steps is to run a check of the TREX landscape. For this purpose, TREX offers a script that generates an archive containing a snapshot of the landscape.

The Python script `landscapeOverview.py` creates a snapshot (without index data) of the TREX landscape in which it runs. The snapshot is an archive that contains HTML pages.

The ABAP program `TREX_LANDSCAPE_OVERVIEW` is the wrapper for the Python script `landscapeOverview.py`. The program calls the Python script, which collects the information and generates an archive. The ABAP program then downloads the archived snapshot to the *SYS* directory on the BIA storage.

The options for the BI accelerator are:

- ▶ SHORT RUN
  Collects only basic information about the landscape, alerts, ping output, and operating system.
- ▶ NORMAL RUN
  Collects what is normally the most useful information about the landscape, alerts, and OS.

▶ GOINGLIVE CHECK

Reports information about BIA sizing, app server ping output, service load, and the BIA system check.

▶ LONG RUN

Executes all available options, for use by SAP service engineers only.

You can start the program from Transaction SE38. The program opens with the screen shown in Figure 5.35. Simply select one of the BIA-SPECIFIC CHECKS and execute. The selection FOR EXPERTS ONLY is for SAP service engineers.

In the unlikely event that you need to ask SAP for support in handling an issue with your accelerator installation, the landscape snapshot is extremely useful in establishing the basic facts that SAP service engineers need to know first. So if you post a message asking SAP for support with an issue, remember to attach a landscape snapshot.

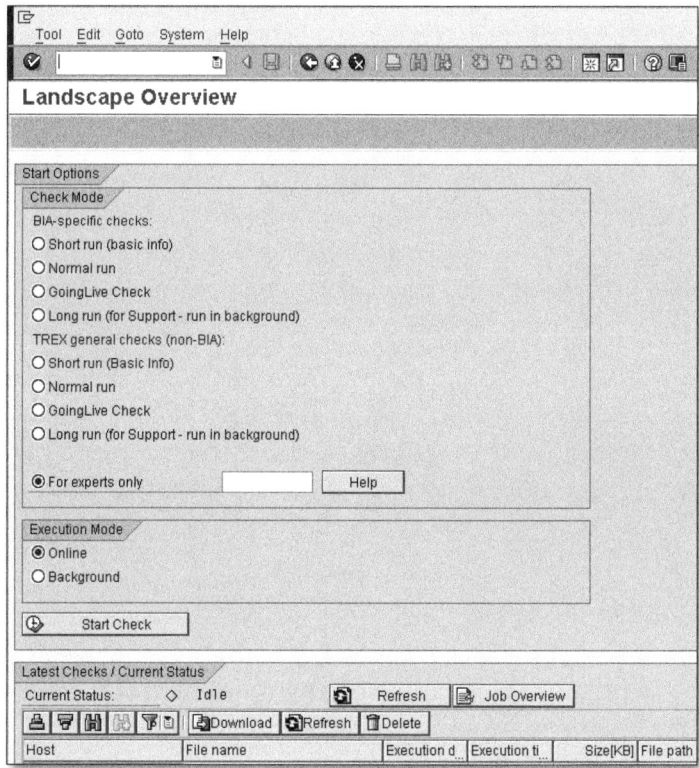

Figure 5.35 TREX Landscape Overview Checks, Initial Screen

5.4.3 Tracing

If errors occur, it can be useful to record system responses in the form of traces. Recording traces may be useful, for example, if you are obtaining different results for a SAP NetWeaver BI query depending on whether you use the accelerator or go to the database.

If you cannot resolve an error condition in the accelerator immediately, you may find it necessary to send a trace to SAP service engineers, who have specialized tools to evaluate these traces.

Because any kind of tracing imposes a performance penalty on the accelerator, it should be activated only to the minimum level necessary for your purposes.

Overview of BIA Traces

Three main kinds of tracing are available in TREX:

▸ Standard tracing, which is detailed logging and includes alert server tracing

▸ Performance tracing, recording data relevant for load and performance testing

▸ Python tracing, generating a line-by-line record of executed code

Standard traces can be recorded at different levels of detail, depending on which trace level is set in TREX for the relevant components. In descending order of detail, the available trace levels are debug, info, warning, error, fatal, none. Standard traces can be started and stopped either via Transaction TREXADMIN or using the TREX standalone administration tool.

Performance traces can also be started and stopped either via Transaction TREX-ADMIN or using the TREX standalone administration tool. The traces can be stored and retrieved for display using the same tools. These traces are useful for performance tuning or for estimating load in the course of checking the sizing.

Detailed Python traces can be made using the standalone TREX administration tool. Python traces allow remote action replays of critical command sequences in test landscapes for debugging purposes. These traces would normally be generated and evaluated by SAP service engineers and are needed only in extremely unlikely cases where it is suspected that errors in the operation of the accelerator require source code debugging.

We now look at the main kinds of trace in more detail. We start with OLAP traces, which are created by an SAP NetWeaver BI tool and are only marginally relevant for the accelerator but are included here for completeness.

OLAP Traces

If a user has encountered an issue during use of SAP Business Explorer for query execution or regarding a data request in the planning modeler, you can reproduce this error by doing the same thing again, and then you can make a trace to record the problem in your SAP NetWeaver BI system. Then you can open a customer message and let SAP experts analyze the trace.

To refer to an OLAP trace in a customer message, it is enough to give the trace ID. SAP experts can access the trace via the service connection, so you do not need to attach the trace.

A specialized trace tool is available to generate a query load for running stress tests, either during validation trials for a new accelerator installation or as a health check during production operation.

You can use the trace tool in your SAP NetWeaver BI system for various purposes:

▶ Recording problems with the frontend or the OLAP engine

▶ Performing regression tests

▶ Creating scalable query execution load

▶ Automated filling of the OLAP cache

To use the trace tool, you need to be authorized to use Transaction RSTT (see Figure 5.36), to define trace packages and trace jobs, and to execute trace jobs.

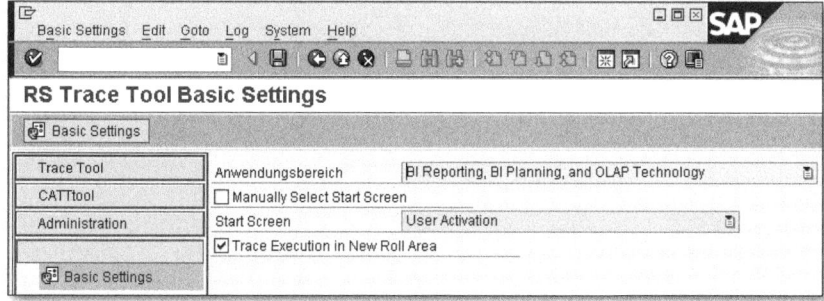

Figure 5.36 Transaction RSTT, Basic Settings

You can use the trace tool to create scalable load in the form of frequent (parallel) query requests to the accelerator, to record the query navigations, and to execute them again later if necessary.

There are three main steps involved in using the tool:

1. **Define the test.**
   As basis for the test, decide on a set of relevant queries and navigations. You need to define at least one trace package for the targeted selection and then define a trace job for scheduled execution of the trace package.

2. **Define the trace package and trace job.**
   To schedule the parallel execution of several traces, you need a trace package for grouping or selecting the traces and a trace job for scheduling the trace package as a standard job. You can either use a local program to define the package and job for the BIA stress test automatically, or you can do so manually, which offers more flexibility.

3. **Execute the test.**
   After you have defined one or more trace jobs, you can trigger multiple trace job executions in the background. You can control the level of load by adjusting the number of simultaneously running background executions of the trace job.

For further details, see SAP Note 998680.

To record an OLAP trace, proceed as follows:

1. Start Transaction RSTT, and activate yourself as a user for trace logging.

2. In the navigation window, in the TRACE TOOL functional area, select the USER ACTIVATION area. The TRACE USER field is preassigned with the current user name.

3. If you are the administrator and you want to activate another user, you can enter the name of the other user in this field. Once you have activated a user, the system displays the activated user and the time of the activation in the Table USERS.

4. Perform the interactions that give rise to the error you wish to record, and continue until the error scenario occurs.

5. To terminate the trace logging, return to the USER ACTIVATION area of the trace tool, and deactivate the user.

To determine the trace ID, proceed as follows:

1. In the navigation window, in the TRACE TOOL functional area, select the TRACE COLLECTION area. The TRACE USER field is preassigned with the current user name.

2. If necessary, add the trace type STANDARD TRACE as a selection criterion for the traces displayed in the trace list.

3. A list of available traces is displayed, in which you can find your new trace.

Standard Traces

You can reset the level of standard tracing for your BI accelerator using Transaction TREXADMIN or the standalone TREX administration tool.

You can set the trace level individually for each component of TREX. Then TREX records a trace for the selected component at the selected level of detail and returns the result in the form of a text file.

TREX Trace Levels

The six standard TREX trace levels are:

▶ **Debug**
This is the most detailed trace level and records almost as much as a Python trace, but it consumes system resources intensively and should only be used for debugging.

▶ **Info**
At this level, not only errors and warnings but also all the information messages generated during operation are recorded.

▶ **Warning**
At this level, not only error messages but also any warnings generated during operation are recorded.

▶ **Error**
This is the default trace level for the accelerator and traces all error messages generated during program execution.

▶ **Fatal**
At this level, only fatal errors generated during program execution are recorded.

▶ **None**
This records nothing and is equivalent to deactivating tracing.

Tracing Queries

In the query monitor, Transaction RSRT, you can execute and debug queries as follows:

1. Select the query for which you want to record a trace.
2. Choose EXECUTE AND DEBUG. The DEBUG OPTIONS dialog box appears. The options are ordered in a hierarchy.
3. Choose BIA SERVER • BIA DEFAULT TRACE.
4. Execute the query against the BIA index.
5. Now repeat steps 1 and 2 but instead of step 3 do step 6.
6. Select DO NOT USE BI ACCELERATOR INDEX.
7. Execute the query with aggregates or an InfoCube.
8. Compare the traces for steps 4 and 7.

If you set the indicator for the BIA default trace, the system automatically activates all the traces listed under this option that log information about the query that is currently being executed.

Changing Trace Levels

You can change the trace level for an individual service in TREX from Transaction TREXADMIN.

To do so, select the INI FILES tab, and double-click on the relevant service (see Figure 5.37). A dialog box appears in which you can edit the trace level lines directly.

In the dialog box, you can edit the *.ini* file for the service. Scroll to section [trace], and then overwrite the relevant words (see Figure 5.38). In ascending level of detail, the trace levels are none, fatal, error, warning, info, and debug. Then save.

Before any change you make to a trace level in this transaction can take effect, you need to restart the selected service. Navigate to the TREXADMIN SERVICES tab, select the service, and choose RESTART SERVICE (see Figure 5.39).

You can also change the trace level for a TREX service in the accelerator very easily from the TREX standalone administration tool.

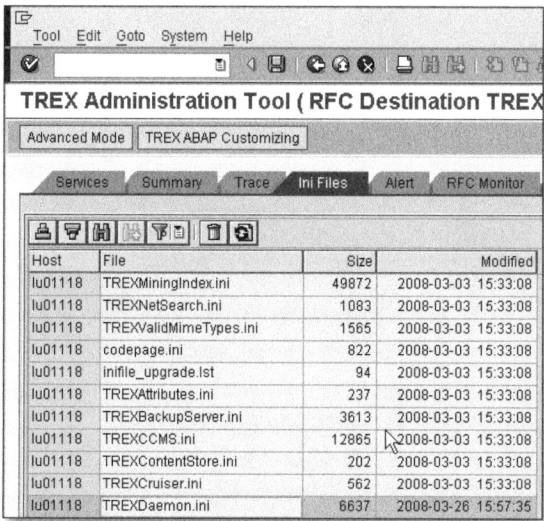

Figure 5.37 TREXADMIN, Select the .ini File

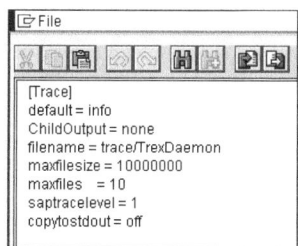

Figure 5.38 TREXADMIN, Edit the .ini File

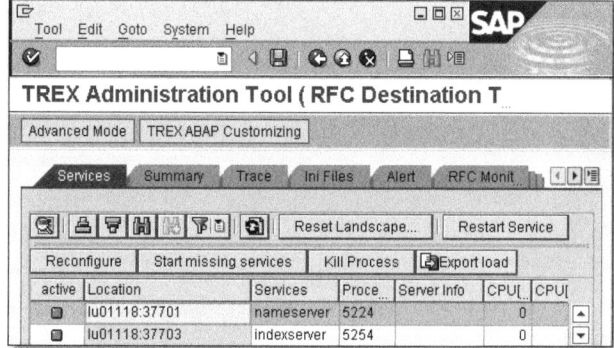

Figure 5.39 TREXADMIN, Restart Selected Service

In the TRACE view, choose TRACE LEVELS. A dialog box appears as shown in Figure 5.40. At the top of the dialog box, select the relevant service, and then select the trace component from the list of components for the selected service.

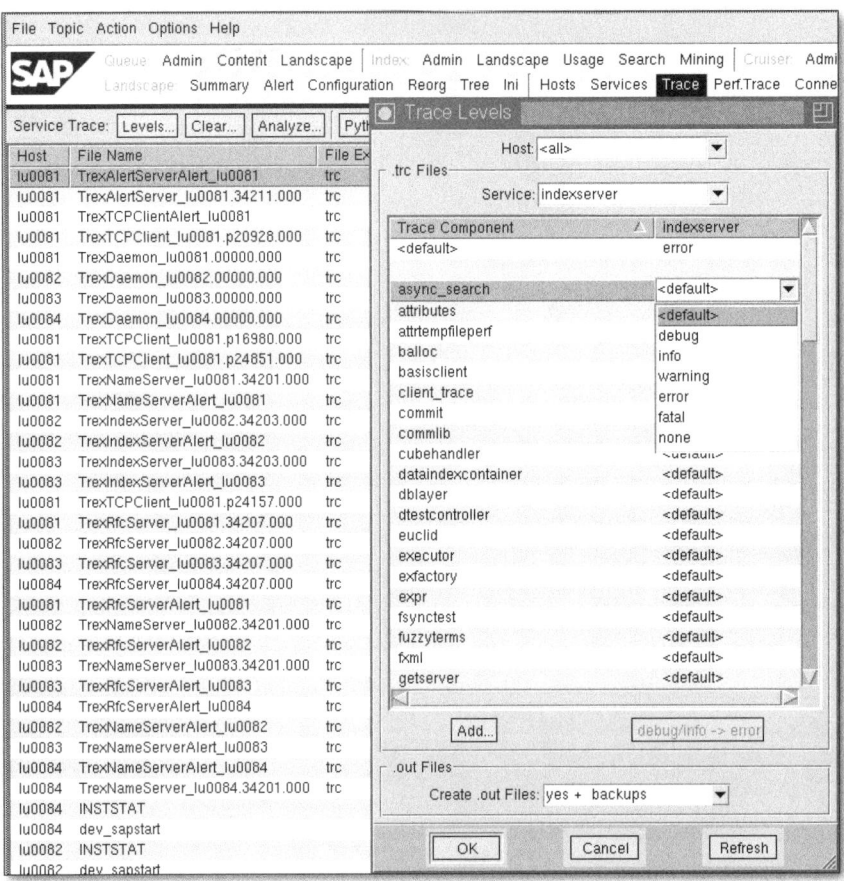

Figure 5.40 TREX Admin Tool, Trace Levels Dialog Box

A drop-down menu enables you to select the desired trace level. As before, in ascending level of detail, the trace levels are none, fatal, error, warning, info, and debug. Then choose OK. That's all. There is no need to restart the service.

Alert server traces form a subset of the standard traces. If standard tracing is deactivated, alert server tracing is deactivated too, independently of the alert server configuration.

One contrast between standard traces and alert server traces has practical importance for administration. Standard traces are automatically limited in size. Older trace files are automatically deleted when the total size of the traces exceeds a preset threshold. By contrast, alert server traces are not deleted automatically. The volume of alert server trace files will grow without limit unless the administrator periodically deletes older files.

Performance Traces

You can activate a performance trace from the BI ACCELERATOR menu in the BIA monitor. From there, the PERFORMANCE TRACE menu offers the following options:

▶ START TRACE RECORDING
Opens a dialog box for entering details and starting the recording.

▶ STOP TRACE RECORDING
Deactivated unless a performance trace is running.

▶ SAVE TRACE FILE
Deactivated unless a performance trace has just been created.

▶ DISPLAY TRACE INFORMATION
Opens an information box with details about the last performance trace recorded.

▶ DELETING TRACE FILE
Deactivated unless a performance trace has just been created. Once you have saved the trace, you can delete the file here in readiness for the next trace.

To start a performance trace from the BIA monitor, choose PERFORMANCE TRACE • START TRACE RECORDING (you may first need to choose DELETING TRACE FILE).

A dialog box appears in which you have the option to start the trace for a particular user and to specify when you want to stop the trace (see Figure 5.41). When you are ready, choose START TRACE RECORDING.

Because performance tracing consumes system resources, we recommend that you do not let performance tracing continue to run for any longer than necessary.

In the status bar, the system shows how long trace recording has left to run. If a trace recording is already running, you cannot start a new one.

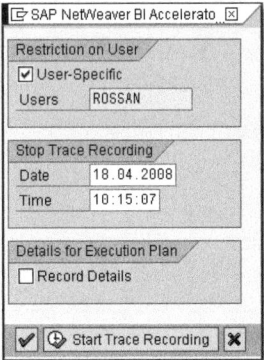

Figure 5.41 BIA Monitor, Performance Trace

If you did not specify a stop time, you can stop tracing later by choosing PERFOR-MANCE TRACE • STOP TRACE RECORDING.

To save a trace file locally, choose PERFORMANCE TRACE • SAVE TRACE FILE. A dialog box appears in which you can enter a file name, specify a target folder, and save (see Figure 5.42).

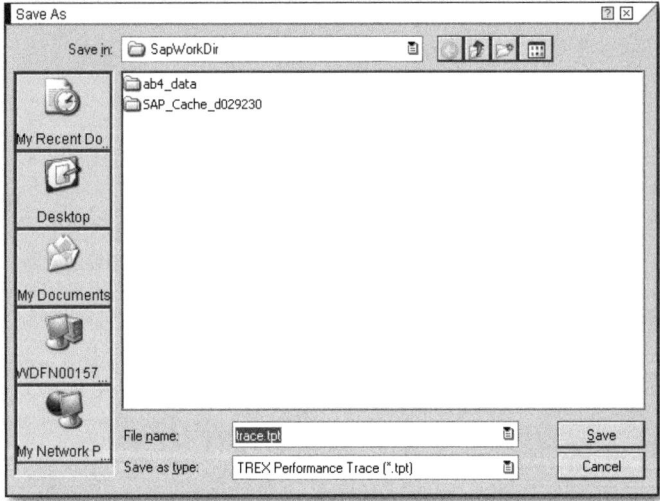

Figure 5.42 BIA Monitor, Save Performance Trace

To display information about the performance trace, choose PERFORMANCE TRACE • DISPLAY TRACE INFORMATION.

The system displays the following key figures for the trace:

▶ Start time

▶ Stop time

▶ Remaining time

▶ Users

▶ File size in kilobytes

To delete a performance trace file either after you have saved it or without saving it, choose PERFORMANCE TRACE • DELETING TRACE FILE.

You can start and stop performance traces for the accelerator very easily from the TREX standalone administration tool. Select the PERF. TRACE view, and choose START. Enter the relevant information in the dialog box, and choose OK (see Figure 5.43). To stop the trace later, choose STOP, and then save. To check the trace, go to TRACE view, and locate it by name or timestamp.

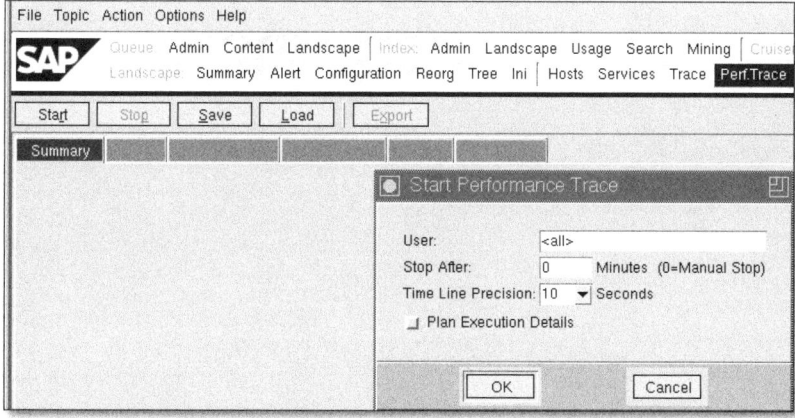

Figure 5.43 TREX Admin Tool, Performance Trace

Python Traces

If you post a customer message reporting a serious issue in your accelerator installation, SAP service engineers may ask you to create a Python trace, which is so detailed that it can be rerun on remote hardware to reproduce error states for debugging or other troubleshooting purposes.

A Python trace records the individual commands executed by the TREX index server. All Python traces are recorded as Python scripts that can be executed again later. Because Python traces can become very large, you can choose to save a Python trace file without displaying or editing it.

You can start a Python trace from the TREX administration tool, by choosing PYTHON TRACE in the TRACE view. The PYTHON TRACES dialog box appears. If you choose SET TRACE, the PYTHON TRACE DETAILS dialog box appears. Both dialog boxes are shown in Figure 5.44.

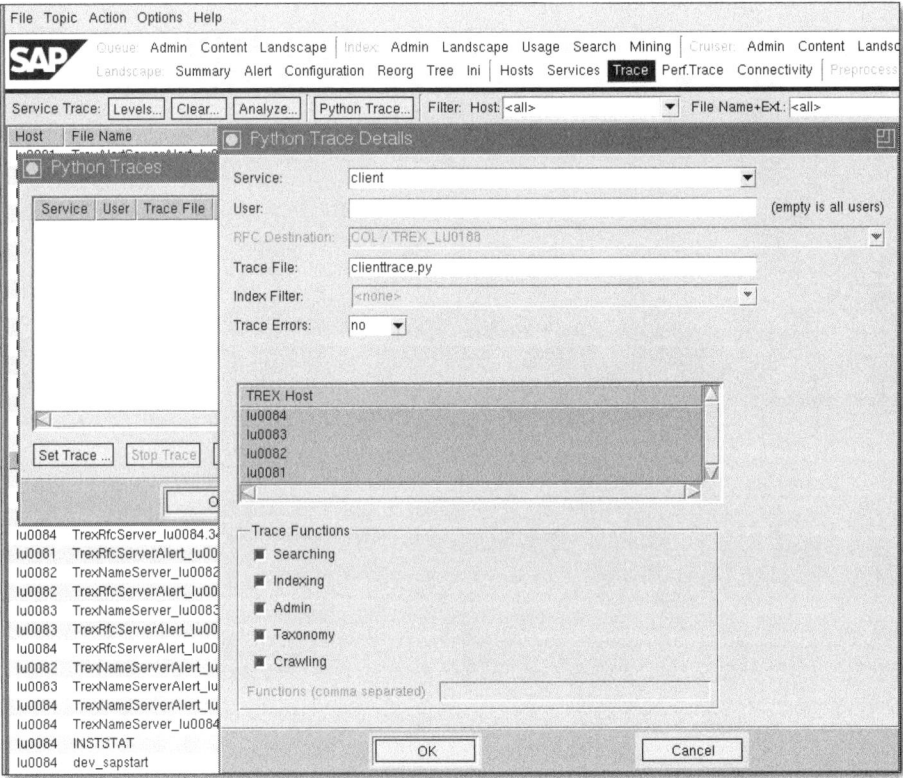

Figure 5.44 TREX Admin Tool, Python Trace

Python traces list every program call in full detail, so that an expert can read exactly what happened during program execution, but the price for this is that the trace files can quickly become enormous. For this reason, and because writing the trace imposes a significant load on the system, you should not run a Python trace unless explicitly requested to do so, and then you should run it only for the shortest possible time. To give an idea of the load here, running a Python trace on an active host for a few hours can create a trace file with a size of many gigabytes.

5.5   Summary

Advanced administration is a huge topic, and the information in this chapter is only a starting point. Most administrators for productive accelerator installations should be able to perform the exceptional and optimization tasks described in this chapter. As for collaboration with SAP, any good administrator needs to be ready if necessary to perform the first steps of troubleshooting in order to assist SAP service engineers. They should also know where to stop and rely on the experts.

6   Success Stories

This chapter presents some success stories resulting from deployment of the SAP NetWeaver BI Accelerator in challenging scenarios. Most of these are in real companies with real business targets to meet.

The first story, in Section 6.1, dramatically demonstrates the scalability of the accelerator. Together with IBM, SAP ran heavy loads on an accelerator installation with 140 nodes working on 25 TB of business data.

The second, in Section 6.2, illustrates the ongoing commitment of the BIA development team to keep on refining the product. In this case, a new approach to multiqueries and some new compression techniques led to a doubling of accelerator performance in certain special cases.

The subsequent success stories report the experiences of leading companies as they introduced SAP NetWeaver BI Accelerator into their corporate SAP landscapes to accelerate reporting on InfoCubes.

6.1   Scalability: Project Jupiter

In 2007, SAP and IBM engaged WinterCorp to monitor and independently report on Project Jupiter, a joint effort by SAP and IBM to conduct large-scale tests of the SAP NetWeaver BI Accelerator against user data volumes at three scale points: 5 TB, 15 TB, and 25 TB. The results demonstrate the ability of the accelerator to address the growing requirements of SAP NetWeaver BI users for ad hoc data analysis on a large scale. Table 6.1 summarizes the system sizes and data volumes.

Scale (TB)	Blades (nodes)	RAM (GB)	Rows (billions)	Data (TB)	Index (TB)	Total (TB)
5	27	432	6	3.9	1.1	5.0
15	81	1,296	18	12.7	1.8	14.5
25	135	2,160	30	20.7	2.9	23.6

Table 6.1 Project Jupiter: System Sizes and Data Volumes

The system landscape provided a complete SAP NetWeaver BI infrastructure on IBM servers and storage systems. It included an SAP NetWeaver BI server running on a 64-processor IBM System p p595 SMP server, an SAP NetWeaver database server on a 32-processor IBM System z9 mainframe running DB2 for zOS V9, the BI accelerator running on a large array of IBM HS21 BladeCenter blades, spanning 2 to 10 blade chassis (each with 14 blade nodes), and a small array of query drivers running on IBM System x servers. The systems were connected in a high-speed Ethernet network.

The attached disk storage was provided by six IBM System Storage DS8300 storage arrays containing a total of 150 TB disk space. The accelerator blades shared high-performance access via IBM General Parallel File System (GPFS) to the storage pool. The GPFS Network Shared Disk (NSD) storage server nodes and the BIA blades were connected via InfiniBand, providing 80 Gbps (gigabit per second) dedicated bandwidth to each blade chassis. The GPFS NSD storage server nodes were connected to the storage system via 20-Gbps fibre channel, with 2 fibre channel connections to each storage server node.

Tests were conducted at three scales. At the 5 TB scale, 2 blade chassis were used, containing a total of 28 blades (27 master nodes plus 1 backup node in case of blade failure). At the 15 TB scale, 6 chassis were used, with 84 blades (81 master nodes plus 3 backups). And at the 25 TB scale, 10 chassis were used, with 140 blades (135 master nodes plus 5 backups). There were no blade failures during the tests, so the backup nodes in fact remained idle.

The system was installed and the tests were run at the IBM System and Technology Group Labs in Poughkeepsie, New York, between July and December 2007.

Data for the project was drawn from two sources. Some data was provided by a large U.S. company that uses SAP NetWeaver BI. This was a 10-year collection of sales, billing, and delivery data divided into 30 InfoCubes with a single MultiProvider to provide a common data view. The rest of the data came from the SAP NetWeaver Standard Application benchmark. This consisted of 48 one-month InfoCubes of sales and distribution data, again with one MultiProvider.

Queries executed against this data involved thousands of variations on 14 complex reporting templates. All queries accessed the data via the MultiProviders and involved joining fact table records with numerous dimensions and characteristics and multiple key figures for aggregation. Many reports touched multiple Info-Cubes. The test driver software was Hewlett-Packard LoadRunner, and query streams were varied up to 800 concurrent streams.

The project involved executing separate tests of load performance, single-user query performance, and multiuser query performance. Resource utilization was also measured to assess load balancing across the accelerator nodes.

The load performance tests measured how quickly data from the attached database could be loaded and indexed in the accelerator. The tests included all 78 InfoCubes at each of the three scale points. Load times ranged from 400 minutes at the 5 TB scale to something over 15 hours at the 25 TB scale, with load rates peaking at 1.28 TB per hour at the 25 TB scale. The increase in load rate was somewhat less than linear at the larger scale points, apparently because the attached SAP NetWeaver BI server providing the data approached saturation.

Single-user tests involved each of the 14 query templates as the system scaled from 5 TB to 25 TB. The test results are summarized in Table 6.2. Adjusted for the increase in volume of data processed, the scaling is close to linear.

Scale (TB)	Records Processed (average, millions)	Response Time (average, seconds)
5	4.7	0.77
15	15.8	0.90
25	25.6	0.92

Table 6.2 Project Jupiter: Single-User Scalability

Multiuser tests involved varying the number of concurrent query streams between 100 and 800 (between 100 and 400 for the 5 TB scale), with each stream running the query sequence from a different start point, so that each in-flight query was processing different data. An inter-query delay of 2 seconds was set to simulate the work of thousands of concurrent users. At each scale, multiuser query throughput peaked at more than 100,000 queries per hour for 200 concurrent query streams. Throughput reached a plateau at higher levels of concurrency because beyond 200 streams the SAP NetWeaver BI server processors became saturated. Overall the average response times remained steady at roughly 4 seconds, with a peak in all tests of less than 9 seconds.

The tests of processor utilization across the 135 nodes of the landscape showed the success of load balancing. In all the tests, the processor utilization varied between 50 and 80 %, with an average at the 5 TB scale of over 70 %, at the 15 TB scale of over 66 %, and at the 25 TB scale of almost 60 %. The deterioration with increasing scale was due first to the difficulty of partitioning data optimally for large indexes and second to saturation in the BI server at high workloads.

The findings were published in March 2008. These are the highlights:

▶ Single user query performance scales quite well as the volume of data processed grows.

▶ Multiuser tests demonstrate linear scalability in both throughput and response time across the full range of data volume tested, from 5 TB to 25 TB.

▶ Throughput in multiuser tests was greater than 100,000 reports per hour at all test scales.

▶ From 100 to 800 concurrent query streams are supported, with optimal results at 200 concurrent query streams — enough to support an active user population in the thousands.

▶ The BI accelerator can load data from an SAP NetWeaver database, deployed on IBM DB2, at rates in excess of 1 TB per hour.

▶ Query activity is effectively parallelized across up to 135 nodes (5 additional nodes were configured as backups, but they were not needed because there were no hardware outages).

The Project Jupiter results show that SAP NetWeaver BI Accelerator can meet the needs of the largest companies. For further details, see the WinterCorp report.

6.2   Colgate-Palmolive Company

Colgate-Palmolive is a leading global consumer products company. Tightly focused on oral care, personal care, home care, and pet nutrition, Colgate serves hundreds of millions of consumers in over 200 countries and territories around the world. With headquarters in New York, the company has 36,000 employees, and worldwide sales were over $13.7 billion in 2007.

Colgate has an extensive SAP NetWeaver BI landscape and was an early adopter of the SAP NetWeaver BI Accelerator. In 2007, they invited the BIA development team to study their data as part of a technical initiative to optimize their deployment of the accelerator in the hope of realizing a greater performance improvement relative to the database.

The background to this invitation was that Colgate saw no big performance improvement for certain particularly challenging queries when they used the accelerator instead of the database. These queries addressed huge but sparse Info-Cubes, and to achieve tolerable performance from the database, Colgate had built optimal aggregates for the InfoCubes. That fact that the accelerator response times were similar to those using the tuned aggregates was no surprise because here the accelerator had to work much harder during query runtime than the database. The BIA team always said that the main benefits of accelerator deployment were in offering fast response for queries lacking suitable aggregates and in reducing aggregate maintenance effort. However, the BIA team saw an opportunity for a radical new approach to executing multiqueries on sparse data (the technical details are explained in Chapter 7).

Together, Colgate and the BIA team measured response times in the Colgate landscape for a set of queries in July 2007. The queries were all executed against tuned aggregates over worldwide data that was broken down by three geographical regions. The queries were then executed using the accelerator. The BIA team studied the results and improved the accelerator coding. After updating the Colgate binaries, the BIA team made a new set of comparative measurements in November 2007. The results were convincing. Overall accelerator response times for these queries (measured in seconds) were on average 179 % better than before. Table 6.3 shows the results.

	BI Accelerator Before (seconds)	BI Accelerator after (seconds)	Improvement (percent)
Region 1	381	157	243
Region 2	67	47	143
Region 3	206	121	170
World	259	145	179

Table 6.3 Response Times Before and After BIA Enhancement

Using the new coding, some additional single-user tests were performed. Response time for the worst 10 queries (including navigations such as drill-downs within a query) measured by database response time were plotted to compare their times using database aggregates with their times using the accelerator. Figure 6.1 shows the results.

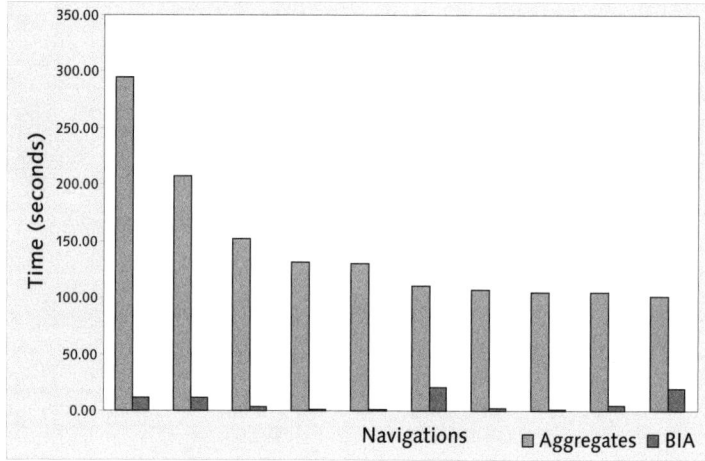

Figure 6.1 Worst 10 Queries for DB Aggregate Time

Further single-user test results for a much larger set of queries were analyzed to plot all the queries for which the response time from the database was greater than 10 seconds and again to compare those times with the times achieved using the accelerator. Figure 6.2 shows the results.

A third plot was made to show the single-user results for the larger set of queries where the response times from the database were less than 10 seconds and again to compare those times with the times achieved using the accelerator. In these cases, many of the queries hit suitable aggregates on the database. However, only in a very few cases, shown by the spike on the graph, was the accelerator response time longer than that of the database. Figure 6.3 shows the results.

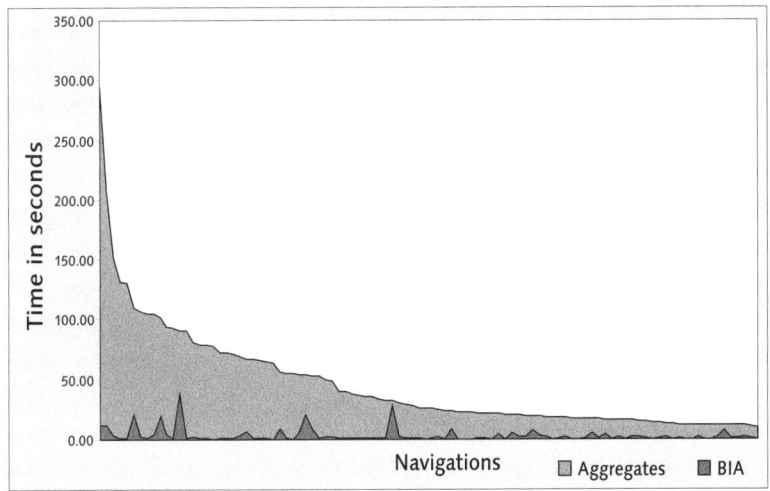

Figure 6.2 Queries with DB Aggregate Times > 10 Seconds

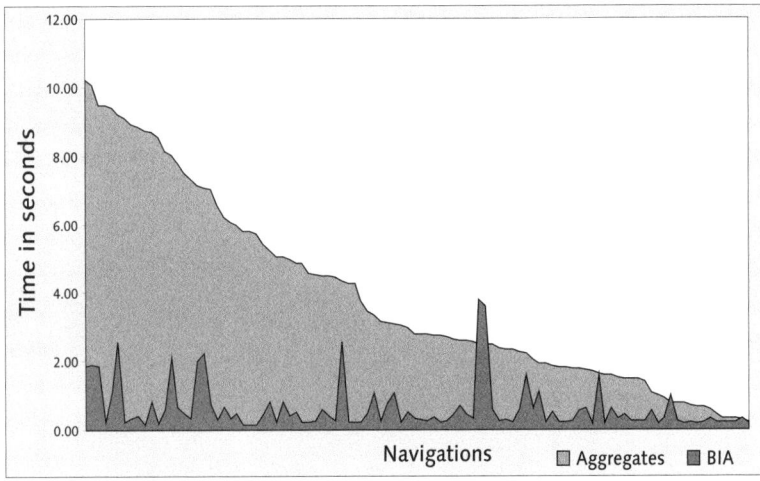

Figure 6.3 Queries with DB Aggregate Times < 10 Seconds

Next, the team looked more closely at one particularly difficult navigation and compared the response times from database aggregates with those from the accelerator. For all the steps, the accelerator improved the results. At the fourth step, a database timeout after one hour was avoided, and the rather long accelerator response time of over 217 seconds was consumed almost entirely by data transfer, with only about 1 % due to the BIA engine itself. Table 6.4 shows the results.

	DB Response Time (seconds)	BIA Response Time (seconds)
Navigation 1	6.56	5.88
Navigation 2	7.48	2.37
Navigation 3	22.05	19.60
Navigation 4	Timeout	217.65 (mostly data transfer)

Table 6.4 Accelerator Avoids Timeout for Hard Query

Next, the total response time for all 37 single-user test cases with 207 navigations was calculated and analyzed. When the database and accelerator results were compared, it turned out that data manager (DM) times, which include the times for accelerator processing, were improved by 860 %. This reflected the success of the new approach to sparse data. Also, the OLAP times, which are independent of the accelerator and depend mainly on the data volumes involved, were improved by 300 %. This reflected the success of the new approach to multiqueries. Table 6.5 shows the results.

	Combined Response Time (seconds)		
	DM	OLAP	DM + OLAP
DB	3,384	757	4,141
BIA	393	252	646
Improvement (percent)	860	300	641

Table 6.5 Overall Response Time Improvements

The performance improvements were in part due to a new (patent pending) procedure for handling complex multiqueries involving the grouping of multiple selections, which among other things greatly reduced the size of the intermediate result sets returned by the accelerator to the SAP NetWeaver BI analytic engine. Because the database could not take advantage of this optimization, the OLAP times using aggregates were longer than those using the accelerator. The new approach to multiqueries involves smart repartitioning of the raw data for the query in memory and enables the BIA engine to do work previously passed to the analytic engine (see Section 7.6.3).

Finally, to ensure that the improvements scaled with number of users, the team performed a load test with 200 users and 2,000 navigations. The team found that all the response times were below 20 seconds, and almost all were substantially below, with many well below 1 second.

In summary, the collaboration here between Colgate and the BIA team was successful. Response times for real company reports running on real business data were greatly improved relative to tuned database aggregates running in a mature company landscape. The initiative improved overall accelerator performance in this scenario by a factor of almost two. This case study shows the intensity with which the accelerator development team is still working to extend the scope of the product.

6.3 Bayer AG

Bayer AG in Leverkusen, Germany, is a world-wide leader in the pharmaceuticals and chemicals industries. The company has more than 300 operating units, which employ 93,700 people on 5 continents. Bayer MaterialScience (BMS) is one of the key Bayer business units, with almost 18,800 employees and annual net sales of €10.7 billion ($13.4 billion) in 2005.

Bayer MaterialScience was seeking approaches to cope with the rapid growth in data volume generated within its SAP NetWeaver BI data warehouse system. The subgroup already had a data volume of more than 2 TB, with a forecast growth of more than 1 TB per annum, reaching 20 TB by 2012. If BMS could collate data and produce meaningful information more rapidly, the company would be well positioned to respond to a fast-changing marketplace.

Bayer Business Services (4,400 employees, €816 million [$1.02 billion] sales), the Bayer group's international competence center for IT-based services, implemented a high-performance information analysis system solution based on SAP NetWeaver BI with the SAP NetWeaver BI Accelerator and IBM BladeCenter technology.

Bayer Business Services decided to add SAP NetWeaver BI Accelerator technology to the existing SAP NetWeaver BI solutions. The SAP NetWeaver BI Accelerator runs on IBM BladeCenter model HS20 blades with Intel Xeon EM64T processors, running 64-bit Linux, linked to the IBM TotalStorage DS4300 storage system. The system is capable of managing 20 parallel user sessions, handling 250 million rows of 500 bytes. The IBM and SAP solution is scalable to a fully populated BladeCenter chassis of 14 blades, able to manage 100 parallel user sessions handling 1 billion rows of 500 bytes. With the addition of the SAP NetWeaver BI Accelerator to the existing SAP solutions, query performance at Bayer MaterialScience has improved significantly.

Harald Sold, Head of Business Intelligence Application Operation, said:

> *Bayer MaterialScience will now be able to expect quick responses for analyses even on complex data sets, delivering query results to the management dashboard more quickly. We will be able to make the best use of the data by providing a more solid and timely basis for management decisions.*

Summing up the value proposition, Mr. Sold said:

> *The ability to collect and analyze data so quickly has a high value to Bayer MaterialScience. With the right information at the right time, managers can better understand the business and the market.*

6.4   German Defense Forces

The German national defense forces (GDF or *Bundeswehr*) include army, navy, air force, joint support service, and central medical services, as well as the territorial defense administration and armaments organization. The organization has around 400,000 employees, all managed in a single hierarchy. Conscription results in high staff turnover, contributing to a rapid rise in human resources (HR) data volumes.

The GDF uses SAP NetWeaver BI to analyze complex data sets for controlling, balanced scorecards, logistics, and HR planning and reporting. With the number of SAP NetWeaver BI users set to double to 4,000, the GDF needed to boost query performance and enable more concurrent user sessions.

Their solution was to implement IBM DB2 with the SAP NetWeaver BI Accelerator to accelerate 100 InfoCubes from the SAP NetWeaver BI system. These cubes have on average 10 key figures and up to 80 million rows, together totaling around 1.5 TB in the database. The SAP NetWeaver BI Accelerator has compressed these cubes by a factor of 12 (comparing the database footprint of the original data with the memory footprint of the BIA indexes). The entire indexing process was completed at an average rate of about 100 million rows per hour.

Lieutenant Colonel Jörg Steinhorst, Standard Application Software Product Family (SASPF) project leader for the GDF, said:

> The advantage of the SAP NetWeaver BI Accelerator is that it can optimize speed and concurrent queries at the same time. Fifty concurrent users can now complete a query in just 30 seconds that previously took 60 seconds for a single user, and 90 seconds during concurrent execution. An even more impressive benefit is that the time-consuming building and maintaining of aggregates in the data warehouse has now been eliminated. This results in both improved response times and reduced effort on data maintenance. For ad hoc queries, we've improved performance by a factor of 116.

6.5   T-Mobile UK

T-Mobile UK, a subsidiary of Deutsche Telekom AG, is one of Europe's leading national telecommunications companies, specializing in GSM cellular telephony. Based in Hertfordshire, United Kingdom, the company employs around 7,000 people and generates annual net revenues of above £3 billion ($4.5 billion); its network handles the traffic of more than 16.9 million customers (including Virgin Mobile).

T-Mobile UK uses SAP ERP to manage its business processes. Nearly all of the company's employees have regular access to SAP applications for everything from high-level financial management to expense claim registration and holiday requests. Around 550 people use SAP NetWeaver BI to analyze the data accrued about daily working practices, company finances, network build, and other business processes. Managers run extensive data queries to discover new ways to increase efficiency and develop better ways of continuously improving processes.

To compete in the UK cell phone market, T-Mobile is continually looking both to cut operational costs and to optimize its revenues by tuning the tariffs it offers to its customers. The ability to analyze real-time business data is key to understanding customer behavior and gaining competitive advantage. The traditional approach to BI had reached its limits, and T-Mobile wanted a faster and more flexible solution.

T-Mobile worked with IBM Global Technology Services to deploy the IBM Systems solution for SAP NetWeaver BI Accelerator. Based on IBM Intel-based BladeCenter technology, IBM System Storage General Parallel File System (GPFS) and SAP NetWeaver BI Accelerator software, average query speed is now up to 150 times faster than before.

Matthias Assmann, Head of Management Information (MI) at T-Mobile UK, said:

> One of the main objectives for the MI team is to support the business by developing solutions in SAP NetWeaver BI that business users in finance and procurement, or those who are involved in building the network, can easily use to get insight out of existing information and data. The problem with our existing solution was that queries could become very slow — we had to spend many hours tuning our queries to ensure good performance, and even then, if a user deviated from the analytical paths we had predicted, response times would lengthen dramatically.

T-Mobile upgraded to SAP NetWeaver BI with the SAP NetWeaver BI Accelerator. As Mr. Assmann said:

> It is a huge improvement; we have seen query response times improve by a factor of 150. Most importantly, with SAP NetWeaver BI Accelerator, it doesn't matter how complex the query is — the response time is constant over the analytical path, and there is no longer any need to second-guess the users' needs or spend time on optimizing query performance. The optimization process could take up to 10 days for some projects. Now we don't have to think about it at all. Whatever queries the users run — even if they follow analytical paths that we did not foresee — the response arrives in seconds. With SAP NetWeaver BI Accelerator, we are not simply saving time and money on development, we are also freeing the business users to think beyond the normal patterns and come up with truly innovative business analysis.

6.6   Rabobank Group

Rabobank Group is a full-range financial services provider founded on cooperative principles, and a global leader in sustainability-oriented banking. The group is comprised of 188 independent local Dutch Rabobanks, a central organization (Rabobank Nederland), and a large number of specialized international offices. The group employs some 55,000 staff and is represented in 42 countries.

User requests for more complex and customized business reporting were causing response times to slow and placing an increasing strain on the IT team, who wanted to balance the need for user-controlled reporting with acceptable response times and minimal impact on IT department resources. They decided to implement the IBM Systems Solution for SAP NetWeaver BI Accelerator, with the accelerator running on IBM BladeCenter servers, supporting some 4,000 users.

Tonnie van der Horst, Manager of IT Strategy and Change within the Group Finance Department, said:

> In certain areas which would previously have required significant development work to optimize the user queries, results are generated a hundred times faster with the IBM Systems Solution for SAP NetWeaver BI Accelerator. Not only does this super-fast response give great service to the Rabobank branches, it reduces or even eliminates the optimization work that needs to be carried out by IT staff. The IBM BladeCenter-based solution has substantially improved our SAP NetWeaver BI performance — for example, one query that previously took over 10 minutes to complete without BIA can now be performed in less than 6 seconds — improving performance by a factor of 120.

Summing up the benefits, Mr. van der Horst said:

> The SAP NetWeaver BI Accelerator software on IBM BladeCenter servers gives flexible, scalable access to data queries in a way that we were unable to deliver before. Report response times are measured in seconds, and users can tailor their queries with no intervention from the IT team, boosting their productivity and reducing the central administration costs.

6.7 Kimberly-Clark Corporation

Kimberly-Clark Corporation makes products to enhance the daily health, hygiene, and well-being of over 1.3 billion people in more than 150 countries. With its well-known global brands, Kimberly-Clark holds the number 1 or number 2 market share position in more than 80 countries. Kimberly-Clark is based in Dallas, Texas, has 55,000 employees, and achieved a 2006 revenue of $16.7 billion.

The company wished to make reporting a mission-critical function, which involved reducing the cost, time, and effort of running comprehensive reports across all lines of business, providing deeper, broader, and faster data-mining analytic functionality for greater business insight, and streamlining ad hoc queries.

Kimberly-Clark decided to leverage its long and successful relationships with SAP and the Hewlett-Packard Company and upgrade its system with SAP NetWeaver BI Accelerator software. A demonstration of the software using Kimberly-Clark's own data showed how SAP NetWeaver BI Accelerator could help the company generate reports up to 100 times faster than before. This proof of concept generated strong support from Kimberly-Clark executives for the project. Further confirmation came from analyst research showing the many business benefits gained from timely access to data. Using its own rapid-implementation methodology, Kimberly-Clark completed a functional upgrade within 3 to 4 weeks and went live with the new software in about 6 months.

With SAP NetWeaver BI Accelerator, business decision making at Kimberly-Clark has improved dramatically. Five installations now handle 5.5 TB of data for 4,500 users and 20,000 queries per day. With greater reporting speed, the company can address more business challenges in the same time. Query speed has improved by more than 60% on average. From a database perspective, the system can now respond to 87% of all queries in less than 1 second and 98% in fewer than 10 seconds. Weekly master data change runs have been reduced from 4 or 5 hours to 10 minutes on one landscape, and report data can be refreshed daily instead of weekly or monthly. SAP NetWeaver BI Accelerator has also helped lower TCO for the existing system. Besides reducing mainframe utilization by 65% in one region alone, the new software lets Kimberly-Clark change master data without additional development activities and has reduced development support activities overall. With scalable BI now available, Kimberly-Clark plans to leverage its investment in other operational domains and give users information that was never possible before.

Phil Nickolai, Senior Manager for Enterprise Business Intelligence at Kimberly-Clark Corporation, said:

> *SAP Net Weaver BI Accelerator has been a role-model implementation. We put it in place and it delivered results immediately. It jump-started our progress more than we expected.*

Illustrating the benefits, Pete Vavruska, Controller, Latin America and Other, Kimberly-Clark Corporation, said:

> *I'm doing drill-downs that I wouldn't have even considered before this enhancement.*

Summing up the benefits, Phil Nickolai said:

> *The real benefit goes well beyond query speed. There's truly been an overall increase in analytical capabilities.*

6.8   WACKER Group

WACKER is a globally active chemical company headquartered in Munich. With a wide range of state-of-the-art specialty products, the WACKER Group is a leader in numerous industrial sectors worldwide and has expertise in fields such as silicone and polymer chemistry, specialty and fine chemistry, polysilicon production, and semiconductor technologies. The group has production facilities at locations in Germany and other parts of the world, with about 15,000 employees on 5 continents.

WACKER uses SAP software, including SAP NetWeaver BI. More than 2,000 people within the company access the SAP NetWeaver BI system. With increased utilization of BI as a key business tool, its results have become more and more time-critical.

In 2007, WACKER carried out a proof of concept for SAP NetWeaver BI Accelerator deployment with the support of IBM Global Technology Services and the IBM System x team. WACKER identified 16 specific queries from their SAP systems and measured existing performance. These 16 queries became the benchmarks for the implementation. All criteria were met or exceeded, and WACKER decided to take the solution into production.

WACKER operates two data centers, one housing the test and development environment, and one for the clustered production system. IBM delivered two IBM System solutions for SAP NetWeaver BI Accelerator: a production system with three blades (two masters and one backup) and a test/QA system with two blades, also designated as the disaster recovery system.

The IBM BladeCenter solution is equipped with BladeCenter HS21 blade servers mounting dual-core Intel Xeon processors. The IBM System Storage DS4700 Express offers high-performance 4-Gbps fibre channel connections for rapidly loading the BIA indexes into the memory of the blade servers. IBM General Parallel File System (GPFS) is used to read and write data in parallel and is key to the high performance delivered by the accelerator.

WACKER created BIA indexes for a total of 103 InfoCubes. Query performance has increased up to 500 % in comparison to native BI query performance without aggregates.

Reinhard Bauer, Team Manager, Business Intelligence and Financials, WACKER, said:

> *The response times were significantly improved with the introduction of the IBM Systems solution for SAP NetWeaver BI Accelerator, and we are able to work much more efficiently and productively. Data can now be flexibly and quickly analyzed at reduced administrative cost, and the need to construct and maintain expensive aggregates was removed.*

> *Particular emphasis should be placed on the scalability of the IBM BladeCenter. Just six months after going into production, the capacity of the IBM Systems solution for SAP NetWeaver BI Accelerator had to be expanded due to data growth and go-live. Thanks to the flexible infrastructure, it was possible to add two additional blades to the BladeCenter without any problems.*

The entire project was implemented, commissioned to production, and completed on time and on budget. The project has been a major success for WACKER and is now being rolled out to more users.

6.9 Summary

The first success story proves that the accelerator technology is readily scalable to scenarios with well over a hundred blade server nodes and data volumes of many terabytes. No hard upper limit has yet been found for the size of a BI accelerator landscape, and the development team expects that much larger landscapes are possible.

The second success story shows that the accelerator offers benefits not only in the classic scenario of queries lacking suitable aggregates but also, now, as the development team continues to invest creative effort to enhance the technology, in direct competition with tuned aggregates. In particular, the handling of sparse data is greatly superior.

The subsequent success stories confirm the message that the accelerator technology brings practical benefits. They add the important further message that investment now in the SAP NetWeaver BI Accelerator brings immediate and visible business benefits. As SAP continues to pursue new technology further, these benefits will only increase.

7   Technical Details

The SAP NetWeaver BI Accelerator is a highly optimized product in numerous respects. To make optimal use of its memory resources, the BI accelerator creates highly compressed index structures from BI InfoCubes. The BIA indexes are compressed using integer coding and other advanced techniques. Each BIA index contains or references a separate table index for each table in the InfoCube on which it is based. Within the table indexes, the table data is stored in separate columns. And tables with many rows are split into parts that are indexed in parallel.

To leverage its CPU and memory resources to the maximum, the BIA software distributes the various indexes it has created over all the available processor cores. For split indexes because the split parts are loaded in memory on separate nodes, the accelerator parallelizes the task of answering queries over all the cores. As a result, an SAP NetWeaver BI system with an accelerator attached can deliver response times that are typically tens and sometimes hundreds of times better than in a normally tuned BI system relying on aggregates.

The rest of this chapter is rather technical.

7.1   Vertical Decomposition

The BI accelerator leverages several ideas to improve query performance. One such idea is to store table columns separately, instead of storing tables over their full width row by row, as in a classical relational database.

The benefit of this approach for SAP NetWeaver BI analytic processing scenarios is that because typical analytic queries only mention attributes from a few columns, only those columns need be touched at all by the BIA engine. It is a general principle of data processing that to maximize performance, it is necessary to minimize the amount of data touched because this pays off several times over by reducing:

- ▸ Bandwidth needed to access the data
- ▸ Latencies to transport the data
- ▸ Memory and cache space to hold the data
- ▸ CPU clock time to process the data

The BIA engine can use column data to find all the instances of a given attribute value very quickly. Figure 7.1 shows the index structures employed.

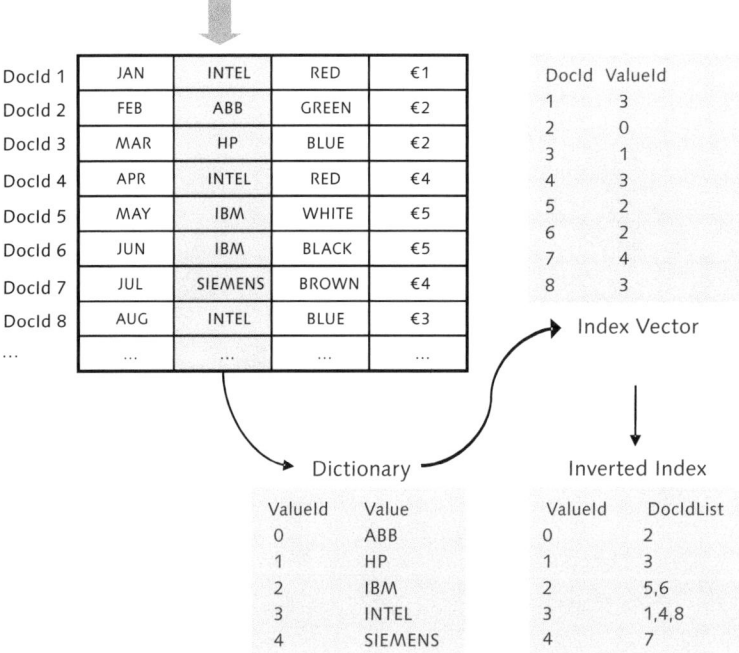

Figure 7.1 From Table Column to Inverted Index

The index vector for a column is generated from the column simply by inserting integer value IDs for the attribute values listed beside the document IDs that number the rows of the table. The inverted index is created from the index vector by listing the value IDs in order, and then for each one, listing the document IDs for the rows in which that value appears in a list called the address vector for that value. So the inverted index is created from the index vector by "inverting" it. This is just like the index in a book (regarding the book as a long vector of words), where for each word (value) a short list (address vector) of page numbers (document IDs) is given. So, given the inverted index, to select the rows with a given value, the BIA engine looks up the value in the inverted index and reads the address vector. Alternatively, if only a count is needed, the BIA engine simply checks the length of the address vector.

By contrast, a database lacking a convenient index for that column would have a harder task. It would have to fetch the first row, read the attribute value entry in the relevant column, go to the next row, read the attribute value, and so on, and most of the data in the table would have to be skipped and then discarded.

This illustrates a wider freedom used in the design of the BI accelerator. The analytic processing to be performed is well defined and highly constrained. Working from first principles, the BIA developers designed the BIA engine to do this task very well. By contrast, a general-purpose database is designed to do more things but often does them less well.

7.2 Parallelization

The BI accelerator achieves speedup by parallel processing at several levels. First, the appliance may contain a large number of processing cores. For example, in an appliance with eight blade servers, where each blade is equipped with 2 processors, and each processor has 4 cores, there are 64 cores available to share any processing load. In this case, any substantial task, such as aggregation of a billion data rows to execute an analytic query, can be parallelized up to 64 ways to achieve a significant speedup compared to serial processing through a single core.

The BIA software is designed to be able to parallelize tasks wherever a clear benefit is foreseen. When the accelerator indexes a large table, it splits it into as many parts as there are cores available in the appliance and indexes the table in parallel through the cores. This is the default behavior, assuming that each core has 4 GB of memory available for the parts allocated to it (the default can be changed by resetting a multiplier parameter to a value other than 1 in the TREX standalone administration tool's REORG view). However, there is an overhead cost for parallel processing because the rows to be indexed must be distributed to the respective cores for indexing. Further, the partial indexes created must be administered as a single logical index, so that the BI system sees a single BIA index. Moreover, during query execution, partial results sets calculated by the separate cores need to be merged for return to the BI system. So the threshold for splitting an index into parts needs to be judged carefully.

The BIA software sets a default threshold for splitting indexes. The default is that if a table is so large that the product of the number of columns and the number of rows is greater than 100 million, the table is split. This is a heuristic value, but it is not feasible to calculate a precisely optimal value for this threshold. Tuning specialists who wish to optimize the threshold more precisely can change the default setting manually in the TREX standalone administration tool.

For split indexes, the benefits of parallel processing are manifest during query execution. On startup, when the indexes are loaded into memory, the parts are loaded into the memory areas allocated to the respective cores so that they can be accessed in parallel for query execution. TREX distributes the indexes and their parts over the landscape using a preset default algorithm. In fact, a variety of algorithms are available, which respectively optimize data volume, expected CPU load, or other criteria. If an SAP expert advises you that it is advantageous to do so, you can select a different algorithm via the TREX standalone administration tool. The indexes and their parts can be reorganized over the landscape whenever changes to the indexes cause an existing index distribution to become suboptimal. TREX monitors the index distribution regularly as a background job and triggers an alert whenever a reorganization run is recommended. Because reorganizing the indexes causes a brief loss of availability, the action is configured to require manual triggering (see Section 5.3.1).

A further level of parallelization is implemented in a patented algorithm used by the BIA engine to aggregate results by means of full table scans. At this level, the parallel processing is more usually called vectorization or block-wise processing. On a traditional database, using full table scans for aggregation would give unacceptable query runtimes. But in the accelerator, the aggregation algorithm runs over only the relevant columns of the table index for the key figures to be aggregated, so the volume of data touched is small enough to allow fast runtimes.

The algorithm is optimized for the accelerator's blade server hardware. Because the key figures are coded using integer IDs with a minimal number of bits, they are small enough to be handled in blocks, rather than individually. This enables the algorithm to optimize the block size for the cache architecture of the chipset used in the blade servers.

During query execution, the filter condition from the query is used to select the key figure values that are to be aggregated. For each value, the combination of dimension values to be used to group them in the final results is used to generate an aggregate key for that value. The key figure values and their aggregate keys are written in blocks into a cache buffer.

The algorithm achieves its speed by aggregating in a single pass over the buffered data. It generates hash keys from the aggregate keys and aggregates any key figures with the same hash key as it writes them to the hash table. It is then a simple matter to convert the hash keys back to the dimensional attributes needed to group the result set.

The aggregation algorithm performs parallel processing by handling the data in cache-optimized blocks. Because it aggregates the key figures in a single run through the data, it features linear scaling: if the column of key figures is twice as long, the algorithm needs twice as long to run through it. This linear scalability is essential to the scalability of the accelerator as a whole, where tasks can be divided to run in parallel over as many cores as are available in the BIA landscape. As test results show, the accelerator shows near-linear scaling over a wide range of practical usage scenarios.

7.3   Smart Compression

The BI accelerator employs smart compression to make optimal use of its memory resources. All the values that appear in the BIA indexes are coded using integer IDs with minimal bit lengths. The BIA engine performs as much as possible of the processing on the integer IDs. Compared with the original values, this reduces the volume of data to be processed by an order of magnitude. This economizes on memory space, cache I/O, and CPU clock time.

Recall Figure 7.1 showing how a column of attribute values is indexed. The first step in the indexing process is to assign value IDs to the attribute values appearing in the column. We define the cardinality k of the column be the number of different values appearing in the column (not its length, which may be very many times greater, due to repeated values). Then the number of bits needed to code the k value IDs for the column is the smallest integer n such that $n \geq \log_2 k$.

For example, if k is 900, then n is 10 because 900 is less than 1,024 (which is 2^{10}), and 10 bits are enough to specify the 900 different values in the column.

The second step is to write the column as an index vector with value IDs for the attribute values. The document IDs are not written because the positions of the value IDs in the vector give them directly. This representation of the column may be an order of magnitude more compact than the original column with text or string values.

The third step is optional but facilitates acccss. It is to invert the index vector, so that the value IDs are listed in order, and the document IDs for the rows containing those values are listed in an address vector beside them. The inverted index is now a list of address vectors, which the BIA engine represents more compactly using difference coding. The engine compresses the numbers further by representing any remaining large numbers using Golomb coding.

Some Basic Compression Techniques

▶ **Dictionary coding**
Given a column of values, which may be text strings or numbers of arbitrary length, a standard trick is to create a dictionary that maps all the values in the column to integer IDs. Further, if there are k different values in the column, we can compress the integers by minimizing the number of bits used to write them. In fact, the integer IDs can be written most compactly using n bits, where n is the smallest whole number greater than or equal to the logarithm (to the base 2) of k.

▶ **Difference coding**
A standard way to present the respective positions in a list of a given value is to write them in an address vector. Counting through the list, we write the positions as numbers in the vector. For example, if a value appears at second, fifth, and tenth positions in a list, the vector is <2, 5, 10>. Now, to reduce the size of the numbers in the vector, each position can be written as the incremental difference from the previous position, so in the example, we would write <2, 3, 5>.

▶ **Golomb coding**
Writing integers in standard binary notation is sometimes wasteful, and mathematical techniques such as Golomb coding can shorten the bit string representation of an integer. Golomb coding uses a parameter g that is set for a range of integers. The Golomb code for a number n with parameter g is the string obtained by concatenating the unary string for the integer resulting from dividing n by g with the binary string for the remainder from the division. For example, if $n = 21$ and $g = 8$, then the code is 110.101 because $21 = 2*8 + 5$, 110 is unary code for 2, and 101 is binary code for 5. In the BIA implementation, there is a global Golomb parameter for each inverted index, and a local parameter for each value in the index, to code its address vector.

More radical compression can often be achieved for tables containing *sparse* data, which occur frequently in the typical InfoCubes filled with business data for which the accelerator was designed. Sparse data contains very many null or repeated values, so that in a multidimensional cube representation, the interesting data points are either scattered thinly over the space or clustered in relatively small subspaces.

The BI accelerator uses a number of additional compression techniques (some with patents pending) that greatly reduce the memory and disk footprint of sparse data. The BIA engine in the accelerator estimates how much each of these techniques would compress a given file and chooses the technique that compresses most, if it achieves a sufficient further reduction over simple dictionary coding.

An important consideration is how far a column of data can be sorted. Each column comes from a table, and the table contains rows of values that belong together. If the rows are sorted by the values in one column, they cannot be sorted freely by the values in another column but only within blocks of identical values from the sorting of the previous column.

Compression is a complicated issue. We call a column sparse either if almost all the entries in the column are the most frequent value (or one of the most frequent values) or if the column has a very small cardinality, and we can attempt to rank columns by how sparse they are. Then we can achieve higher compression factors if we sort the rows first by the sparsest column, then by the next sparsest column, and so on. In fact, this is a tricky optimization problem with no easy solution, and, in practice, it is sufficient — and faster — to use robust heuristics for compression.

Some Advanced Compression Techniques

▶ **Prefix coding**
Prefix coding involves sorting a column containing sparse data to bring all the appearances of the most frequent value to the top. All these repeated values can now simply be deleted and replaced with a single integer that says how many repeated values were deleted. The engine can easily reconstruct the full column from the truncated column plus the integer. This technique brings most benefit if the column can be sorted freely. Imagine that a column has a million rows but a cardinality of a thousand, and the most frequent value appears 900,000 times. Using dictionary coding, the column needs 10 bits per row, to give a lightly compressed file size of about 1.25 MB. Using prefix compression as well, assuming the column can be sorted to bring the most frequent values to the top, the short column needs just 125 KB, and the number of erasures can be coded as a 20-bit integer. This gives a further compression factor of about 10 relative to dictionary coding alone.

▶ **Sparse coding**

Sparse coding starts with a truncated column obtained by using prefix coding on the most frequent value in the column. The engine shortens the truncated column further by deleting all the remaining appearances of the most frequent value, and writes a bit vector for the truncated column recording which values were deleted. The accelerator can easily reconstruct the column with the help of the bit vector and the prefix. Sparse compression works well even if the column cannot be sorted.

▶ **Cluster coding**

Cluster coding resembles prefix coding. The main difference is that it works in cases where a column contains more than one frequent value. The column is first sorted to cluster any repeated appearances of distinct values as much as possible. Then it is divided into blocks with a standard size. Any block that contains a unique distinct value is compressed to a single entry. A vector is written for the column that specifies for each block in turn whether it has been compressed or not. This technique works best if the column can be sorted freely.

▶ **Indirect coding**

This technique is useful in cases where a column contains more than one frequent value but cannot be sorted freely. The engine divides the column into blocks and creates a vector for each block containing short IDs that refer to a small lookup dictionary for the block. The block dictionary for the entire column is just the series of block dictionaries for the individual blocks in the column. The engine writes pointers from the block vectors to their respective small dictionaries. These pointers give column offset values for the lookup in the block dictionary. The coding overhead is higher than for the other methods but is often acceptable.

▶ **Run length coding**

Run length coding is very simple. It does not use blocks or dictionaries and has very little overhead code. It is useful in cases where columns can be sorted freely but contain multiple frequent values. As the column is written, any runs of repeated values are skipped, and only the positions of new values are noted. The technique is fast in both directions and can achieve large compression factors in columns with long runs of repeated values.

The BIA engine uses a variety of advanced techniques to work with sparse data. Altogether, such compression techniques bring substantial runtime benefits. The resulting table indexes are extremely compact flat structures that can be loaded quickly and occupy minimal space in memory. The computational overhead to decompress the indexes in query runtime is often negligible in comparison with the cost of the rest of the query processing.

7.4 SAP NetWeaver BI InfoCubes

The BI InfoCubes with which the BI Accelerator works have a specific structure. An InfoCube is a multidimensional view of business data that allows users to view a combination of attributes simultaneously. The fact (F) table and dimension (D) tables are specific to an InfoCube. The X, Y, and S tables contain master data and can be shared with other InfoCubes.

Figure 7.2 shows a simplified form of a typical extended star schema representation of a BI InfoCube. At the center of an InfoCube extended star schema, a fact table contains one or more columns of dimension identifier (DIMID) numbers representing characteristics and one or more columns of key figures. Characteristics are called view attributes in the TREX metamodel. Key figures are numerical values.

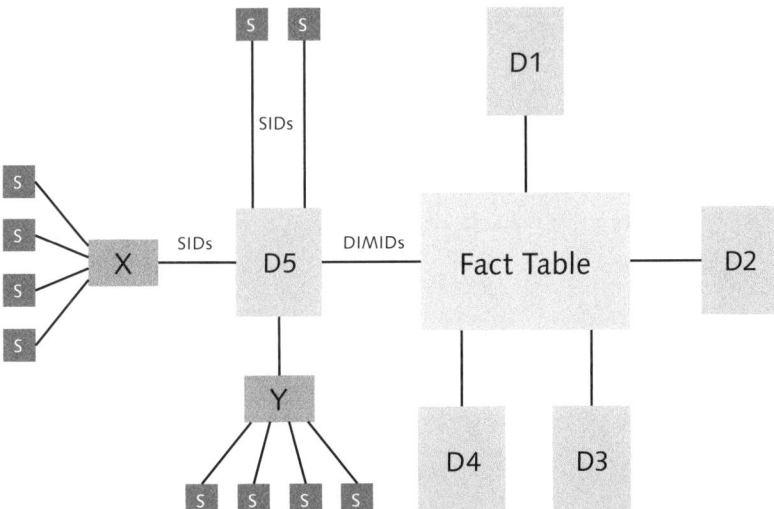

Figure 7.2 Star Schema Representation of an SAP NetWeaver BI InfoCube

Around the F table are dimension tables, or D tables, mapping DIMIDs to master data identifiers (surrogate IDs or SIDs, not to be confused with SAP system IDs, also called SIDs). These SIDs join to master data key values in surrogate tables, or S tables. In some cases, the join paths are indirect and go via navigational attributes in intermediate X or Y tables. X and Y tables are similar to each other, except that attributes in X tables are time-independent, and attributes in Y tables are time-dependent.

In some cases, if a characteristic has too many values to fit in a reasonable-sized D table, it can be defined as a line item and assigned its own dimension.

In SAP NetWeaver BI, there are three ways to connect attributes to the F table:

▶ Mappings from an S table to an X (or Y) table, from the X (or Y) table to a D table, and from the D table to the F table. Here, the mappings between S and (X or Y and) D tables are via SIDs. Mappings from the D table to the F table are via DIMIDs.

▶ Mapping from S to D tables via SIDs (directly, not via X or Y tables) and from the D table to the F table via DIMIDs.

▶ Mappings from S tables directly to the F table via SIDs. These are called line item dimensions. This is the only case where SIDs appear in the F table.

The BI system selects the appropriate way automatically. The default is the first way.

Master Data

In an InfoCube, the F and D tables are specific to the InfoCube but the X and Y and S tables contain master data and can be shared with other InfoCubes (see Figure 7.3).

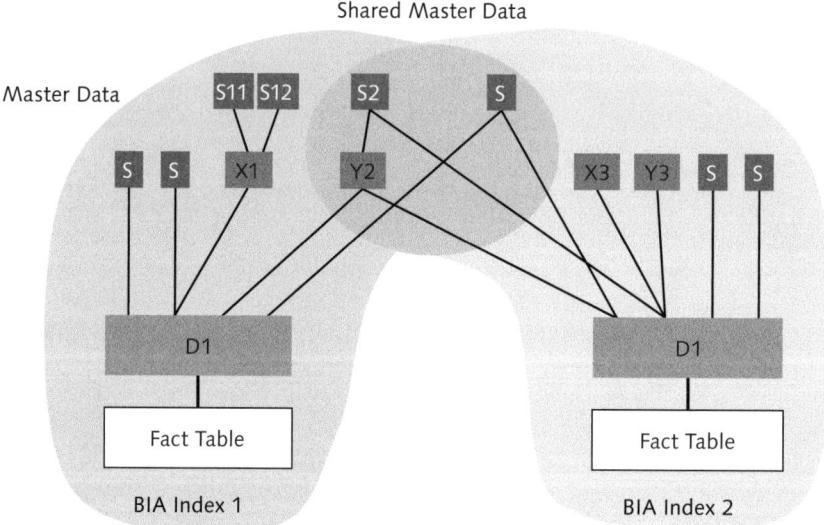

Figure 7.3 Shared Master Data

Master data is business information that is needed often and in the same form. For example, the master data for a cost center contains the name of the cost center, the person responsible for the cost center, and the corresponding hierarchy area. Similarly, the master data for a vendor contains the name, address, and bank information for the vendor. The accelerator stores master data tables once only and lets multiple BIA indexes access them.

Master data templates define how master data is created. A master data generator uses a template to create master data. The details here are unchanged by deployment of the accelerator.

In SAP NetWeaver BI, a master data ID (surrogate ID or SID) is an internal key of integer type for a master data characteristic. Master data IDs and characteristic values are stored in master data tables (also called S tables).

An X or Y table is a table for assigning the SID of a characteristic to the SID of the navigation attribute for the characteristic. A navigation attribute is an attribute that a user can select in a query. Attributes in X tables are time-independent, and attributes in Y tables are time-dependent.

SAP NetWeaver BI also makes use of P and Q tables for time-independent and time-dependent master data, respectively. P and Q tables are not needed in runtime and are used only to store display attributes, which specify how to format screen elements. The SAP NetWeaver BI Accelerator does not index P and Q tables.

SAP NetWeaver BI transactions RSDDBIAMON and RSDDV enable administrators to see which BIA indexes use shared master data tables.

7.5 BIA Indexes

The index structures created by the BI accelerator are based on the TREX metamodel, which defines the metadata for the indexes.

7.5.1 TREX Metamodel

The logical structure of a star schema for an InfoCube can be represented as a join graph over a set of tables. TREX creates a table index for each table and represents the join relations in the join graph by means of join conditions, where each join condition specifies exactly which table field in one table is mapped to which table field in another. This representation schema is called the TREX metamodel because it enables any given InfoCube to be modeled in logical terms that the TREX engine can understand.

Figure 7.4 shows part of the star schema for an InfoCube as a join graph on the left and the part of the BIA index structure that represents it in accordance with the TREX metamodel on the right. The latter represents the star schema as a join graph, and the TREX engine computes joins over the graph during query runtime. Below the star schema is a part of a typical SAP NetWeaver BI query written in a form that can be interpreted using the structures shown.

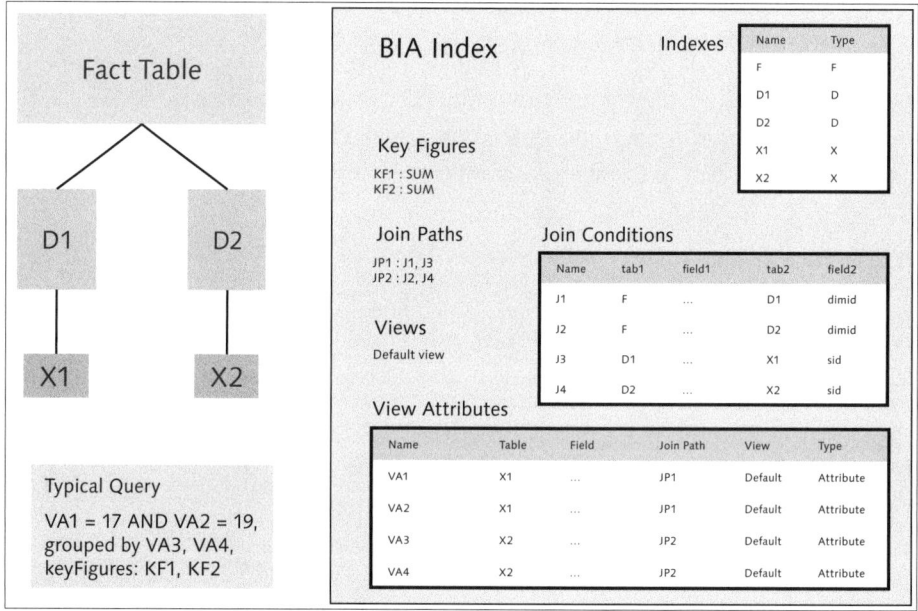

Figure 7.4 Star Schema and TREX Metamodel

The star schema includes a fact table F joined to two dimension tables D1 and D2, which are respectively joined in turn to two X tables X1 and X2. TREX represents the tables as indexes F, D1, D2, X1, and X2. Between the indexes, TREX defines the following join conditions:

- ▶ Join J1 from F.field11 to D1.field12
- ▶ Join J2 from F.field21 to D2.field22

- Join J3 from D1.field31 to X1.field32
- Join J4 from D2.field41 to X2.field42

TREX defines the following join paths JP1 and JP2 over the join graph:

- Join path JP1 from F via J1 to D1 and from D1 via J3 to X1
- Join path JP2 from F via J2 to D2 and from D2 via J4 to X2

TREX defines the join graph as the default view with F as the anchor table. TREX may define key figures KF1 and KF2 and view attributes VA1, VA2, VA3, and VA4 for the BIA index.

Example

Consider a business scenario with the following interpretation of this formalism:

- KF1 = Number of cars sold
- KF2 = Value in Dollars
- VA1 = Sales region, where value 17 = U.S.
- VA2 = Calendar year, where value 19 = 2007
- VA3 = Engine class (cubic capacity)
- VA4 = Model name (company brand)

TREX can now use the accelerator index to answer a query like this:

Tell me the number of cars (KF1) and their Dollar value (KF2) sold in the U.S. (VA1 = 17) last year (VA2 = 19), grouped by engine class (VA3) and model name (VA4).

7.5.2 BIA Index Metadata

The TREX metamodel defines BIA indexes. This new concept of a BIA index is quite different from the concept of index used in the world of database systems. The TREX structures are called BIA indexes because the TREX engine of the SAP NetWeaver BI Accelerator handles them logically rather like it handles inverted indexes in the context of search over textual documents. However, a BIA index is a more complex structure that contains several table indexes, one for each table in the original InfoCube. The BIA index joins these together in accordance with the join conditions to select sets of results in response to a query.

In the TREX usage, a BIA index is a logical model of an SAP NetWeaver BI Info-Cube. Its metadata consists of the following specifications:

▶ **Indexes**

This is a list of index names and their corresponding index types. The index types are F, D, S, X, and Y, corresponding respectively to fact tables, dimension tables, surrogate ID tables, and X and Y tables. Their logical relationships are represented as join conditions and join paths.

▶ **Join conditions**

This is a list of joins, consisting of their names and the mappings of index1.field1 to index2.field2. Join conditions specify the relationships between the indexes. The joins are inner joins, in accordance with standard database theory.

▶ **Join paths**

This is a list of all the join paths in the join graph for the BIA index. A join path is a series of join conditions that start at an anchor table and end on an index. In the extended star schema, the anchor table is the fact table. It defines the keys of the objects (rows) and contains the target information that a user can access by means of a view.

▶ **Views**

This is a list of view names, anchor tables, and view attributes. Each view presents a subgraph of the join graph with the anchor table as key. The default view is the full join graph, and its anchor table is the fact table.

▶ **View attributes**

This is a list mapping view attribute names to indexes, fields, join paths, and views. View attributes are the attributes that appear in views. If no view is specified, the view attributes appear in the default view. Each view attribute is linked to the anchor table via a specified join path.

▶ **Key figures**

This is a list of key figure names matched with their default aggregations and return types. The available aggregation functions are sum, min, max, and count. The accelerator can handle key figures of type cumulative or non-cumulative.

The BIA index consists of this metadata specification plus the data in the named indexes.

7.6   Query Execution

When the BI accelerator receives an analytic query against a given InfoCube from the attached BI system, a sequence of events is triggered:

1. The RFC server routes the request to the master name server for the BIA landscape.
2. The name server identifies the BIA index needed to answer the query and routes the request to the index server assigned as master for that BIA index.
3. The BIA engine on the master node creates a query plan.
4. The master index server distributes the query plan to all the nodes in the BIA landscape.
5. On each node, the node BIA engine reads the plan and identifies which plan operations it is tasked to perform.
6. As soon as a node gets the relevant input, it performs the tasked plan operations. If the relevant index parts are not already in memory, they are loaded from the attached storage.
7. The master index server collects the results of the plan operations and returns the results to the attached BI system.

It may be interesting to look more closely at the processes of creating a query plan and executing plan operations.

7.6.1   Query Plans

The execution of an analytic query breaks down into execution of a set of plan operations, for such steps as search, join, aggregate, or merge. Each plan operation requires certain input data and generates certain output data. Some of the operations use as input the output of other operations and therefore must be performed in serial order. Other operations may be performed in parallel. Each operation needs to be performed on a node, for example, the node where the required index data resides.

A query plan is a table containing a list of plan operations and specifying for each one which node it should run on, what input data it needs, and what output data it generates. The plan is determined uniquely by the query and the metadata for the corresponding BIA index. The plan can always be represented as a graph in which the vertexes are plan operations, and the edges are input or output data. An example is shown in Figure 7.5.

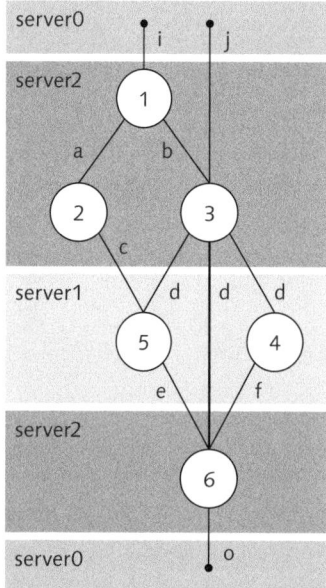

Figure 7.5 Simple Query Plan Represented as Graph

In this example, there are three nodes, called server0, server1, and server2. There are six plan operations with identifiers 1–6. And there are initial inputs i and j, intermediate output/inputs a, b, c, d, e, f, and final output o. The graph shows that plan operations 2 and 3 can be performed in parallel, as can operations 4 and 5. Otherwise, the execution is serial.

The BIA engine on the node hosting the logical cube index writes the plan and distributes it to the other nodes. Each node reads the plan and executes its own part of the plan as soon as it can. No further coordination between the nodes is needed. The logic of the query plan ensures that the correct serialization occurs, and the result is output as soon as possible.

Query plans are often very complicated and hard to reconstruct manually. Any BIA administrator who is curious about how the TREX engine handled a given query can display the query plan as an automatically generated color-coded graph from the TREX standalone administration tool, as long as the appropriate freeware graph generator is installed (the tool gives details).

7.6.2   Plan Operations

The plan operations (denoted in TREX source code with the prefix "pop") used by the accelerator are sufficient for all the analytic queries that can be executed on a BIA index. They include pops for searching in a given index, joining certain table fields together, aggregating given key figures, merging given partial results sets, building result sets, and other more technical operations such as caching. The pops are implemented as classes in C++ with input and output parameters. For each pop in the plan, the BIA query executor creates an object and executes it in a new thread.

7.6.3   Multiquery Optimization

A multiquery is a set of related queries that share common subexpressions. The execution of multiqueries can be optimized by finding evaluation plans that exploit these common subexpressions by sharing common results. Previous approaches to multiquery optimization for relational databases assumed that the common subexpressions were materialized. However, performance can be improved if the subexpressions are not materialized.

For many multiqueries, the previous approach was to perform preprocessing of the queries to represent them in a form that the database can handle and then perform post-processing of the database results to calculate what the user requested. Average response times for these multiqueries were often unsatisfactory and worst-case times increased without limit.

Example: Multiquery Optimization

Consider the following multiquery.

For product P, return the revenues for:

1. January 1, 2007

2. Month of January 2007

3. First quarter 2007

4. All of 2007

The traditional approach here is to define a database multiquery with the global restriction "product P" (part 0) conjoined to a disjunction of the four clauses "date 20070101" (part 1), "date between 20070101 and 20070131" (part 2), "date between 20070101 and 20070331" (part 3), and "date between 20070101 and 20071231" (part 4), to be grouped by date.

In response, the database returned an intermediate result set divided into 365 groups. This excessively complicated result set needed further processing to give usable final results.

In the BIA implementation, the query is reformulated so that the BIA engine does not generate a large intermediate result set. The new idea is to use a more sophisticated algorithm to define the required parts of the result set.

In the example, we define the following partition of the result set:

P1: Product P and date 20070101

P2: Product P and dates 20070102 to 20070131

P3: Product P and dates 20070201 to 20070331

P4: Product P and dates 20070401 to 20071231

We now ask the engine the same query as before but now to be grouped by partitions P1 through P4.

We then ask the engine to group the partitioned results into part containers as follows:

P1 (January 1, 2007): parts 1, 2, 3, 4

P2 (rest of January): parts 2, 3, 4

P3 (first quarter): parts 3, 4

P4 (rest of 2007): part 4

This is a minor extra step for the engine.

The partitioning functions allow the engine to group the results during a single pass through the data. In this example, the functions ensure that the engine does not waste time allocating results to 365 groups (for the days of the year).

Finally, the results are compressed to eliminate duplicates (in a process called FEMS compression in the Technical Operations Manual) before they are returned to the application. This greatly reduces network time compared with returning huge intermediate result sets, including multiple copies of any rows determined to be in more than one of the final result groups.

Compared with previous approaches, the new approach (for which an SAP patent is pending) offers much better average response times and much better worst-case behavior.

7.7   Deploying the Accelerator

In principle, the BI accelerator can be deployed quickly. To a first, crude approximation, all you need to do is create some BIA indexes, ensure that process chains include roll-ups to them, and enjoy the shorter response times. You can learn to be more relaxed about optimizing the data model of the InfoCube, and you can forget the chore of building database indexes and aggregates. Because the complexity of the query and the size of the result set have a much larger impact on the query runtime than the number of records selected in the InfoCube, you can easily do the following:

▶ Index even your biggest InfoCubes — or at least any for which you need fast responses.

▶ Design reasonable queries — the main constraint is to keep them simple and selective.

▶ Relax guidelines for analyzing data — you can let your users drill right down to the facts.

In summary, compared with BI colleagues still working directly on the database, you can afford to devote less time and effort to maintenance and performance optimization.

However, with a slightly more sophisticated approach, you can achieve much more. You can use deployment of the accelerator as an opportunity to reconsider your data warehousing practices. Once you have an accelerator, many previous InfoCube design guidelines become irrelevant. For example, you can design your InfoCubes without having to worry so much about performance. You can even design an InfoCube to store fully detailed data, down to the line items. Once the accelerator has indexed the InfoCube, you can enjoy accelerated query performance right down to the line items.

The revolution in data warehousing practices enabled by the accelerator technology is only just beginning.

How BIA Can Impact the Data Staging Process

Consider a scenario involving a DataStore object for sales order line items and an InfoCube for sales order information at a more aggregated level. Users can slice and dice the data in the InfoCube and can call a special report if they want more detail.

Response times for accelerated queries are best when the result set is small; otherwise, the network takes too long to return the results. But the response times are good even if there are vast numbers of records in the InfoCube. So in this scenario, you can store the sales order line items directly in the InfoCube. Users can still run the same reports as before, but they no longer need to run a special report to look up a particular line item. All the information is in the InfoCube.

Once you no longer use the DataStore for reporting, and assuming the data source provides delta information, you can now optimize the DataStore object for writes. Now that you no longer activate this object, you reduce data latency. This frees up disk space because the write-optimized DataStore object has no log table.

In this way, deployment of the accelerator is an opportunity to improve the whole data staging process.

7.8   Summary

The BI accelerator creates BIA indexes for InfoCubes and then accelerates the execution of analytic queries by holding the indexes in memory and performing the query processing in parallel and entirely in memory, without delays for disk access during query runtime. Because the BIA index structures are highly compressed relative to the InfoCubes, this approach allows all the relevant data from the InfoCubes to be held in memory without wasting hardware resources. The accelerator performs any aggregation required to answer a query during query runtime, to deliver both flexibility and performance in a hitherto impossible combination. And because more mass data can now go into InfoCubes, the new approach extends even to data warehousing practices.

8   References

Most of the best sources of up-to-date knowledge about the SAP NetWeaver BI Accelerator are online. To ensure that you access the latest information, check the SAP Community Network page on the SAP NetWeaver BI Accelerator at:

www.sdn.sap.com • SAP NetWeaver Capabilities • Information Management • Business Intelligence • BI Accelerator

In October 2008, this page included links to:

▶ BI Accelerator in SAP NetWeaver 7.0 (SAP, 69 slides, June 2008, PDF, 3 MB)

▶ SAP Business Intelligence Accelerator (IDC, 9 pages, October 2005, PDF, 154 KB)

▶ SAP Solution Brief: SAP NetWeaver Business Intelligence Accelerator (SAP, 4 pages, January 2007, PDF, 95 KB)

▶ The SAP NetWeaver BI Accelerator: Transforming Business Intelligence (Winter Corporation, 22 pages, September 2006, PDF, 1.4 MB)

▶ Large-Scale Testing of the SAP NetWeaver BI Accelerator on an IBM Platform (Winter Corporation, 14 pages, March 2008, PDF, 1.8 MB)

▶ Installation Guide: SAP NetWeaver 7.0 BI Accelerator (SAP, 47 pages, Version 2.1, September 2007, PDF, 1.1 MB)

▶ Update Guide: SAP NetWeaver 7.0 BI Accelerator (SAP, 15 pages, Version 1.4, June 2008, PDF, 529 KB)

▶ Technical Operations Manual for SAP NetWeaver BI Accelerator (SAP, 181 pages, Version 1.4, October 2008, PDF, 1.3 MB)

All these sources were used in the preparation of this book. The page also included links to much more online material about the accelerator.

On the public SAP website, you can navigate as follows:

www.sap.com • Large enterprises • Platform • SAP NetWeaver • Business Information Management • Customer References

In October 2008, this page panel included links to several success stories, including:

▶ Bayer Business Services (IBM, 4 pages, May 2006, validated March 2008, PDF, 150 KB)

▶ Bundeswehr (IBM, 2 pages, January 2007, PDF, 128 KB)

▶ ConAgra Foods (IBM, 4 pages, October 2007, PDF, 594 KB)

▶ Rabobank (IBM, 4 pages, September 2007, PDF, 183 KB)

▶ T-Mobile UK (IBM, 4 pages, May 2007, PDF, 261 KB)

Another source of success stories is the IBM site at *www.ibm.com*, where a search for "BI accelerator" in October 2008 yielded as first hit a page with links to several BI accelerator success stories, including:

▶ Lionsgate (IBM/SAP, 4 pages, September 2008, PDF, 237 KB)

▶ WACKER Chemie (IBM/SAP, 12 pages, March 2008, PDF, 1.23 MB)

▶ Kyocera Mita Corporation (IBM/SAP, 4 pages, April 2008, PDF, 215 KB)

Yet another source of success stories is the HP site at *www.hp.com*, where a search for "BI accelerator" in October 2008 yielded as first hit a page with a link to the following BI accelerator success stories:

▶ Coop (HP, 2 pages, January 2008, PDF, 92 KB)

▶ Kimberly-Clark (HP, 4 pages, August 2007, PDF, 251 KB)

The following additional references need to be documented here.

The citation at the beginning of Chapter 1 is from Joe Hellerstein, Professor of Computer Science at the University of California, Berkeley, and appeared in the Computing Community Consortium (CCC) blog (*www.cccblog.org*), in an entry titled "The Data-Centric Gambit" dated October 20, 2008.

The background information for Figure 1.1 came from a study posted online by John C. McCallum (*www.jcmit.com*) and is used with permission.

Several passages in this book are based in part on information from blogs, indeed on more blogs than it is possible to list here. However, it is worth emphasizing that the blogs on the SAP Community Network form an especially valuable resource. This resource is constantly being updated with new information that will be relevant to anyone professionally concerned with the BI accelerator.

Another source for the more technical parts of this book is the large and constantly growing collection of SAP Notes available through the SAP Help Portal. These notes are for experts only and are hard to read and apply correctly. But they are an invaluable resource for anyone professionally concerned with the BI accelerator. The collection is searchable (the engine for which on the SAP side is a large TREX installation) using keywords and other search criteria. Some of the detailed information in this book will eventually become outdated, but an intelligent search in the SAP Notes should soon enough give you the current facts.

The SAP NetWeaver EIM BI and TREX teams are fortunate to have benefited from the contributions of many talented colleagues. Relevant publications from permanent (professional) or temporary (student) members of the SAP NetWeaver EIM BI and TREX teams include:

▶ Gerhard Hill, Andrew Ross: *Reducing Outer Joins*. The VLDB Journal, August 2008 (*www.springerlink.com/content/74j0264538002714/*).

▶ Thomas Legler, Wolfgang Lehner, Andrew Ross: *Data mining with the SAP NetWeaver BI Accelerator*. Proceedings 32nd International Conference on Very Large Data Bases, Seoul, Korea, September 2006, pages 1059–1068.

▶ Thomas Legler, Wolfgang Lehner, Andrew Ross: *Der Einfluss der Datenverteilung auf die Performanz eines Data Warehouse*. Proceedings 12. Fachtagung Datenbanksysteme für Business, Technologie und Web, Aachen, pages 502–513, March 2007. Only available in German language.

▶ Christian Lemke, Kai-Uwe Sattler, Franz Färber: *Kompressionstechniken für spaltenorientierte BI-Accelerator-Lösungen*. Submitted to: 13. GI-Fachtagung Datenbanksysteme für Business, Technologie und Web, Münster, March 2009. Also available in English as: *Compression Techniques for Column-Oriented BI Accelerator Solutions*.

▶ Peter Sanders, Frederik Transier: *Intersection in Integer Inverted Indices*. Proceedings 9th Workshop on Algorithm Engineering and Experiments (ALENEX 2007), pages 71–83. SIAM, January 2007.

▶ Pascal Schmidt-Volkmar: *Betriebswirtschaftliche Analyse auf operationalen Daten*. Gabler Verlag, 244 pages. Dissertation, University of Duisberg 2008. Only available in German language.

▶ Frederik Transier, Peter Sanders: *Compressed Inverted Indexes for In-Memory Search Engines*. Proceedings 10th Workshop on Algorithm Engineering and Experiments (ALENEX 2008), pages 3–12. SIAM, January 2008.

A   Glossary

ABAP (Advanced Business Application Programming) The proprietary SAP high-level programming language. ABAP is object oriented and offers advantages relative to Java and other languages for business applications. It is the primary language for programming SAP business applications.

API (application programming interface) A source code interface that a software system provides to support requests for services that are sent to it by external applications. The two main TREX APIs support calls in ABAP and Java, respectively. The BI accelerator communicates via the ABAP API with the attached SAP NetWeaver BI system.

B (byte) A unit in information science that denotes 8 bits of data, where each bit is a binary digit, either 0 or 1. By contrast, the unit for bits is b (lowercase, not uppercase). Read as an 8-bit binary number, a byte can code numbers 0 to 255 because $2^8 = 256$.

BI (Business Intelligence) A generic set of capabilities for supporting the analysis of business data in order to enable business leaders to make more informed strategic and tactical decisions. The SAP Business Intelligence package is called SAP NetWeaver BI and is bundled with the SAP NetWeaver technology platform.

BIA A deprecated acronym for SAP NetWeaver Business Intelligence Accelerator in substantive usage but is used as a con-venient prefix in compound terms such as "BIA hardware" or "BIA indexes." It is not a registered name or trademark of SAP.

Business Objects, an SAP company The world's leading BI software company. The company offers a broad family of tools and applications to help teams optimize business performance. See Section 2.2.

CCMS (Computer Center Management System) The central SAP system management infrastructure. It can be accessed via transaction RZ20.

CPU (central processing unit) The logic engine at the heart of every chipset that does the bit-level work in all information processing hardware. The main metrics for CPUs are clock rate, counted in cycles per second or Hz, and flops, or floating point operations per second. The input/output rates for moving data through the CPU and the associated level 1 and level 2 cache sizes are also significant metrics for evaluating performance.

CRM (customer relationship management) A set of information processing capabilities for managing the dealings between a business and its customers or prospective customers, from first contact to final archiving. The main SAP CRM capabilities are part of SAP Business Suite, SAP Business All-in-One, and SAP Business ByDesign, and they run on the SAP NetWeaver platform.

D table (dimension table) A category of tables in an SAP NetWeaver BI InfoCube that is joined directly to the central fact table via dimension identifiers (DIMIDs).

DataStore object An object defined in SAP NetWeaver that stores consolidated and cleaned-up transaction data at the basic document level. A DataStore object describes a consolidated dataset from one or more SAP NetWeaver BI InfoSources. A DataStore object consists of a key and data fields that can also contain character fields. You can use a delta update to update data from a DataStore object into InfoCubes or other DataStore objects in the same system or in a different system. In contrast to mul-tidimensional data stores for InfoCubes, data in DataStore objects is stored in trans-parent, flat database tables.

DB (database) Often used to denote not only a stored collection of data records but also a database management system (DBMS). In this sense, the database includes all the software for managing fac-tors such as performance, concurrency, integrity, and recovery from hardware fail-ures. The SAP NetWeaver BI Accelerator dedicated storage is not a database in this wide sense but simply file storage on disk.

DBMS (database management system) See DB and RDBMS.

Display attribute An attribute defined in SAP NetWeaver BI for screen elements. The current values are bold, invisible, right jus-tified, leading zeros, two dimensional, and fixed font.

DW (data warehouse) A repository of an organization's electronically stored data. Data warehouses are designed to facilitate

reporting and analysis. In an expanded def-inition, data warehousing includes tools for business intelligence; tools to extract, trans-form, and load data into the repository; and tools to manage and retrieve metadata.

E table Like an F table, this is a fact table compressed within SAP NetWeaver BI. It is irrelevant to the accelerator.

EIM (enterprise information management) A set of capabilities, including business warehousing, business intelligence, Knowl-edge Management, master data manage-ment, and so on. In SAP, all this is part of SAP NetWeaver EIM.

ERP (enterprise resource planning) A set of information processing capabilities for sup-porting the day-to-day running of an enter-prise, including financials, controlling, pay-roll, human resources, production planning, materials management, vendors and subcontractors, customer master data, and more. The main SAP ERP capabilities are part of SAP Business Suite, SAP Business All-in-One, and SAP Business ByDesign, and they run on the SAP NetWeaver plat-form.

ETL (extraction, transformation, and load) The three-step process of moving data from an operational system to a data warehouse.

F table (fact table) The central table in an SAP NetWeaver BI InfoCube, and the cen-tral table in the star schema representation of an InfoCube.

FTE (full time equivalent) A measure of the amount of work required or performed for a task, in person-years, where this is reck-oned as person-hours divided by the maximum number of hours a person may normally work in a year.

Fujitsu Siemens (Fujitsu Siemens Computers) A leading European IT infrastructure provider and an SAP-certified hardware partner for the delivery and deployment of the SAP NetWeaver BI Accelerator.

GB (gigabyte) A unit in information science that denotes 1 billion (10^9) bytes of data. Often, the unit is used loosely to denote 2^{30} bytes of data (where 2^{30} = 1,073,741,824), for which the correct unit is GiB (gibibyte).

GHz (gigahertz) A unit of frequency that denotes 1 billion (10^9) hertz, or cycles per second. In IT, it is used primarily for clock rates governing CPU operations.

Golomb coding A standard mathematical technique for compressing the binary representation of integers used in the accelerator to reduce the data volume occupied by the integer presentations of attribute values and key figures. The Golomb coding $G(n, g)$ for a given number n using the Golomb parameter g is the string obtained by concatenating the unary string for the integer resulting from dividing n by g with the binary string for the remainder from the division. For example, if the given number $n = 21$ and the Golomb parameter $g = 8$, $G(21, 8) = 110.101$, which codes the fact that $21 = 2*8 + 5$, where 110 is unary code for 2 (with 0 as end marker), and 101 is binary code for 5.

GPFS (General Parallel File System) A high-performance file system based on either shared disks or clustering developed by IBM that provides concurrent high-speed file access to applications executing on multiple nodes of clusters. As well as providing fast and high-bandwidth data access from a single node to many nodes and providing high availability features, GPFS includes management and administration tools. It has been available on Linux since 2001.

GSM (Global System for Mobile communication) A widely used digital mobile telephone system. GSM digitizes and compresses data, then uses a variation of Time Division Multiple Access (TDMA) to send the data down a channel with two other streams of user data, each in its own time slot, in a frequency band of either 900 MHz or 1,800 MHz.

HA (high availability) A generic system design goal and associated implementation that ensures a predetermined numerical level of operational continuity during a specified period. A system is available when a user community can access the system and do their work in it, and is unavailable otherwise. Downtime denotes periods when a system is unavailable. The cumulative duration of unplanned system downtime over a period of a year is used to calculate a percentage availability level. For example, a "three nines" (99.9 %) HA level corresponds to a tolerance of less than nine hours of unplanned downtime per year, four nines (99.99 %) less than one hour per year, and five nines (99.999 %) about five minutes per year.

HDD (hard disk drive) A persistent, non-volatile data storage medium. Data bits are written to tiny magnetic domains on hard disks and later read from the disks via the same read-write heads. Hard disk storage is both much cheaper and much slower than solid-state storage (RAM).

HP (Hewlett-Packard) A long-established company in the field of IT and data processing, and an SAP-certified hardware partner for the delivery and deployment of the SAP NetWeaver BI Accelerator.

HP-UX (Hewlett-Packard Unix) A flavor of the well-known operating system UNIX. Although most SAP software is enabled to run on a range of operating systems, including HP-UX, the SAP NetWeaver BI Accelerator is delivered on preconfigured hardware to run specifically on Linux.

HTML (Hypertext Markup Language) The language used to specify both the content and the format of web pages. Essentially, it consists of text strings representing natural language content enriched with formatting tags within <...> brackets.

HTTP (Hypertext Transfer Protocol) A communications protocol used to transfer or convey information on intranets and the World Wide Web. Its original purpose was to provide a way to publish and retrieve hypertext pages. HTTP is a request-response protocol between a client and a server.

IBM (International Business Machines) A long-established company in the field of IT and data processing, and an SAP-certified hardware partner for the delivery and deployment of the SAP NetWeaver BI Accelerator.

InfoCube (SAP NetWeaver BI InfoCube) A multidimensional data cube used in an SAP NetWeaver BI system for online analytic processing.

INT4 (4-byte integer) An SAP data type that can represent integers up to 2^{32} (or 4,294,967,296 in decimal) using 4 bytes (32 bits).

Intel (Integrated Electronics Corporation) The world leader in semiconductor and microprocessor technology. SAP cooperated directly with Intel when building the SAP NetWeaver BI Accelerator in order to ensure that the BIA engine extracted the maximum possible performance from the Intel Xeon CPUs used in the BIA hardware.

I/O (input/output) Used to describe data flow rates in a hardware landscape, particularly flow rates in and out of a central processing unit, cache memory, random access memory, or hard disk storage. The bandwidth of I/O is typically measured in megabits per second (Mbps) or gigabits per second (Gbps).

IT (information technology) A generic term for the entire technical area concerned with digital information processing on electronic hardware. The IT department in a company is typically responsible both for computing and communications hardware and for the technical management of the related software. In relation to the accelerator, the company IT department would be responsible for maintaining both the hardware (in cooperation with the hardware partner) and the software (in cooperation with SAP).

Java EE (Java Enterprise Edition) A platform for developing portable, robust, scalable and secure server-side applications in the Java programming language. The Java EE platform differs from the standard edition of Java in that it provides Web Services, component model, management, and communications APIs for implementing SOA. The Java EE 5 SDK is available for download at the Sun Microsystems website.

JRE (Java Runtime Environment) Provides the libraries, the Java Virtual Machine, and other components to run applets and applications written in the Java programming language. The JRE tools are available for download at the Sun Microsystems website.

KB (kilobyte) An informal unit in information science that stands ambiguously for 2^{10} bytes or a thousand (10^3) bytes of data (because 2^{10} = 1,024). Strictly, the correct unit for 1,000 bytes is kB (lowercase k) and the unit for 1,024 B is KiB (kibibyte).

KF (key figure) A numerical quantity of interest listed in an SAP NetWeaver BI Info-Cube fact table that can be aggregated in the course of executing an OLAP query. Typical key figures include fact table entries for revenue in a given currency unit or for number of items sold in a given period.

Knowledge Management The branch of SAP NetWeaver EIM concerned with the management through a portal interface of documents containing unstructured information, which is to say information conveyed via text whose structure is not further analyzed within the Knowledge Management application.

KPI (key performance indicator) A term used in TREX for the TREX performance parameters, such as CPU load or memory usage, displayed in the TREX standalone administration tool. See Section 5.3.1.

LAN (local area network) The physically networked collection of machines in a local area such as a company landscape. Nor-mally, a LAN is understood as a cabled network where the cables are plugged into the machines. The cables in a company intranet might be based on gigabit Ethernet, which would support a communications bandwidth in the gigabit per second (1 Gbps) range and enable a 100 MB file to be transferred between two machines in about 1 second.

LRU (least recently used) A generic name for an algorithm in data processing that decides which of a given set of files to swap out of memory on the basis of when each of the files was most recently used, as indicated by a timestamp, such that the file with the oldest such timestamp is swapped out first.

MB (megabyte) A unit in information science and denotes 1 million (10^6) bytes of data. Often, the unit is used loosely to denote 2^{20} bytes of data (where 2^{20} = 1,048,576), for which the correct unit is MiB (mebibyte).

NAS (network attached storage) File-level data storage with a network connection to various clients. In the case of the BI accelerator, the clients for the data are the blade servers, and the NAS is a part of the BIA appliance. NAS hardware is similar to a traditional file server equipped with direct attached storage. The NAS server provides only data storage, data access, and management functions. The NAS unit may contain one or more hard disks in a RAID configuration. NAS uses file-based protocols such as NFS, OCFS, or GPFS.

Navigational attribute An attribute that you can select in an SAP NetWeaver BI query.

NFS (Network File System) A network file system protocol developed by Sun Microsystems and IBM in 1984. It allows a user on a client computer to access files over a network as easily as if the network devices were attached locally. If the BI accelerator storage uses NFS, all the blade servers have the same view of the BIA shared file hierarchy, but one of the BIA blades controls access to the files. In a clustered NFS solution, file access is controlled within the attached storage unit, not from a blade.

OCFS (Oracle Cluster File System) A shared disk storage file system developed by Oracle Corporation and released under the GNU General Public License. OCFS version 2 is integrated into the Linux kernel.

ODS (operational data store) An integrated, volatile, current-valued, detailed-only collection of data to meet an enterprise requirement to store the latest transactional information. In an SAP data warehousing landscape, it provides a temporary store for transactional data before the data undergoes the extraction, transformation, and load (ETL) process that packs the data into BI InfoCubes.

OLAP (online analytic processing) A term for the numerical analysis, such as slicing and dicing and aggregation, of structured data from multidimensional cubes. SAP NetWeaver BI contains an OLAP engine that either relies on the attached database for support or, now, leverages the SAP NetWeaver BI Accelerator.

Polestar (BusinessObjects Polestar) A tool for information discovery that combines the analytic power of BI with the performance boost of the SAP NetWeaver BI

Accelerator to provide quick answers to business questions. See Section 2.2.2.

PSA (persistent staging area) A transparent database table for the initial storage of requested data. SAP NetWeaver BI creates a PSA for each DataSource and source system. Data in the PSA is unchanged from the source system.

P table A master data table for time-independent master data. It contains the following fields: the master data characteristic, the compound characteristics of the master data characteristic, all time-independent attributes, and fields CHANGED and OBJEVERS. These fields form the key.

PuTTY This is a terminal emulator application for building secure connections via SSH, which is free, open-source software that SAP Service engineers can use over SAP remote service connections to accelerator blades in order to run the TREX stand-alone administration tool.

Q table A master data table for time-dependent master data. It has the same fields as a P table.

RAID (redundant arrays of inexpensive or independent disks or drives) A storage technology using multiple hard disk drives (HDDs) to maximize performance and availability. The key idea behind RAID schemes is that they divide and replicate data among multiple HDDs so that if any one disk fails, redundant copies of any data on it can be retrieved automatically from one or more other disks in the array. Different RAID configurations offer different levels of high availability (HA).

RAM (random access memory) The volatile, addressable solid-state memory built into the server hosts used to run applications. In a 32-bit environment, the addressable space is at most 2^{32} bytes, which is about 4 GB. Because each blade server in a typical accelerator appliance has 16 GB of installed RAM, the accelerator software runs exclusively in a 64-bit environment, with an addressable space of up to 2^{64} bytes, or about 16 exabytes (EB, where 1 EB = 10^{18} B).

RDBMS (relational database management system) A database management system that is based on the relational model. Relational databases are the most common kind of database in use today. In a relational database, the database tables store ordered sets, called tuples, of related data values as records, where a table row stores the tuple for one record. The table columns correspond to the respective attributes or characteristics, each of which has a specific value in each tuple.

RFC (Remote Function Call) A proprietary SAP technology for calling ABAP functions remotely over a network connection.

RFID (radio frequency identification) A new technology enabling the automatic identification of objects by attaching small tags to them. The tags are transponders that store information about the objects and can be interrogated remotely using radio waves. RFID allows companies to track materials and products more precisely than ever before but also requires much more data processing capacity.

RSA1 This SAP NetWeaver BI transaction for the Data Warehousing Workbench, a tool for controlling, monitoring, maintaining, and modeling data in SAP NetWeaver BI.

RSDDBIAMON This SAP NetWeaver BI Accelerator monitoring transaction is the primary administration and monitoring tool for a BIA installation.

RSDDV This SAP NetWeaver BI transaction is the primary SAP interface for creating and maintaining the BIA indexes for BI InfoCubes.

RSRV This SAP NetWeaver BI transaction is the launch point for consistency checks and performance tests on a BI accelerator. From here you can also delete and rebuild BIA indexes, adjust them after InfoCube activation, and rebuild master data indexes.

RSTT This SAP NetWeaver BI transaction is a tool for the tracing of automated stress tests for an SAP NetWeaver BI system with an accelerator, where the tests are based on a generated query load.

RZ20 This SAP NetWeaver transaction is the access point for the monitor sets in the central SAP system management infrastructure (CCMS).

SAP (Systems, Applications and Products in Data Processing) The company that created the SAP NetWeaver BI Accelerator. In German, the name stands for "Systeme, Anwendungen und Produkte in der Datenverarbeitung." The acronym is not normally spelled out. SAP is the world's largest business software company.

SCM (supply chain management) A set of information processing capabilities for managing the dealings between a business and all the companies in its supply chain.

The main SAP SCM capabilities are part of SAP Business Suite, SAP Business All-in-One, and SAP Business ByDesign, and they run on the SAP NetWeaver platform.

SE16 This SAP NetWeaver transaction is a data browser for displaying the contents of system tables.

SE38 This SAP NetWeaver transaction is the ABAP editor for displaying and changing ABAP code.

SGML (standard generalized markup language) A metalanguage in which one can define markup languages for documents. SGML is a descendant of an IBM markup language developed in the 1960s and provides a variety of markup syntaxes that can be used for many applications.

SID (system identifier or surrogate identifier) This ambiguous acronym stands for the system identifier for an SAP system, which is a set of three characters (uppercase letters or, in the second or third positions, numerals) used to denote the system at operating system level, as well as for logons and so on. In SAP NetWeaver BI, the surrogate identifier for a master data item is the integer value used within BI InfoCubes to stand for the data item. The surrogate ID is generally much shorter than the data item.

SOA (service-oriented architecture) A new paradigm in IT architectures according to which standardized services are used as modules to build up more complex applications in a loosely coupled environment supporting a model-driven approach to the design and deployment of application processes.

SOAP (simple object access protocol) A protocol for exchanging XML-based messages over computer networks, normally using HTTP. SOAP forms the foundation layer of the Web Services stack.

SLES (SUSE Linux Enterprise Edition) The commercially packaged flavor of the open source operating system Linux that is marketed by the Novell Corporation. SLES has been selected for use in the SAP NetWeaver BI Accelerator appliance.

SLG1 This SAP NetWeaver transaction is the entry point for analyzing application logs in an SAP system. For example, a user can display the indexing job logs for creating and filling BIA indexes in this transaction.

SMART (SAP Strategic Marketing Asset Repository and Toolset) An online resource designed to provide access to SAP sales and marketing materials, including advertising, collateral, presentations, demos, and more.

SM59 This SAP NetWeaver transaction where SAP system users can configure the RFC connections in their SAP landscape. The RFC connection between an SAP NetWeaver BI system and an attached BI accelerator is of type TCP/IP.

SMTP (simple mail transfer protocol) A technical standard for e-mail transfer over the Internet. It is a text-based protocol. The message is transferred to a remote server using a procedure of queries and responses between the client and server.

SSH (Secure Shell) A network protocol that allows data to be exchanged using a secure channel between two networked devices.

SSH uses public-key cryptography to authenticate the remote computer and allow the remote computer to authenticate the user.

Sun (Sun Microsystems) A well-established company in the field of IT and data processing, and an SAP-certified hardware partner for the delivery and deployment of the SAP NetWeaver BI Accelerator.

SUSE (a Novell trademark) The name behind SUSE Linux Enterprise Edition, the flavor of Linux used by the SAP NetWeaver BI Accelerator. Novell acquired the company Suse Linux AG in 2004.

TB (terabyte) A unit in information science that denotes 1 trillion (10^{12}) bytes of data. Often, the unit is used loosely to denote 2^{40} bytes of data (where $2^{40} = 1,099,511,627,776$), for which the correct unit is TiB (tebibyte).

TCO (total cost of ownership) A business acronym denoting the lifetime costs accumulated from all sources as a result of owning a given product. For example, one can say that the BI accelerator offers superior TCO compared with previous solutions relying on commercial database systems.

TCP/IP (Transmission Control Protocol/Internet Protocol) A protocol suite for communication over an intranet or the Internet. The TCP/IP reference model consists of four layers. Each layer provides a well-defined service to the upper layers based on using services from lower layers. Upper layers are logically closer to the user, while lower layers are closer to the physically transmitted bit strings.

TREX (text retrieval and information extraction, "T. rex") The unofficial name for the engine software at the heart of the BI accelerator. The acronym is a historical legacy and is not normally spelled out. It is not a registered name or trademark of SAP.

TREXADMIN The TREX administration transaction is the intended first point of contact to a BI accelerator installation for an administrator who wishes to interact with the TREX software, for example, to change a TREX parameter setting.

VA (view attribute) An attribute (in TREX terminology) or a characteristic (in SAP NetWeaver BI terminology) that appears in a view of the data in a BIA index (TREX) or an InfoCube (BI) and can be used to select data in an OLAP query and to display the results.

VNC (Virtual Network Computing) Remote control software that allows you to interact with one computer desktop (the VNC server) using a simple program (the VNC viewer) on another computer desktop anywhere on the Internet. SAP Service engineers can use VNC over SAP remote service connections to BIA blades to run the TREX standalone administration tool. VNC is available from RealVNClimited (*www.realvnc.com*).

WLAN (wireless local area network) A radio-based local area network (LAN). WLAN utilizes spread-spectrum or orthogonal frequency-division multiplexing (OFDM) modulation technology to enable communication between devices within the area where the radio signal is sufficiently strong and clear.

Xeon (the Intel Xeon processor) The CPU used in the accelerator blade server hardware. The Intel Xeon processor offers high levels of processing performance for the TREX engine at the heart of the accelerator. When coupled with suitable Intel chipsets, the Intel Xeon processor provides high memory bandwidth, high memory capacity, and high I/O bandwidth, to create a balanced platform that delivers excellent price-performance, scalability, and flexibility.

XML (extensible markup language) A simplified subset of standard generalized markup language (SGML) designed to offer more power for online usage than Hypertext Markup Language (HTML) by enabling the user to define new tags.

X table (time-independent attribute table) A table contained in some but not all Info-Cubes that is positioned in the star schema between a D table and one or more S tables and maps a navigational attribute to a set of surrogate IDs.

Y table (time-dependent attribute table) Like an X table except that its navigational attribute is time-dependent.

ZB (zettabyte) A unit in information science that denotes 1 billion trillion (10^{21}) bytes of data. This is a little over twice the estimated amount of data generated worldwide in 2008 (according to EMC Corporation).

B   The Author

 Andrew Ross joined SAP in 1999 and joined the TREX team in SAP that developed the SAP NetWeaver BI Accelerator in 2003. He has participated in the development of the accelerator from its first conception in 2004. Since unrestricted shipment began in 2005, he has held numerous lectures and workshops on the accelerator and created several iterations of online learning materials introducing it to both business and technical audiences.

In his first year at SAP, Andy worked as an information developer for Technical Core Competence in Walldorf, Germany. In 2000, he prepared training materials for SAP University. In 2001, he became a certified SAP support engineer.

Andy is British and grew up in southern England. He holds four degrees from Oxford and London: Master of Arts, Master of Science, Master of Philosophy, and Master of Letters. For further details of his life and works, visit his personal website at *www.andyross.net*.

Andy could not have written this book without the support and inspiration provided by his colleagues in the SAP NetWeaver EIM teams TREX and BI. He dedicates this book to them all.

Index

A

ABAP   25, 49, 186, 243
ABAP client   53
Activating delta indexing   175
Agassi, Shai   19
Aggregate   26, 33, 36, 41, 43, 76, 120, 237
  Aggregate strategy   38
  Building aggregates   37
Aggregation   17
  Aggregation algorithm   50, 222, 223
Alert server   53, 111, 138
Alert Server Configuration   112
Alert server trace   194
Anchor table   231
Appliance   10, 17, 39, 47, 48, 55, 221
  Appliance model   39
  Backend appliance   42
Assmann, Matthias   212

B

Backup   62, 125
Backup and recovery   62
Backup blade server   57, 60
Backup mode   61
Basket analysis   32
Bauer, Reinhard   216
Bayer AG   209
Bayer Business Services   209
Bayer MaterialScience   209
Best practice for accelerator backups   126
BI analytic processor   120
BI compression   36
BIA   243
BIA engine   49
BIA index   231
BIA index backup   125
BIA Index Maintenance Wizard   98, 176
BIA load monitor   124
BIA snapshot   62, 126, 161, 162
BIA system check   89
Binary large object (blob)   53

Blade server   41, 45, 46, 47, 48, 71, 127, 221, 222
Bundeswehr   210
Business Intelligence   243
Business Objects, an SAP company   26
BusinessObjects
  Enterprise   27
  Polestar   27, 28, 108
  Voyager   27
  Web Intelligence   27
  Xcelsius   27, 35

C

Call center   30
CCMS infrastructure   54
CCMS monitoring   83
CCMS monitoring framework   84
Central gateway   140
Change run   76, 121, 122
Changing a check set   155
Changing trace levels   192
Characteristics   37, 227
Check matrix   148
Check set   154
Client-server paradigm   21
Cloning a BIA instance   71, 127
Colgate-Palmolive   205
Composition Environment   24
Compression   223
  Cluster coding   226
  Difference coding   224
  Golomb coding   224
  Indirect coding   226
  Integer coding   224
  Prefix coding   225
  Run length coding   226
  Sparse coding   226
Compression technique   45, 50, 224, 225
Consistency check   144, 159
Creating a new check set   154
CRM   243
Crystal Reports   27

255

Master the functional professional migration of SAP BW 3.5 to SAP NetWeaver BI 7.0

Find out how to migrate data flows, reports, and authorizations

Use the many valuable tips from real-life projects on effort estimating and project progression

Daniel Knapp

SAP NetWeaver BI 7.0 Migration Guide

SAP PRESS Essentials 50

SAP NetWeaver BI 7.0 includes major changes from earlier releases, making migrations a challenging task, but with this book, consultants, developers, power users, and project teams will find the knowledge needed for technical and functional NetWeaver BI 7.0 migrations. Using real-life examples and highlighting SAP-recommended approaches, you'll work through data, authorizations, report migration and more. Both the automatic and manual aspects of report migration are highlighted, with particular attention to the radically revised Web reporting.

181 pp., 2008, 68,– Euro / US$ 85
ISBN 978-1-59229-228-8

>> www.sap-press.de/1852

Fundamental knowledge and in-depth administration advice

Expert advice on key areas like planning, administration, and development

Includes extra chapters on backup, recovery, restoration, SAP NetWeaver BI, and more

Michael Höding, André Faustmann, Gunnar Klein, Ronny Zimmermann

SAP Database Administration with Oracle

Oracle is one of the most significant, but also one of the most complex, DB platforms available for SAP systems---so why hasn't someone written a book on how to configure the interaction? Well, here it is: With this in-depth reference book, administrators get much needed background knowledge, as well as complete details on architectural and software/ logistics issues, in addition to step-by-step instructions for all of the most important administration tasks. Every aspect of system landscape planning and maintenance is covered, helping administrators hone their problem solving skills. Bonus chapters deal with Java, SAP NetWeaver BI, and the highly complex issues of Backup, Recovery, and Restoration.

818 pp., 2008, 89,95 Euro / US$ 89.95
ISBN 978-1-59229-120-5

>> www.sap-press.de/1386

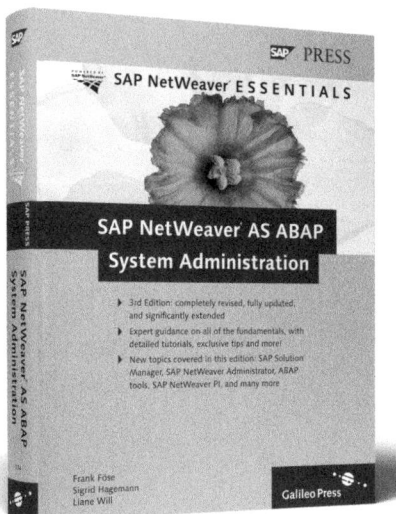

3rd Edition: completely revised, fully updated and significantly extended

Expert guidance on all of the fundamentals, with detailed tutorials, exclusive tips and more!

New topics covered in this edition: SAP Solution Manager, SAP NetWeaver Administrator, ABAP tools, SAP NetWeaver PI, and many more

Frank Föse, Sigrid Hagemann, Liane Will

SAP NetWeaver ABAP System Administration

This completely revised, updated and extended edition of our best-selling SAP System Administration book provides administrators and SAP Basis consultants with the core knowledge needed for effective and efficient system maintenance of SAP NetWeaver Application Server ABAP 7.0 and 7.1. With the help of this book, you'll master fundamental concepts such as architecture, processes, client administration, authorizations, and many others, while you learn how to optimize your use of the system's key administration tools. You'll profit from step-by-step tutorials as well as proven tips and tricks with this comprehensive book, which is also suitable to help you prepare for the certified SAP Technical Consultant exam.

646 pp., 3. edition 2008, 69,95 Euro / US$ 69.95
ISBN 978-1-59229-174-8

>> www.sap-press.de/1643